Other Books by Ruth Rouff

Pagan Heaven
Ida B. Wells: A Woman of Courage
Great Moments in Sports

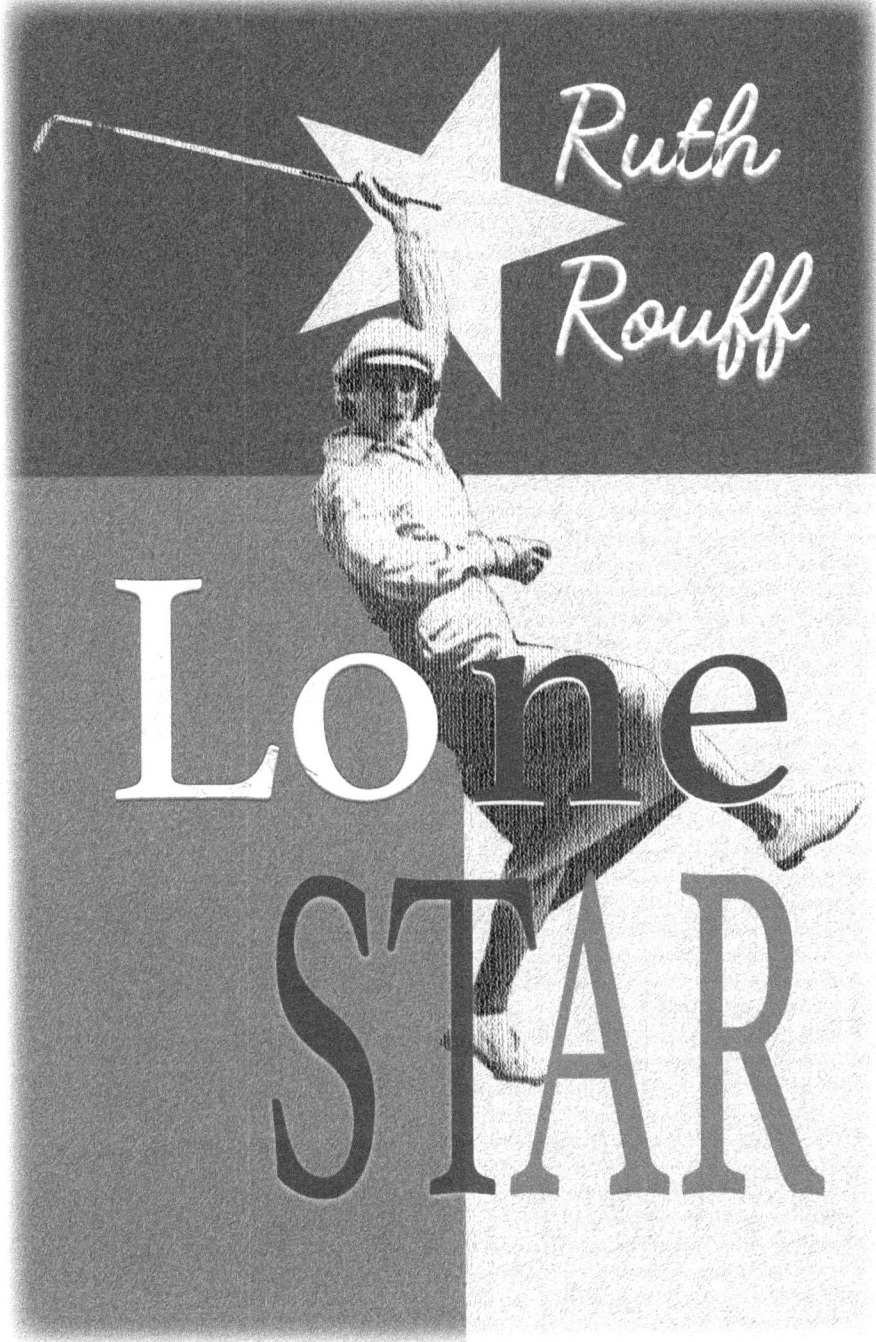

Ruth Rouff

Lone STAR

BInk
Bink Books
Bedazzled Ink Publishing Company • Fairfield, California

paperback 978-1-949290-87-5

Cover Design
by
Sapling Studio

Bink Books
a division of
Bedazzled Ink Publishing, LLC
Fairfield, California
http://www.bedazzledink.com

In Memory of Steve and Lynne

1

"WHERE DID I get that t'ing!" Mama Didriksen cried out as her sixth and by far most rambunctious child, Babe, returned home from the butcher shop empty-handed. Mama put down her potato peeler, rose from the kitchen table, and regarded the child now squirming before her.

Was Babe a changeling left by the trolls? That's how the old folks in Norway would have explained her, with her wild ways. The sweet, docile baby girl she had given birth to ten years earlier had been stolen and a mischievous changeling set in her place.

"Babe, tell me what happened to the stew meat!" Mama demanded.

No one called Babe by her given name of Mildred Ella. It just didn't fit her personality. As the youngest of six children, Babe had been called Baby from the beginning. The name had changed to Babe after her younger brother Arthur was born. Now her playmates, the neighborhood boys, called her Babe in emulation of Yankee slugger Babe Ruth.

"Mama, a great big dog jumped up on me and grabbed it out my hands," Babe said. "I tried to chase him down, but he was too fast."

What Babe neglected to say was that while she was returning home from the butcher shop, some boys called to her from the now vacant trolley-barn lot off Doucette Street and asked her to join them in a baseball game. Unable to resist the siren song of play, Babe laid down the package of stew meat she had purchased, on a tree stump bordering the lot. Because Babe was so good, the boys vied to have her on their team.

Babe played only for a few minutes, maybe a quarter of an hour, went to bat, hit the ball into the outfield, between fielders, and rounded the bases. But this detour was enough for a wandering mongrel, a brown-spotted hound, to raise his nose to the air and smell the meat, then amble over, plant his front paws on the tree stump, and tear open the butcher paper.

"Hey Babe! That dog's got your package!" one of the boys shouted, pointing in the dog's direction. Babe, who was by now finishing her tour of the bases, turned and raced hollering over to the dog, but he was already licking his chops.

"Get out of here!" Babe cried, shooing the now satisfied mongrel away. What remained was only the bloody butcher paper, a testament to her carelessness.

"Yep, that mutt was so big, he practically knocked me down,' Babe told her mother.

But Babe was an awful liar; something about the playful light in her hazel eyes betrayed her.

"You was playin' ball, I bet? Like you always do. You put that meat on the ground, eh?"

Babe looked down.

"Well, not exac'ly on the ground . . . on a tree stump."

With a quickness that belied her stoutness, Mama picked up a wooden spoon that was sitting nearby on the table. She grabbed Babe by the wrist, spun her around as if waltzing with her, and gave her three brisk smacks on the bottom.

"Ouch!" Babe cried. Really, the smacks didn't hurt all that much, not nearly as much as some of the injuries she had sustained while playing. Mama always did have a sweet spot for her, she knew, even though she now ordered her to the porch front bedroom she shared with two of her sisters.

"And don't come out 'til supper," Mama said.

Babe obeyed, rubbing her bottom.

"I DON'T KNOW where I got that t'ing," Mama repeated to her husband Ole when he returned home from work.

"What'd she do now?" Ole knew without asking which child Mama Hannah was referring to—their daughter Babe, already known as "the worst kid on Doucette Street."

Mama told him about the stew meat, and he sighed and shook his head.

"*Barn i disse dager*," he told himself. "Kids these days." Hannah had already spanked the child and sent her to her room. That punishment was enough for him, a naturally genial man, especially for daughters.

"Well, no meat for supper." He sighed. "Beans again, I guess."

It was kind of funny about the dog. It was also disappointing, but it wouldn't be the first time the family ate beans. Ole sat down in his favorite chair and put his feet up on a footstool he had made of spare pine. Then he took a big black pipe from his shirt pocket and filled it with tobacco from a pouch in his other shirt pocket. He lit the pipe, inhaled, and then gazed at the smoke as it dissipated into the air. *Just sit down and relax. Let everything go.*

Meanwhile, Mama Hannah went back to the kitchen and began cutting up onions. Even though Babe's carelessness still aggravated her, it was hard for her to stay angry at the girl. True, Babe was wild, but Hannah Olson had once had a wild streak too, or at least an athletic one. Before she married Ole, she had been an excellent skater and skier back in Norway—a girl who could glide along shimmering, ice-covered lakes and streams and schuss down snow-covered slopes. So much for that. She had met Ole Didriksen at a neighborhood dance. He was a cheerfully industrious young man who periodically shipped out as a ship's carpenter, and who talked glowingly of America—where there was plenty of work.

As they continued seeing each other, Hannah decided that she liked Ole, probably even loved him. He was quite a talker, telling wild stories of being caught in terrible storms and having to cling to the main mast while rounding the treacherous Cape Horn and of narrowly escaping the clutches of pirates and the jaws of sharks, and Hannah suspected that some of these stories might even be true. So, she put aside the tedious work she did for her family, as well as her girlish pleasures, and married him.

Three children followed while they were still in Norway. Then, when Ole was away on one of his ocean voyages, he found a town where he knew he would never again feel the chill and despair of long dark winters, a town he thought would be suitable to raise his family—Port Arthur, Texas, on the Gulf of Mexico. There was work for him in bustling Port Arthur, much of it due to the bubbling black largesse of Spindletop—the world's greatest oil geyser, which lay nearby. Great oil companies like Texaco and Esso were being founded because of Spindletop, not that Ole ever wanted to get into the oil business. He was a craftsman at heart. But the people moving in, due to the oil refineries, would certainly have a need for a skilled carpenter. So, Ole wrote home to Hannah of his intentions, lived frugally in a rooming house, saved his money, and then built a house. He beckoned his wife and children to join him three years later.

Despite the glowing picture of Port Arthur Ole had presented in his letters, Hannah was shocked when she got off the boat.

"*Badstue!*" she exclaimed as the coastal humidity hit her. *Badstue* was Norwegian for sauna. And the stench from the oil refineries made her eyes sting. What was even more difficult to get used to was, whatever the season, there was never any real respite from the heat, never any frozen streams and lakes and snow in Port Arthur. Nor was there in the nearby city of Beaumont, where the Didriksens moved soon after a hurricane hit Port Arthur, badly damaging their house. Instead of peaceful snow-capped mountains looming on the horizon, there were spidery black oil derricks, gushing out millions of barrels of crude a year, husbanded by the incessant activity of men and machines.

"The smell of America," Ole called the stench.

"Ole said he liked the climate. No more cold winters," Hannah reflected one day. "What I wouldn't give for a cold day now. A little ice." The oven where she was baking bread was giving off heat, causing the kitchen temperature to rise toward a hundred. She wiped her sweaty brow with the hand towel she kept on the table. Sometimes she felt like a stick of butter, melting on a skillet.

Nonetheless, Hannah was not the type of woman to harp on the negative. Truth to tell, she did take special pride in Babe—"min bebe"— her "changeling," her sixth little American. If the girl was considered a hellion by her neighbors, if last year she broke three ribs and cut open her leg when jumping off a half-built house on a dare; well, she could also beat the boys at their games, run faster, jump higher, play baseball and basketball with greater prowess. What was the American expression?

"More power to her," Hannah thought.

"STEW WITHOUT MEAT, ugh," Babe's older brother Louis said as he dolloped a portion of the meatless dinner onto his plate.

"There's plenty of beans in it," Mama told him. One could always afford beans.

Ole pointed his fork at Louis. "Just be grateful you got something to eat. Besides, we'll have meat tomorrow." He would be paid ten dollars tomorrow for a cabinetry job for some rich people. They could splurge on a chicken or two.

But tomorrow had not yet come. Although Mama had managed to give the stew a little meat flavor by adding a can of beef stock, this wasn't enough in her children's minds.

Babe looked guiltily around the dinner table. She knew that neither of her parents had told her brothers and sisters she was the reason they had no meat in the stew. They hadn't had to. When Babe's older sister Lillie found Babe alone in their room, Babe told her what had happened, and Lillie snitched to her twin, Louis, who told all the others.

Now her siblings—Ole Jr., Dora, Esther Nancy, the twins Lillie and Louis, and even little tow-headed Arthur—known as Bubba—cast sour looks at her, rubbing it in as only aggrieved children can.

"I'm still hungry," Bubba whined after he had eaten a bowl of stew.

"Here, have some more," Mama told him.

Babe felt terrible. The cheers she had received at hitting a home run that afternoon were cold comfort to her now. As she ate her dinner, she consoled herself with the fact that someday she would make it all up to her family. She imagined them all living like pashas she had seen in the movies; servants fanning them with ostrich feathers. Forget stew; they would have steak!

Because she, Babe Didriksen, world's greatest athlete, would earn enough money to support them all in grand style. The fact that no woman before her—the world over—had done as much as earn a living as an athlete registered not at all in her mind. She, Babe Didriksen, was someone absolutely new in the world. She would find a way.

2

"C'MON, BABE, BE on our team," tall, skinny, freckled Billy Mallory said. The kids stood in the vacant trolley lot that doubled as their baseball field. Weeds stood along the perimeter of the field. Way out in left field was a rusting green trolley car, rodent-infested, missing windows, and partly obscured by weeds. Out in right field was the abandoned chassis of a 1908 Ford Model A, minus the wheels, engine, and anything else that might be of value. Anything hit over these long stationary objects was considered a *de facto* home run.

Although Billy Mallory had spoken up first, stocky Fred Stoltz, who was a somewhat better athlete than Billy, also wanted Babe on his team.

"I'll give you two sticks of gum if you join our team," Billy Mallory said.

Fred had nothing to offer her except his athletic prowess and half a Lucky Strike. Babe didn't smoke—yet. The rather bent sticks of paper-encased gum that Billy pulled out of his back pants pocket decided it. That was the way to do things, Babe was fast learning . . . get them bidding for you, giving you things. It was ironic, since these boys were still at the stage where they despised most girls. Babe despised most girls too, with their sissy ways and fragile aspect.

Sometimes when their class was standing in line, waiting to enter South End Junior High in the morning, Babe would lightly punch a girl in an adjacent line. She didn't know exactly why she did it. Maybe she really was a changeling like her mother said. She didn't mean to hurt the girl. It was just that something about the girl attracted or offended her so much that she just had to hit her.

"Ouch!" the girl would cry out and turn around looking for who had hit her. She knew, dollars to donuts, it was Babe. But Babe would be innocently staring at something, anything, the flagpole to their left, pretending not to know what her victim was talking about.

One day a girl who Babe punched, Marjorie Ann Phillips, yelled "ouch!" jumped out of line and bravely complained to the teacher, Mrs.

Brownmiller, who was standing at the top of the school steps with a whistle on a lanyard around her neck, supervising the students' entry into the building. The students called Mrs. Brownmiller "George Washington" behind her back, both because of her white hair, her stature—over six feet tall—and the fact that she took her supervisory duties so seriously.

Now Mrs. Brownmiller marched down the steps, pulled Babe out of line by her shoulder, and questioned her.

"I did not!" Babe heatedly denied hitting Marjorie Anne, and although several of the kids had seen her do it, none of them wanted to risk Babe's wrath by tattling on her. Their silence didn't matter. Mrs. Brownmiller saw through Babe just as Babe's mother had.

"Mildred, you have earned after-school detention in my room," Mrs. Brownmiller told her. "Today," she added, quite unnecessarily. Kids were always earning detentions and having to serve them the same day. It was too much trouble for the teachers to keep track of detentions otherwise, with every school day bringing a new batch of miscreants.

"What?" Babe cried. Then she shrugged. Wiping down the blackboards, sweeping out George Washington's classroom, and emptying the trash can after school wasn't such a big deal. It was better than learning math. Too bad she couldn't exchange one for the other.

The occasional detention wasn't much of a deterrent to Babe. When she really felt like it, she still gave the girls some whacks and pinches. What most bothered Babe about her female classmates was the way they hung out in little groups. They would gather in their silly little groups and from their glances her way, she knew they were talking about her, making fun of her for her boyish ways. Though she despised these girls, their opinion still mattered to her. It was a vicious cycle. They would make fun of her, and she would play right into their caustic comments, cursing more, hitting them during gym class and at recess.

One afternoon on the way home from school, one bright day in April, Nancy Hickock called Babe a particularly vicious thing after Babe had taunted her.

"I'm the teacher's pet, huh? Well, you're not even a girl, you're a freak," Nancy said. "Like they have in circuses."

Not knowing what else to do, Babe scooped up a handful of mud from the curb and threw it at Nancy. Nancy gasped as the mud splattered her pretty pleated skirt. Babe let out a braying laugh, a laugh so loud it startled her sister Lillie, who was walking about three yards ahead of her.

But seeing Nancy fume in her muddy skirt was worth it to Babe even when, less than half an hour later, Nancy's mother marched over to the Didriksens' house and angrily presented Mama with the soiled garment.

"This mud will never come out," Mrs. Hickock complained.

"*Uff da*!" Mama cried in Norwegian. She made Babe apologize to Mrs. Hickock and promise to sew Nancy a new skirt.

"What did that little girl say to you that made you so mad?" Mama asked after Mrs. Hickock departed.

Babe repeated the remark about being a freak.

"You're not a freak. Don't never listen to nonsense like that," Mama said. Anyhow, better a tomboy than a *Savner Priss . . .* a prissy girl. She had never liked prissy little girls, even back in Norway.

Fortunately, Babe was good at sewing, too; Mama had made sure all her daughters knew how to sew. So, Babe peddled away with her knobby knees at the sewing machine in one corner of her parents' bedroom, fashioning the new skirt, pleats and all.

THE NEIGHBORHOOD BOYS were Babe's solace. They were all lower-class boys in patched pants and rumpled, hand-me-down shirts, risk takers, tough talkers, showoffs, roustabouts like her papa, who had gone to sea when he was nine years old, or so he claimed. Rather than despise Babe, they admired her for her gumption.

Like today: when Ray Alsop, who was *only* the best boy athlete in the entire neighborhood, tried to sneak a fastball by her, Babe slugged it as far as any of them had ever seen a baseball fly in Beaumont, far over the wrecked trolley car. When she walked, she flowed like mercury. When she ran, it was the perfection of running—Ty Cobb around the bases—and nearly as fast. She could shoot baskets, hit baseballs, jump hurdles, she could do everything with authority. She could even hunker down in the dust and beat the boys at marbles.

It was the boys—Billy, Axel, and Joe, mostly—who taught her to swear. Words like *ass* and *bastard* and *shit*. Actually, they didn't *teach* her to swear; she picked up certain choice words from hearing them so much. Everyone knew what an ass and a bastard and shit were. But the swear word that most intrigued Babe was the word *fuck*. The boys used that word a lot when older people weren't around. "Fuckin' this and fuckin' that." So she started using it.

"Look at that kid." She snorted, gesturing to a plump boy dressed in a neat blue jacket, knickers, and tie, a regular Little Lord Fauntleroy, who was holding his mother's hand while walking past the Rexall drugstore. "He's too fuckin' old to be holdin' his mama's hand like that."

Billy, Axel, and Joe frowned.

"A nice girl like you shouldn't use that word," Billy said, looking sternly down on her, hands on hips. For Babe *was* a nice girl in their eyes.

"But why shouldn't I say fuck?" Babe asked.

Billy snickered. Joe looked perplexed. Axel rubbed his head in consternation. He had only recently gotten over a bout of ringworm that had forced him to have his head shaved, and he was still a little self-conscious about it.

"Ask your mama," he finally volunteered, and the other boys seconded him.

Babe felt cheated, the same way she had when she was six and her mama told her she could no longer walk around the house without a shirt on. It was so hot in the house sometimes that she didn't want to wear a shirt. She didn't see why her older brothers Ole Jr. and Louis could and she couldn't and said so.

"Idiot, it's cause one day soon you'll grow tits like Mama," her oldest brother, Ole Jr., had told her.

The thought appalled her. She loved Mama dearly, but she sure as heck didn't want to look like her. Her mama was stout by now and yes, her bosom was ample and sagged nearly to her waist, like twin loaves of dough.

Instinct told Babe that asking her mama what "fuck" meant would not be wise. One memorable day, however, Babe said fuck in front of her older sister, Lillie. The two shared a bedroom along with their older sister Esther Nancy. Their bedroom was actually half of the enclosed front porch (the boys slept in the other half) which their father had built onto their house to allow for more room. They had to lower the window blinds when they were dressing to keep the neighbors from seeing in, but it was cooler at night when there was a breeze coming through the open windows.

This afternoon older sister Esther Nancy had gone directly to her babysitting job after school. Babe and Lillie were taking off their school dresses and putting on their worn, frequently mended, at-home clothes. Lillie was the opposite of Babe in many ways, conventionally pretty and blond, nice, not at all a troublemaker. Still, the sisters got on well, with Lillie admiring her two years younger sister for the boldness she lacked.

"That girl Pauline is a fuckin' idiot," Babe said. Pauline, one of her classmates, had recently accused Babe of being too tomboyish. Such comments were a frequent litany to Babe's ears, and she had grown tired of it.

Lillie gasped.

"Don't you ever say that word again," she told her.

"You mean fuck? Why not? The boys all say it."

"That's no reason." Not able to resist a little sisterly needling, Lillie added, "You don't even know what it means."

Babe had to acknowledge this was true.

"I asked the boys and they wouldn't tell me."

"Thank God for small favors."

Babe was eleven now. She wore a pair of Louis's old shorts and one of his old shirts around the house. Lillie wore a pinafore that had been Dora's.

"Wait a couple years and I'll tell you," Lillie added. Lillie was a tame girl herself. Still, she knew Babe was innocent about s-e-x. The little Lillie knew about the topic had come from Dora and Esther Nancy. Where they had gleaned the information they had, she didn't know. From some other girls, she guessed. It was like the game, "Whisper Down the Lane." You never knew just how accurate the information you were getting was. Like hand-me-downs, it was threadbare by the time it got to you.

"No, I want to know now."

"Okay, you asked for it."

Lillie rose, with a dramatic flourish shut the bedroom door, came back to the bed they shared and told her in a low voice. Such matters shouldn't be broadcast because you never knew when a Didriksen brother—Ole Jr. or Louis, or even little Bubba—little pitchers have big ears—was about.

Babe was so shocked by what Lillie told her that her face turned red. Her mouth looked like she had bitten into a lemon.

"No!" she cried. "That can't be right."

"It is right. How do you think babies get made? The stork? The man puts his thing inside the woman, between her legs where you pee."

To Babe, this procedure sounded painful, like getting stabbed. On the other hand, her mother never seemed to be in pain, at least not in that way. And she and Papa must have . . . she didn't want to think about it.

"Nothin' like that is *ever* goin' to happen to me," Babe vowed.

"It will too," Lillie said. "You'll see. You'll meet a boy you like and get married and first thing he'll want to do is . . ."

"I will not!" Babe was indignant. On the other hand, maybe there was more to it than Lillie knew, some redeeming feature. She couldn't imagine what that would be. Babies? They didn't appeal to Babe either.

"Well, let's not argue about it. Mama wants us to mop the kitchen floor. Let's go."

3

MONEY WAS SCARCE around the Didriksen household. Most men in the neighborhood worked for the huge Magnolia Oil Refinery, but Ole Didriksen—disdaining refinery work and with a certain old-world pride in craftsmanship that had been handed down to him from his carpenter father, did not.

"The oil business is dirty work. "No skill in it. Anyone can do it." He smiled at his wife. "You don't want me comin' home stinkin' like an oily rag, do you?"

She admitted she didn't. Ole made decent money as a carpenter and furniture refinisher when he was employed, but sometimes there were gaps between jobs. This time the gap was long, so Ole had to go to sea again as a ship's carpenter to earn money to send back to the family. In his absence, all the children helped out. Babe sewed burlap potato sacks, a penny a sack. She was good at sewing the sacks and one day surprised her employer by earning sixty-seven cents in an hour. Saving ten cents for herself, Babe bought candy—Haribo Gold Bears with their five juicy flavors were her downfall—and Black Jack chewing gum. She proudly gave the rest of her earnings for the afternoon to her mother.

In a rare moment of repose, Mama was sitting at the kitchen table, sipping tea. Her hands were red from doing laundry—her family's and the neighbors.

"Mama, if I dropped out of school, I could work fulltime," Babe mused aloud.

Her mother had already thanked her for the coins she had earned and put them in an old coffee can she kept in a kitchen cabinet. Babe knew how hard her mother worked when she took in washing because Babe sometimes helped her. Mama's pink face became so red as she pulled the steaming wet clothing from the ringer washer that Babe feared she would have a stroke, like one of the neighborhood women had.

Now Mama was sitting down at least, letting the bread dough she had been kneading rise, a linen dish towel covering it. It had a wholesome smell, even before baking. Babe took a leftover Norwegian meatball from the ice box and grabbed the last piece of another loaf of bread to make an open-faced sandwich, a quick snack before dinner.

Mama did not begrudge her daughter the sandwich. However, she did balk at Babe's idea about school.

"Don't be foolish," Mama replied. "Me and your papa don't come all the way to America so you kids can quit school. In America everyone gets free school. Anyhow, we're not starving."

That was true, especially since their neighbors the Hansons, Scandinavians like them, had been bringing over large roasts once a week or so and sitting down to eat with them now that Ole was away. Because the two families ate together, it was considered a social occasion and not charity.

"Yeah, but I'm not good in school," Babe countered. "No matter how hard I try, I always get C's, or even worse. So why bother?"

The fact that Babe had just gotten a D on an American history exam was much on her mind. All those names! All those dates!

Mama took a sip of lukewarm tea. "It don't matter what your grades are. When you're out in the world no one is gonna ask about your grades. They won't care. But they will ask if you got a high school diploma. Having a diploma means you saw something through to the end. That's what people want: hard workers who can finish a job."

"Okay, Mama." Babe sighed before taking a hearty bite of her sandwich.

She guessed what her mother said was true. As she ate, she thought maybe she might get an office job with a high school diploma . . . help out her family that way. That way her mother wouldn't have to take in wash. But as much as Babe tried to envision herself sitting in some office taking shorthand dictation from some droning man and typing away on a machine, she couldn't. She would much rather be outdoors somewhere, anywhere, playing sports.

THEY WERE GROWING up now. Everyone knew the facts of life. In Hygiene class, the girls had been given cloying little pink booklets explaining menstruation, complete with illustrations of one's "plumbing," as Babe called her inner workings. At first she dreaded getting The Curse, but then she observed the methodical way her older sisters put up with it. They had sewn masses of rags for the purpose and instructed her how the rags were to be attached to one's undergarments with safety pins and then washed out—boiled with lye.

Everyone knew there were commercial products—euphemistically called napkins or sanitary pads—available by now on the shelves of the drugstore and even at the local Woolworth's, but the Didriksen girls, except for oldest sister Dora, who by now had graduated high school and found steady office work, couldn't afford them. Even if Babe could, she would have been embarrassed to purchase one of the boxes. She sure as hell didn't want some pimply faced Rexall clerk knowing her business.

Then Lillie told her that Rexall Drugs had a box that you could put money in when you took a box of menstrual pads off the shelf. It was the honor system. No need to deal with a clerk. Lillie was saving her money to start buying Kotex every month. No more boiled rags. Babe filed this information for future reference. And when she finally got the curse, she saw she could live with it. Better yet, it didn't interfere with her athletic endeavors, except for swimming when you had to tell the gym teacher you were on the rag. And Babe didn't see the need to fake cramps to get out of gym class like she suspected some of the other girls did. You would have thought their guts were falling out the way some of them moaned and rubbed their stomachs and generally carried on. In contrast, Babe's period sometimes made her slightly uncomfortable, that was all.

Other things had changed. Many of the boys she once played sports with were now seeing girls.

"What do girls see in those fellows?" she asked herself.

Of course, it was natural for her mother to love her father, but that was different. She couldn't imagine any of the boys she knew growing up to become hale and hearty men like her father. They were all awkward things now, with squeaky voices and pimply complexions and sparse facial hair. Neither did she identify with the girls. That is, she had no desire to wear frilly clothes and brassieres and girdles and experiment with face paint and wait around like a dog in heat for some boy to notice her. She scarcely needed a brassiere. She worried about these things, about being different from the rest of the girls, but not a lot. Keeping busy helped.

4

DUE TO ALPHABETICAL seating, an absent-minded, blond-haired girl named Candace Dilford sat directly behind Babe in English class. As a result, Candace had plenty of time to muse upon Babe's cropped hair as Mrs. Scurlock, their English teacher, lectured about *Beowulf*—a narrative that did not arouse Candace's enthusiasm.

Suddenly Candace had an idea, though not about *Beowulf*. She leaned forward in her seat.

"Babe, you have such pretty chestnut hair. Can I curl it for you?" she whispered as the class was considering the nobility of Beowulf's abrupt, though not unexpected, demise at the claws of the dragon.

"Nah, Candace, I don't have time for that kinda thing," Babe tossed over her shoulder. She was sitting back in her seat, legs out, sleek brown arms folded over her chest. *Beowulf* wasn't the worst thing they had studied in English. She liked adventure stories, even if they a thousand years old. Besides, according to Mrs. Scurlock, *Beowulf* was set partly in Denmark, which was close to Norway. That made him a Scandinavian, like her. "You and the girls can do that stuff."

Candace was a little miffed. It seemed like such a good idea to curl Babe's hair for her. It would make her much more attractive. The girl did have possibilities—good skin, neat figure, pretty hazel eyes, if she'd only take advantage of them.

"Okay, but if you change your mind, let me know."

Babe was surprised by Candace's offer. She was a pretty, popular girl who didn't have to talk to her at all.

One day Ole Didriksen, who was back home from the sea, flush with money and gainfully employed once more in Beaumont, was reading the *Beaumont Journal*. Though reading English was still a chore for him, a story about the 1928 Olympic Games in Amsterdam caught his eye. For the first time ever, these Olympics were to feature track and field events for *kvinner*—women.

"Babe, maybe you can be in these Olympics when you get older," Ole said.

Babe was sitting on the couch doing a school assignment.

Unlike some men of his generation, Ole had nothing against women athletes; in fact, Hannah's grace as a skater had mightily appealed to him before their marriage.

"What, Pop?"

He handed Babe the sports section so she could read about the 1928 Olympics for herself. She was a much better reader of English than he was.

She put down her homework and read the *Beaumont Journal* article, several times over in fact, as if letting its import seep into her pores.

BABE AND LILLIE were standing outside their home at eight on a Saturday morning when it was still relatively cool. That is, the dew on the grass had not yet evaporated in the blazing Texas sun and the temperature had not yet topped ninety. Both were wearing sleeveless shirts and shorts. Lillie was still yawning while Babe was pointing down the street.

"See all them hedges?" Babe said to Lillie. Box hedges from two to three feet high divided each modest property along Doucette. "I'm gonna jump all of 'em, while you run along the sidewalk. That way I'm gonna be ready for the hurdles in the 1932 Olympics."

"What do you need me to run for?" Lillie asked.

"You gotta set the pace. You know, make it more like a real race." Babe noticed Lillie's reluctant expression. "I'll treat you to a Co' Cola later on."

"Okay."

To Lillie, Babe's goal of becoming the world's greatest female athlete didn't seem that farfetched. Babe was already the best girl athlete at Beaumont High, maybe even the best girl athlete in the state.

Out of the corner of her eye as she was running, Lillie saw Babe hurdling the hedges with those graceful legs of hers. They weren't particularly long, but the way they cut through the air—fluid as sunlight through water.

They raced in tandem down the street before Babe pulled up short at one hedge, which was too tall for her to hurdle. Babe regarded the offending hedge with a frown. Then, without hesitation, she knocked on the owners' door. Lillie stood on the sidewalk behind her. A paunchy, balding man in a sleeveless t-shirt came to the door. The man, who wore a thick, dark moustache, held a newspaper in one hand. The smell of fresh-brewed coffee wafted around him.

"Hi, Mr. King, you know me, Babe Didriksen from down the street? I'd like to cut your hedge down a little, even it out a little with the others on the street, if you don't mind."

"Why?" Mr. King asked, incredulous that a kid, a girl no less, would want to do yardwork for him. She must want to be paid.

Smiling, Babe explained her intention of practicing for the 1932 Olympics, particularly the hurdles.

"The Olympics, eh? They let girls in now?"

"Yep, they just started," Babe confirmed.

Mr. King looked at the overgrown hedge and then regarded Babe.

He had heard from his son Mickey, who also attended Beaumont High, that she was a fine athlete. The Olympics. They were taking girls now. Wouldn't it be something if a kid from this neighborhood did something like that?

"I'll even pay you twenty-five cents to cut it," Mr. King said. "There's clippers in the tool shed behind. And a sack for the clippings near the lawn mower."

By the time Babe finished trimming the hedge, with Lillie gathering the clippings into the canvas sack, the sun was high overhead, and the temperature had risen ten degrees. Looking over their work, Mr. King fished around in his trousers and gave Babe an additional fifty cents.

By now the girls' clothes clung to them like a second skin and sweat dripped down their faces. But Babe almost beat Lillie jumping hedges home.

When they were once again in front of their house, Lillie was panting. Babe, however, danced around, arms extended.

"Oh you, don't crow." Lillie smiled. "You haven't won anything yet. Besides, you owe me a Coke."

"I'll make it an ice cream sundae," Babe said, well pleased with her efforts.

THOUGH MOST OF the boys were still nice to Babe, she got the feeling they didn't want her around much anymore. They were growing hair on their faces, getting muscles and deeper voices and acting in strange, furtive ways. Playing together on the ballfields of Beaumont was becoming a thing of the past as more and more of them got part-time jobs. Some of them dropped out of school and got jobs: at the Magnolia, of course.

One afternoon Babe made the mistake of walking up on a group of boys, old friends, when they were huddled in a dusty, trash-strewn alley not far from the new Safeway. There was a scurry of motion, a flash of skin. The boys looked flushed, a little angry as they turned to her.

"Don't walk up on us like that," a fellow named Jerry admonished, red-faced.

After that, Babe stayed away from her former playmates, for the most part.

Sometimes other boys knocked against her in the hallowed hallways of Beaumont High. In general, these were the lowliest, scrawniest, homeliest boys, the ones most eager to prove themselves. When they knocked against her, she knocked against them. One day she tripped one, a mean little guy named Earl Pomeroy, and sent him flying, scattering his papers all along the hallway like so much litter while other kids stepped around him and laughed.

"Why you little bitch!" Earl told her. But he knew better than to retaliate. Babe was one tough cookie. Besides, she had brothers.

BARELY TRYING, BABE became a member of the Beaumont High School Miss Royal Purples basketball team. She felt proud putting on the purple and white school uniform. Gradually, she made friends with her teammates—Jackie Bridgewater and the others. Jackie was a decent player and didn't talk too much about boys, so Babe was friendly with her. But never too friendly. Sometimes she couldn't believe her teammates' awkwardness, their slowness, the way they missed easy shots. The sad part was that they thought they were good. It wouldn't be nice to tell them otherwise. But she was always somewhat apart from them, as if rubbing elbows with them would only dull her luster.

Babe had stopped giving little punches on the arms to certain girls a couple of years earlier. She noticed that the boys often still gave each other punches in friendship, like little explosions of pent-up energy. The boys took it all in stride, often punching back or giving noogies, but not the girls. Babe had learned by now that you couldn't roughhouse with girls. You had to keep a certain distance.

"Stir the batter until it's smooth and creamy, until all the lumps were out," Miss Whitaker was saying. Babe and her classmates were baking vanilla sponge cake in cooking class. Miss Bernice Whitaker was their teacher.

Babe didn't really need to learn this skill, as she had learned to bake cakes years ago in her mother's kitchen. But some of the girls, whose families could afford cooks or who were simply spoiled rotten, evidently didn't know their baking soda from their yeast. All this aside, Babe liked Miss Whitaker.

"Hey, Little Sugar, have I mixed this batter long enough?" she asked. She knew she had but liked to get her teacher's attention.

"Mildred, you must not call me Little Sugar," Miss Whitaker said. Miss Whitaker, a pretty, birdlike young woman just out of East Texas State Teacher's College, was not much older than her students. "If the principal happens by and hears you call me that, we'll both be in trouble."

"Okay, Little Sugar, I won't call you that anymore." Babe smiled.

Just then a few of the girls shrieked and pointed to one corner of the room. Their shrieking aroused the others, some of whom climbed onto the nearest chair. Babe looked behind her and noticed a sleek brown rat scurrying around among the desks. While the rest of the girls were screaming and standing on chairs, Babe raced to the corner where the rat had headed. Finding a battered pot in one of the cabinets, Babe took it, got down on her hands and knees, and trapped the rat in the pot.

"I got it!" she cried out.

As the girls got down off their chairs, she raised the pot off the floor, freeing the rat and causing another panic. The girls once again started screaming and climbed back up on their chairs, as Babe nearly choked with laughter. Miss Whitaker, who stood there speechless, hands on hips, wasn't amused and gave Babe a D for the class.

Babe's favorite teacher outside of gym class was Ruth Scurlock, her English teacher. Babe wasn't particularly good in English, especially in grammar, but she tried her best. Besides, she knew Mrs. Scurlock was married to Bill "Tiny" Scurlock, the sports editor for the *Beaumont Journal* because she asked her one day after class. Babe religiously read the *Journal* sports pages. When Mrs. Scurlock told her that, yes, Bill Scurlock, was her husband, Babe's attitude toward English class changed. She didn't want Mrs. Scurlock telling her husband what a knot-head her student Babe Didrikson was—teachers gossiped, you know—so she buckled down and did her assignments, even reading dry as dirt stuff like poems by Alfred "Lord" Tennyson.

Although Babe had no real problems with her teammates in basketball and other sports, the girls in her gym class were a different story.

"That Babe is getting a little too cocky," Enid Adams said to her friend Marjorie Tighe one morning in the girl's locker room at Beaumont High.

Enid was gingerly feeling her right shoulder, which was starting to throb. In gym class just a few minutes earlier, Babe had elbowed Enid aside while scrambling for the basketball, causing the off-balance girl to tumble hard to the parquet floor. Now the girls had showered and were putting on street clothes, though even the perfume girls like Enid liberally put on after showering couldn't entirely mask the dank locker room smell. Then again, it seemed to Enid that *some* girls weren't nearly as diligent as they should be about laundering their gym tops and bloomers.

"Well, you have to admit, Babe is the best girl athlete we have," Marjorie Tighe said.

"But that's just it. Girls shouldn't *be* athletes," Enid returned as she hitched her uplift brassiere. She was a full-busted girl and proud of it. "Having to take gym class is bad enough but *wanting* to get hot and sweaty like that. It's not ladylike."

Marjorie wondered why Beaumont High even had girls' sports teams if girls weren't supposed to play sports. But she was too in awe of Enid to raise this point.

Finished dressing, they brushed their hair in unison, like two cats grooming themselves. Enid pulled out her compact and lipstick from her shoulder bag and re-applied her make-up. She was a member of the Kacklers Klub, a school club whose sole purpose was to support Beaumont's male athletes. Marjorie, who was dating a second-string guard on the basketball team, wanted to join and knew she would need Enid to help her get in.

"What's worse is that Babe plays like a boy," Enid continued after putting back her compact and lipstick. "She didn't have to go after the ball that hard. And she always plays like that, even when it doesn't mean anything."

"I guess, but she sure seems to be getting a lot of attention for it."

"Well, she shouldn't."

Enid frowned at Babe, who was standing by a nearby bench, about to step into a shapeless shift, probably handsewn. If you squinted at her, she looked like a boy. She was as thin and lacking in curves as any boy. Her face, arms, and legs were browned by the sun. She didn't wear a brassiere, just some undershirt-type thing, since her breasts were no more than nubs.

Her face was not pretty. Chin jutting. Nose like a hawk. It was true that her eyes were kind of pretty—deep set and hazel with light flecks in them, but the way that silly immigrant mother of hers cut her hair was terrible: bowl-cut, framing her bony face like . . . like Beowulf's iron helmet.

Enid put her compact and lipstick back in her pocketbook. Then she walked over to Babe. She had a seductive walk when she wanted to use it. She had modeled it after the movies' "It Girl," Clara Bow. Rumor had it that Enid and her boyfriend, Carter Elder, had gone all the way. But that may have just been scurrilous gossip, as both attended a Baptist youth group and had sworn to clean Christian living.

"Hey, Babe," Enid said.

Babe, who was seated on a bench and pulling up her rumpled white socks, looked up at Enid, startled that she would even address her. She knew Enid was a member of the Kacklers, one of the most prestigious clubs at Beaumont High.

"Hullo, Enid," Babe said warily. "Sorry about flooring you back there."

"Oh, that's all right," Enid said dismissively enough, "You were just going for the ball."

Enid had delicate white skin, with a kind of pearly sheen to it. She had been considered "delicate" as a child and had barely survived the Spanish flu. As a result, she had grown used to being pampered by her parents, siblings, and the servants.

"I was wondering if you wanted to go to the movies with Marjorie and me this Friday night."

"Me?"

Babe could hardly believe this was happening. Enid had barely said two words to her all school year. Maybe she should have elbowed her earlier.

"*Beggars of Life* is playing," Enid said smiling.

"Haven't heard of it."

"Richard Arlen is in it. So is this new girl, Louise Brooks. It's supposed to be good."

Babe said nothing. She wondered about Carter, Enid's steady. She thought it was awful fishy that Enid was inviting her to join them at the movies.

Enid read her mind. It wasn't hard, considering how unsophisticated Babe was and how sophisticated she was. Enid's mother was a big club lady, both literally and figuratively, drenched in feathers and tulle, who had schooled her daughter well in the social graces.

"Carter is driving to Dallas Friday afternoon to visit his cousin, so Marjorie and I are going to the movies alone—girl's night out. It'll be a relief in a way. You know how boys are sometimes," she said in a confiding manner, although she was confident that Babe had no idea what boys were like. How could she? What boy would want to date her?

With that, Enid placed a well-manicured hand on Babe's shoulder. Her silver charm bracelet jingled like a pirate's treasure, and she smelled like lavender, even against the dank backdrop of the locker room.

Babe accepted Enid's invitation to the movies. How could she not?

"I didn't know Carter was going to Dallas," Marjorie whispered to Enid, having overheard the conversation while standing nearby.

"Hush up," Enid told her. And winked.

THE GIRLS PLANNED to meet in front of the Jefferson Theater at seven-thirty, just in time for the evening showing of *Beggars of Life*. A couple of days prior to the event, Babe had taken the trolley down to the theater in Beaumont's town center and looked at the colorful posters for the coming attraction. They showed a beautiful young actress named Louise Brooks, with slicked-down dark hair and wearing a boy's rough shirt, jacket, and rakish cabby cap standing between the similarly clad Richard Arlen and Wallace Beery. All three looked like roustabouts, roughnecks, not sissies at all. Babe thought she would enjoy the picture.

That night as she lay in the double bed she shared with Lillie, Babe allowed herself a rare treat: to dream about Enid. Nothing too specific; just to reach out and touch that soft, white creamy skin. Babe's guiltiest secret was that she allowed herself to "like" certain actresses. That was far safer than "liking" girls around her, whom she instinctively knew would not "like" her in the same way. Babe's deepest, darkest secret: she pretended she was John Gilbert kissing Greta, intoxicated by her, enfolding her in her arms. What came next, she had difficulty imagining. It didn't matter; a kiss would be enough. Now, could she really dream that a real girl, someone she knew, liked her that way?

When Friday evening came, Babe dressed up in her finest dress, chocolate-colored linen, which she had sewn by hand from a McCall's pattern and which everybody told her looked good on her. She borrowed beige pumps from Lillie, who was surprised that Babe was going to the movies with anyone but one of her siblings. Then Babe took the trolley through the hot evening air to the Jefferson Theater. Trying to control her excitement, she searched the crowd gathered near the jutting marquee for Enid and Marjorie.

It was a large Friday night crowd, half of Beaumont High there with dates. The "rich" boys straining to look nonchalant in seersucker or linen jackets and ties and stylish shoes; the working-class boys standing stolid in neatly pressed white or checked shirts with dark or khaki pants and shoes or boots not so stylish. All the girls in their best pastel dresses— some wearing hats, some fanning themselves, some not. Small groups of Negroes, also in their Friday night finery, some fancier dressed than the whites, stood around the perimeter of the crowd, waiting to buy tickets for their balcony seats.

But wouldn't you know it? Among the crowd nearest the box office, was Enid standing with Carter. Enid's dark eyes lit up and she waved when she saw Babe, while lean, lanky Carter was gazing abstractedly over the crowd. Marjorie was standing off a few yards away from Enid with her boyfriend, Tommy Swanson. Babe barely noticed Marjorie and Tommy. She was already steamed.

"Hi, Babe. Guess who didn't have to go to Dallas after all." Enid grinned, reaching out with one gloved hand to beckon Babe. At the same moment, she leaned into Carter and wrapped her right arm around his.

Carter was tall, blond-haired, son of a Magnolia Oil vice president. Although he played wide receiver on the football team, Babe, who had attended several Royal Purple football games, judged him to be not that talented a player.

"Hullo, Babe," Carter said.

From Enid's blood red smile and triumphant eyes, Babe knew that Carter never planned to go to Dallas at all, that Enid had set this all up to sucker her. Why she would do so, she didn't know. Babe had never done anything to her except to accidentally floor her in a basketball scrimmage in gym class. Was that so terrible?

"Babe, honey, you look surprised. Don't worry. Carter won't bite, will you Cart?" She turned and placed her hands on Carter's chest. "Carter, why don't you be a gentleman and buy Babe's ticket too?"

"Sure," Carter said. He didn't mind paying for her ticket if Enid would go off with him to their own special place after the show. It was the same place they usually went to, the grounds of an abandoned whiskey distillery on the outskirts of Beaumont. What they did there wasn't a sin if they fully intended to get married.

"I pay for my own tickets," Babe snapped.

And with that she turned on her heel, made her way through the crowd, and walked home. Forget about the damn trolley, forget about the heat. As she walked, her borrowed pumps bit into her heels like alligators, and the humid air clutched her in its oily embrace.

For the first time in her life, she noticed that the houses along her route got smaller and less impressive, and yes, shabbier—the closer she came to home: proud stone dwellings with swelling lawns and manicured gardens and long driveways guarded by grinning Negro lawn jockeys gave way to stucco and clapboard dwellings, some well-maintained despite their modest appearance, some with rotting windowsills, unpainted porches, and crab grass lots. Not that her own house was ever anything less than well-tended, Ole and Hannah Didriksen made sure of that, *av Gud*. But it was still, with its tacked-on front porch, undeniably humble.

Once inside the movie theater, Carter said to Enid, "Well, that was kinda odd. The way she looked at me. Wonder what got into her?"

"I don't know," Enid said rather airily. "She is an oddball. I don't know why I ever invited her. I guess I just felt sorry for her. She never has dates."

Marjorie, who had witnessed the whole thing, walked into the theater with Tommy and the rest of the group.

Back at home, Babe kicked off her shoes, which had caused angry blisters on her heels, tore off her dress, and tossed it in a ball on the floor. She lay face down on her bed in her underclothes, clutched the pillow, and thought. Fortunately, a breeze came through the windows. You couldn't call it a cool breeze, more like a puff of warm air, but it was better than nothing.

Lillie came in an hour later, stared at Babe lying supine on the bed.

"I thought you were going to the movies," she commented.

"I changed my mind and came back. I think I got a stomach bug."

"Let me feel your forehead," Lillie said, sitting down on the bed and reaching out her hand.

"Lay off, let me alone," Babe grumbled, twisting away from her on the warm mattress.

"Okay. Want me to bring you some water? Soda pop?"

"No, I'm okay."

Lillie noticed Babe's dress on the floor by the bed.

"Why did you throw this on the floor? It's your best dress."

Babe grunted. What good were dresses anyway? Clown suits on her.

Lillie picked up the pretty linen dress, smoothed it out, and carefully hung it in the closet. Then she went out to join her family in the living room. They were drinking soda pop and playing Hearts.

A FEW MONTHS later, Babe's biology class was at work at the green-topped lab tables toward the back of the room. They were dissecting frogs that had been pickled in formaldehyde. Their teacher, Mr. Albert Fortunato, a short, darkly handsome man in his early thirties, who the students not unfondly called "Wop of Fortune" behind his back, was instructing them, diligently pointing out the frog's internal organs as the students opened the poor creatures up with their scalpels.

"That's the liver," he'd say pointing to some disgusting-looking blob. "That's the stomach." Mr. Fortunato liked to wear a white lab coat when he led his students during biology lab.

The room stank of formaldehyde. Some of the girls were emitting polite little sounds of disgust—ughs and eeks—at having to dissect the rubbery frogs, while many of the boys looked grim.

"Poor critters," one of the girls, heavy-set Dolores McNair, said. A few minutes earlier, Paula Loveday had gone to the ladies' room after telling Mr. Fortunato that she was going to be sick. She had returned by now, holding a moist hankie over her nose.

Babe lowered her scalpel and detached her gaze from the rubbery carcass in front of her. She raised her hand, and also asked Mr. Fortunato for permission to go to the ladies' room. Mr. Fortunato liked Babe because she gave him no trouble. Given permission, Babe took her time in the ladies' room. Ambling back to class, she glided near where Enid Adams had her pocketbook slung over her chair near the front of the classroom. Babe looked toward the rear of the large classroom at the lab tables, where the students were now making detailed drawings of the dissected frogs, which Mr. Fortunato would collect and grade. Then she rejoined them.

A day later, just after lunch, Enid reached inside her pocketbook to fish around for her lipstick. There, amongst the compact and comb and keys and lipstick and breath mints and Kleenex and yes, a little tin of *Sheik* condoms because you couldn't count on Carter to remember them, she felt something cold and rubbery. Her scream of disgust and outrage echoed through the Girls' lavatory and out into the halls.

"Someone put a frog's leg in my pocketbook," she told the girls who ran to ask her what had happened.

But these girls weren't even in her biology class. Enid knew who had done it, and gossip being what it was, she knew that soon everyone in the school would know what she had found in her purse. But if she ratted out Babe, Babe would only deny, deny, deny it, saying she had no reason to do such a thing. And Enid couldn't very well bring up the subject of the movie theater, could she? It wasn't really worth it. Just flush the horrid thing down the toilet.

"Hi kiddo, how ya' doing?" Babe grinned at Enid in the hallway the next day before homeroom.

A sickly look on her face, Enid raised her nose in the air and veered away from Babe like a fly from a swatter. That was just fine with Babe, who reminded herself that she had never liked Enid in the first place.

5

ONE AFTERNOON, MRS. Beatrice Lytle, the coach of the Royal Purples, noticed Bill "Tiny" Scurlock, sitting among the crowd in the gym bleachers taking notes on their game against the Vidor Lady Pirates. But she didn't tell her players, not wanting them to become distracted.

The next time Tiny Scurlock appeared at a Royal Purples game, he lumbered down from the bleachers—watching the huge man descend was like watching the approach of a slow-moving boulder—and introduced himself. Although he congratulated the team for their win, the way his eyes shone when he looked at Babe made it clear to the rest of the girls that he only wanted to talk with her. So they drifted back into the locker room.

"Young lady, you are an excellent athlete," he said as the two stood by the sideline. She had that specific gravity, that density of muscle and sinew that all fine athletes had, as different from the run-of-the-mill human body as gold was from clay.

Babe shrugged. "Thank you, Mr. Scurlock. But why shouldn't I be excellent? I'm only playin' against girls."

Bill laughed, a little taken aback by the distinction she made.

"I mean I used to play against boys—the boys in my neighborhood. They're tougher. They'll throw an elbow at you, no sweat."

"I understand," Bill said.

Right there, Babe decided to like Bill "Tiny" Scurlock. From his benevolent smile, it was clear that he wasn't put off by her boyishness. She also liked that he was a big man. It was the squirts that often gave her trouble.

"Well, that was an awful nice writeup you did of me in the *Journal*. If I had known you were watching the game, I would'a played better."

"Truly deserved, Babe," Tiny said. "What's more interesting, I got a call from Colonel Melvin McCombs of Employers Casualty Insurance. He reads my column, and he says when the championships roll around in Houston, he's going to scout you for their girls' team."

Babe knew that a lot of companies sponsored athletic teams comprised of their employees. Women's basketball was big throughout the South and Midwest, and it was great publicity to sponsor a winning girls' team. That the Royal Purples would take part in the state championships was a foregone conclusion by now, with Babe on the team.

"That's great news!" said Babe, hardly believing it at first. But then again, why not? She knew she was the best player in the state. And if she got a job at Employers Casualty, she could help out her folks and play basketball all at the same time.

As Babe walked home from Beaumont High School that day, her feet barely touched the pavement. In her mind, she was flying toward the basket and there was nothing to block her way.

6

A GLOB OF saliva fell to the pavement from the top floor of the Rice Hotel in downtown Houston. The globule narrowly missed hitting a hatless man in shirt sleeves who seemed oblivious to the fact that he had been targeted.

"Nearly got that one," Babe said, snapping her fingers at the near miss.

It was the 1930 girls' high school basketball championships in Houston, and Babe was leaning out her team's hotel window. She was spitting on the people below her, seeing how many she could hit. She aimed again, and a man in a straw hat felt something, took off his hat, and looked at the wetness on the crown in puzzlement. Then the man looked up, but Babe's head and shoulders had already disappeared back into the hotel room.

Her teammates, who were sharing the room with her, tittered at her behavior, but Mrs. Beatrice Lytle, their coach, who was chaperoning the team together with Mrs. Ruth Scurlock, took a stronger tack once she noticed what Babe was doing.

"Babe, stop that this minute."

"Aw, Coach, I'm only seeing how good my aim is."

"Get away from that window."

Lytle glared at Babe as she turned around.

What everyone said was true. Even though Babe was dressed in a blouse and skirt like the rest of the girls, she did look like a boy. Perhaps she should have been a boy. There was nothing feminine about her, no softness whatsoever, from her hard, angular face to her small but noticeable Adam's apple to her lithe, cowpuncher's body. In fact, Babe's angular face, piercing eyes, and thin lips reminded the coach of the movie cowboy, William S. Hart.

Coach Lytle was an old hand with girl athletes and had been coaching Babe since ninth grade. During that time, she had half-expected Babe to become more feminine as she matured, like most of the other girls. Getting the curse changed a lot of them, settled them down, reminded them of their future as child-bearers. But not Babe. She was the same raw-boned kid she had been a few years earlier, only a few inches taller and a few pounds, all muscle, heavier. All the same, she was by far the best athlete Beatrice Lytle had ever coached. *Would* ever coach, probably.

Now Babe looked at Coach Lytle and grinned that lop-sided piratical grin. It was hard to stay mad at her. Nonetheless, she had to be chastised.

"Young lady, you have a lot to learn about deportment. We're here representing Beaumont High School, and we must show people that we're not hicks, that we Lady Royal Purples know how to act. And being a lady *certainly* doesn't mean spitting on people from hotel windows."

Babe loved the way Coach Lytle emphasized the word *certainly* and knew she would re-use it when relating this incident to her siblings. But just then Ruth Scurlock walked into the hotel suite. She had gone down to the hotel lobby to purchased several copies of the Dallas newspapers. Ever the English teacher, she wanted the girls to keep up on current events, even when they were away from home. As she stood by the door, one of the girls whispered to her what had happened.

"Aw Coach I know," Babe conceded. "I'm so ashamed." But she didn't look ashamed. A smile still played on her lips. The other girls in the room giggled, Babe's insincerity was so palpable.

Coach Lytle again shook her head and cast a "what are we to do" look at Ruth Scurlock, relieved that her co-chaperone wasn't the hotel manager.

The next day Babe easily carried her team to the state championship; her aim in shooting baskets being far better than her aim had been from the window of the Rice Hotel.

7

"I DON'T LIKE the idea of you quitting school," Mama Didriksen said.

Amid the sweet, slightly acrid smoke from Ole Didriksen's black pipe and the pleasant smell lingering from a roast chicken dinner, the Didriksens were having a living room conference. Babe had been asked to sign with the Golden Cyclones, the girls' semiprofessional basketball team managed by the Employers Casualty Company of Dallas. It was partly Tiny Scurlock's doing. He had pumped Babe's image so much to Colonel M.J. McCombs that the Colonel was practically on tenterhooks to see Babe play in the high school championship. Then again, McCombs would have been a fool not to want to see her, the Golden Cyclones having narrowly lost the national championships the year before.

"Aw, Mama, I can come back and take my final exams in June and still graduate, that's what the principal said," Babe said.

"And who is this man? Colonel Mc . . . who?" Ole asked, who had hitherto been silent. As usual he was sitting in his easy chair. His hair was gray now, and his face wrinkled and browned by the fierce Texas sun.

"Colonel Melvin Jackson McCombs. He runs the sports teams for ECC . . . basketball and baseball."

"A grown man around a bunch of girls, I don't know." Mama fretted. She was sitting next to Babe on the well-worn couch, apron still around her waist.

"Don't worry. He has a lady who chaperones—looks out for us," Babe replied. "Her name is Mrs. Henry Wood. You can call her on the telephone. Tiny says it's all on the up and up."

By now Babe's parents knew who Tiny Scurlock was and respected him as an educated man.

"And you're sure you can still graduate?"

"That's what Principal Dixon says."

Mama turned to her husband.

"What do you think, Papa?"

Ole considered, steadily puffing on his pipe.

"He could be sending smoke signals," Babe thought, like the Indians she had seen in westerns.

Ole finally put down his pipe.

"Dallas, that's a big step," he said. He would miss Babe if she left town. But hadn't he come to America to see his children advance in life? And Babe was a child after his own heart. She had the same adventurous spirit he had in his youth when he had shipped out and sailed around Cape Horn, scarcely fifteen years old. Here Babe was seventeen. He knew she'd do great in whatever sports she played. She always had.

"They'll pay me to type and play on their teams. Please say yes," Babe pleaded.

"But you don't know how to type, do you?" Mama asked hopefully.

"I took it one term in school. I know how well enough."

Mama feared she was being selfish, but she would especially miss having Babe live with them. Oh, she loved all her children, but there was something special about Babe, something that was—*forfriskende*—refreshing, like the brisk breezes coming off the harbor in Oslo.

Reluctantly, Mama had to admit that "min Bebe"—her Babe was ready for Dallas.

Ole put his own seal of approval on the matter when he said, "Goddommit, let her go."

A few days later, Ole dressed up in his best blue serge suit and escorted his daughter Mildred Ella "Babe" Didrikson on the overnight train to Dallas.

8

COLONEL MELVIN J. McCombs stood chatting with Bill "Tiny" Scurlock, who had come up to Dallas to see how Babe was getting along. The two men stood on the grassy perimeter of the regulation track at SMU's Ownby Stadium. They were watching the Employers Casualty Team prepare for their upcoming AAU meet to be held the next day. In particular, they were watching Babe Didrikson throw the javelin. She was dressed now in scant white track shorts and a white sleeveless shirt that revealed her finely wrought shoulder muscles and arms.

"That girl swears she never picked up a javelin before joining us and now look at her," McCombs was crowing.

They watched as Babe reared back and tossed the javelin, which whizzed through the sunny air with a snakelike hiss and then buried its head in the grass many yards away.

"Perfect form," McCombs said. "She could be a hood ornament."

"A hundred and twenty feet if it's an inch," Tiny said.

"I taught her how to hold that thing and how to step into it," McCombs said. "But the rest is sheer talent. You should see her in the high jump."

"How high?"

"Five feet easily."

Tiny Scurlock whistled.

"I'll be surprised if she doesn't set a U.S. record," McCombs said.

"U.S. record? She'll set a world record, and soon."

As Tiny envisioned all the world's attention focused on the young woman he took to be his discovery, Babe noticed the them watching her, lay down the javelin in the grass, and strode over to them.

"Hi, Old Top," she said to Tiny, giving him a friendly slap on his back. It was like smacking a boulder.

Babe and Tiny had been corresponding ever since Babe left for Dallas, Babe informing him in not-too-grammatically correct English of her feats for ECC and Tiny assuring Babe in perfect English that he was keeping her name before the public back in her hometown.

"I can see you're getting along pretty well here, Babe. That was a beautiful toss."

Babe made a wry face. "I would do better if I hadn't stepped on pieces of broken bottle some fool left in the bathhouse the other day."

Tiny Scurlock looked shocked.

"It's true," McCombs said. "We had to take her to the doctor the other day. He dug around with a forceps and got the glass out—then cleaned out the wound. Must have been painful, but your gal here took it like a trooper."

"Aw, it wasn't that bad," Babe said. Unlike the girls at home who carried on when they got so much as a hang nail, she prided herself on her ability to withstand pain. "Though I gotta say that mercurochrome stung."

Later, as McCombs walked off to coach some of the other girls who were practicing, Babe turned her back on their doings to talk with Tiny. By now he had become not only her friend but her *de facto* publicity agent, writing features about her in the *Beaumont Journal* and wherever else he could place them.

"Tine, you really oughta start subscribing to the Dallas papers," Babe said. "They're printing lots of stories about me these days."

A less tolerant man might have taken offense at Babe's self-centered suggestion, coming as it did from one so young. But Tiny was more amused than anything. One had to make allowances for greatness.

"Maybe I will," he told Babe.

"Say Tine, are you gonna stay for the meet?"

"That's why I'm here."

"Good."

It would mean at least one person from Beaumont cheering her on. Although Babe made a practice of sending over half her salary of seventy-five dollar a month back to her parents, they still weren't able to attend. Work had again slowed down for Ole, who had recently been having shoulder problems.

By now Tiny was wilting from the heat; his white shirt soaked with perspiration. He wiped his brow with the handkerchief he pulled from his pants pocket.

"Let's go over to the shade," he suggested.

Tiny sat down heavily on a wooden bleacher seat beneath a tree. He had been meaning to go on a diet for the past twenty years.

"You know, Tine, I got a letter from the Kansas City Life Insurance Company asking me to play for their team."

Tiny tried to shield his eyes with his hand. He had left his sunglasses in his car yet again.

"But, Babe, you've only been playing for Employers Casualty a few months. You know you have to wait a year before you can switch teams."

"Yeah, but it's frustrating. Here's the thing Tiny, Kansas City is willing to pay me eighty dollars a month and a bonus of twenty-five dollars a victory in regular games and fifty dollars per victory in city tournament games and a hundred dollars a victory in national games." She rattled off the figures like an accountant. "Wouldn't I be a fool not to take that?"

"Well, I don't know. Wouldn't that make you a professional?"

"No, it's all been approved by the Western AAU. I checked." Babe had begun to take the economic aspect of her athletic career very seriously. It wasn't all fun and games; it was dollars and cents and contracts where you had to read all the small print no matter how boring it was. It was worse than English class.

"So, take it after you play a year for ECC."

"I will if McCombs don't pay me more."

Tiny knew Babe's family was poor and that she was sending money home to them. She had written to him that she had recently bought her mother a new Kenmore stove from Sears, paying for it on the installment plan. He also knew that she spent very little on herself. If she was becoming something of a hustler, it wasn't for her own sake.

The next day at the tournament, Babe ran, hurdled, and leaped into the sky, setting a U.S. record in the high jump. She also came in first in the baseball throw, shot put, and javelin, leading her track and field team to an easy victory. She felt she could have done better but given her foot injury, which still throbbed a bit, it was not a bad outcome. Anyhow, what was an ECC victory? She had bigger things in mind.

9

"WOULDN'T IT BE grand," McCombs mused as he gazed at the framed photo of his most current Golden Cyclones team hanging on the wall near his desk, "to present Babe as a one-woman team?" Besides being an All-American basketball player two years running, she was easily his best track and field athlete. And after studying the records of the women who would be her competitors on other teams, he figured that no one was likely to beat her in any number of events at the AAU Nationals, to be held in a few months at Northwestern University in Evanston, Illinois.

McCombs sat back in his swivel chair. A copy of the *Dallas Morning News* lay open to the sports section in front of him. He had noticed in the box scores that Babe Ruth had hit another home run, his fifteenth, and the season was still young.

McCombs picked up his fountain pen, tried for a few minutes to think of an alliterative moniker comparable to the Sultan of Swat for his Babe, and wrote them down one after another on a yellow legal pad. Texas Tornado? Battling Babe? Dallas Dynamite? None seemed exactly right. McCombs put down his pen. Let the myth makers sort that one out.

A day later, McCombs had his secretary summon Babe into his private office. She had been sitting at her desk in the department's main office where all the steno and typist girls sat, typing some insurance correspondence or other. When she walked into his office, she walked past paneled walls adorned with framed photos and trophies of successful ECC teams of the past. McCombs raised a beckoning hand, inviting Babe to sit down. Since it was during the workday, she was dressed in her usual work clothes: a home-sewn blue pinafore over a white blouse, white ankle socks, never stockings, scuffed oxfords. As usual, she wore not even a spot of makeup, and her neatly combed chestnut hair was as short as a boy's.

McCombs looked at Babe and thought: Plain Jane. He knew she was sending much of her salary home to her parents—she told him so, but couldn't she spend just a little more on herself? From the way she dressed, one would have thought he wasn't paying her generously, in fact more than many a head of household in these troubled times. If he hadn't known she would get ticked off at the idea, he would have suggested she buy some pretty clothes for herself and start wearing makeup, for God's sake. But he refrained.

"Don't kill the goose that lays the golden eggs," he reminded himself.

Babe slouched in her chair before him. She was hoping he wouldn't lecture her on some dumb mistake she might have made in her work. Typing correspondence and columns of figures all day was yawn inducing, and sometimes her mind drifted to bigger and better things.

"Now, Babe," McCombs began and told her of his idea of her being the sole representative of ECC at the upcoming AAU Nationals/Olympic tryouts. He presented the whole thing to her as carefully as he could, so she wouldn't feel too much pressure.

"That's a great idea," Babe said, now bolt upright in her chair. It was as if she were a radio, and someone had turned her on. "I'm your best track and field athlete, easy. I can beat anybody."

"I thought you might be a little startled by the idea."

"Ha! I love it."

Now the problem for McCombs would be breaking it to the rest of the athletes on the women's track and field team that they would not get the opportunity to compete at the AAU Nationals and therefore have no chance of competing at the Olympics.

This little problem didn't seem to have occurred to Babe. Although she was by now friendly with some of the girls on the team, as she saw it, she was by far the most gifted of them. Thus, she deserved every chance at glory she could get. Babe left the meeting with McCombs in a rapture, eager to tell her family and Tiny Scurlock the news.

McCombs called a Friday afternoon meeting with Babe's teammates in the company conference room. Already surprised to be meeting in such an important-looking room, the young women were not happy after McCombs announced his plans for Babe.

A talented sprinter named Mary Casey spoke up.

"But, Colonel, some of us could qualify for the Olympics if we had the chance," Mary said.

"I understand what you're saying, Mary," McCombs replied. "But look at it this way: having Babe as ECC's sole representative will be sure to generate enormous publicity for women's sports. That will benefit you all in the long run."

Based on their downcast expressions, this did not seem to mollify the group.

"Besides, it's only for this year's championship," McCombs added. "You can take part in the nationals next year."

The girls wondered if he thought them stupid. Everyone knew this was an Olympic year.

"Maybe Babe will bow out of some events if we tell her we want to compete," another athlete, a hurdler and long jumper named Clara Gunnison, suggested.

Mary Casey smirked.

"Babe is out for Babe," she said. "Fat chance she'd agree to that."

McCombs said nothing.

Clara reluctantly conceded that. So what could they do? They were ECC employees—clerks and typists—and McCombs could fire them at will. She and the other girls suspected that McCombs was not particularly concerned about publicizing women's sports. He wanted to publicize ECC, that was all.

Before ending the meeting, Colonel McCombs told them he was giving them all a raise, a "generous raise," he called it, of twenty-five cents an hour. That was nice, but missing the nationals wasn't. So they were stuck.

"Good luck at the nationals," a few of them told Babe before she departed for Evanston. But there was no warmth in their words.

"Thanks, gals," Babe said. She understood the girls' resentment of her and felt bad about it. But what was she supposed to do? Disappoint the boss?

10

AS A VOICE over the loudspeaker announced Babe as the sole representative from Employers Casualty Company, she ran onto the field waving her hands and grinning.

"Who is that tough cookie?" one young woman asked, an athlete from Connecticut. She was standing with her team, which had already been introduced to the crowd at the AAU Nationals.

"That's a girl?" Another athlete smirked. "I thought it was a boy."

"That's Babe Didrikson, from Texas," a tall, talented high jumper named Jean Shiley said. Jean hailed from Haverford, a wealthy suburb of Philadelphia. She had read about Babe in the newspapers. "She thinks she's the last Coke."

Now Babe addressed the gathered athletes.

"Ah'm gonna lick you all single-handed," she proclaimed, her East Texas drawl more pronounced than usual.

There were disbelieving murmurs from the crowd of athletes. Many of the girls came from families who prided themselves on their gentility, and it was considered in poor taste to promote oneself like Babe did.

"We'll see about her beating us all," Jean Shiley said. She hadn't taken the train all the way from Philadelphia to return home empty-handed.

AS BABE TOSSED and turned in her hotel bed that night, her stomach felt as if someone were tying it in a sailor's knot. Normally not one to complain about physical discomfort, she couldn't help but cry out.

Mrs. Henry Wood, the ECC "team mother" or chaperone who slept in the room's other twin bed and who had accompanied Babe on the train from Dallas, awakened.

"Dear me, what is the matter?" she asked, turning on the nightstand light and blinkingly gazing over at Babe.

"My stomach is killing me." Babe looked at her pleadingly, all bravado gone from her eyes.

Mrs. Wood knelt over Babe and felt her forehead, which didn't seem feverish. Then she put her hand on her stomach, which seemed to flop around beneath her palm.

"I hope you're not having an appendix attack." Mrs. Wood picked up the hotel room phone and was put through to the hotel doctor, who hurried over. He was a short, thin balding man who looked as if a strong wind would blow him over. He carefully examined Babe, who had by this time had recovered a little of her usual jauntiness.

"Will I live, Doc?" she asked.

"I was worried it was appendicitis," Mrs. Wood explained, somewhat embarrassed to have roused the man in the middle of the night. "My younger sister had that and nearly died when it ruptured."

"It's not appendicitis, it's just a case of excitement affecting the nerve center in her diaphragm," the doctor concluded.

"Well, that's a relief."

"Try to relax a little," the doctor said to Babe.

"I'll try, Doc." Though her stomach pain subsided, when she closed her eyes it was as if the starting gun had just sounded and she had to move, move, move. She didn't fall asleep until four. Then, a few hours later, Mrs. Wood didn't have the heart to wake her until the last possible moment. As it was, Babe had to switch into her sleek white track outfit in a cab, with Mrs. Wood holding a hotel blanket around her.

Babe had never seen so many reporters and photographers. They shadowed her every move, but she loved it. From the sawdust of the long jump pit to the javelin throw to the high jump to the hurdles, they went where she went. And these weren't your small-time reporters. These were sportswriters from the nation's most important papers. In addition to Tiny Scurlock and the usual friendly gang from East Texas, there was Arthur Daley of the *New York Times*, George Kirksy of the *United Press*, and Grantland Rice of the *New York Tribune*. Grantland "Granny" Rice was syndicated and with his elegant prose, the acknowledged dean of American sportswriters.

It was Tiny Scurlock himself who introduced her to Grantland Rice. He, Tiny, wasn't about to miss his protégé's appearance on the national stage, having driven from Beaumont to St. Louis and then taken the train from there to Chicago. But he knew how important Grantland Rice could be to Babe's future.

"Young lady, I've heard so much about you," Rice said in that Tennessee drawl of his, extending a hand.

Right away Babe decided she liked Grantland Rice. He was a courtly Southerner, a former Vanderbilt University athlete—a Commodore—of some renown. Best of all, Babe already knew that "Granny" as she soon started calling him, tended to paint athletes in heroic terms. It was he who had dubbed the great Notre Dame backfield the "Four Horsemen of the Apocalypse." Who knew what heroic language he would use to describe her?

Enthralled that Babe had entered the competition as a one-woman team, Rice asked her, "Babe, when you were a kid, was there anything you didn't play?"

"Yeah, dolls," she replied. That tickled him.

Racing from event to event, barely recovered from being winded, Babe won six of the ten events she entered that day. Some of her competitors complained that officials delayed the start of events for her, but the way Babe looked at it those were the breaks, kid. If you had the guts to compete in all these events, you should be given a little leeway.

Babe broke four world records in the span of an afternoon. She only tied Jean Shiley in the high jump, but in Babe's view that was because Shiley had an advantage over her; she was three inches taller. It gave Babe a special satisfaction to win against who she considered the high-toned girls. The girls. Her against them. The way they easily clustered around each other, gabbing and laughing, reminded her of back in high school. They had friends and probably boyfriends, but she had trophies and world records. And someday, she hoped soon, she would have moolah, enough moolah to put her family on Easy Street for good.

That night after her fabulous victory, Babe and Mrs. Wood and Colonel McCombs and Tiny Scurlock went out to celebrate at Benny's on the Loop, a ritzy Chicago restaurant. Everyone told her Chicago was the place to order steak, so she treated herself to a nice, juicy Delmonico. She hoped she was done for good with hamburger. Anyway, McCombs was picking up the tab.

"Here's to the Olympics," Babe toasted, clinking her fluted champagne glass against the champagne glasses of her older associates.

The champagne wasn't bad. Babe liked its dry, subtly sweet taste and the little buzz it gave her, but she knew it was too early to go whole hog on celebrating. That could wait until after Los Angeles.

For Jean Shiley, the long train ride back to Philadelphia was hardly a celebration, for she had wanted to win the high jump outright. But as Jean nibbled on a package of crackers she had purchased in the dining car, she guessed she could live with a tie for now. It would be only a month or so until she would be competing in the Los Angeles Olympics.

11

"OH GOD, HERE she comes again," Evelyn Hall said to her teammate Rose Johnson on the Los Angeles Limited. The two were playing gin rummy and talking with the teammates facing them in the opposite seat: Jean Shiley and Lillian Copeland.

From behind them came the sound of running footsteps on plush carpet.

"Heavens," Rose said, rolling her eyes.

It was Babe Didrikson racing down the aisle yet again. As she passed the card players, she shouted out, "Watch for that Lillian. She cheats."

"What does she think she's doing?" Rose asked.

"She says she's training," Jean replied as Babe disappeared into the next car.

"That's nuts. No one trains on a train. Pun intended," Lillian said. Lillian was a sprinter out of Ohio State and no slouch herself when it came to training.

"Wouldn't it be awful if someone tripped her?" Rose suggested. "Next time I could just reach out my foot and . . ."

In fact, she did place her foot in the aisle but promptly withdrew it when Jean Shiley gave her a disapproving look. All the girls respected Jean, who was attending Temple University in Philadelphia on scholarship and whom they had voted team captain.

It was a long train ride to Los Angeles, even with planned stopovers in Denver and Albuquerque. The scenery, pleasant at first, had become numbingly monotonous, especially as the train rolled through the Great Plains, where trees were sparse and flat fields ran on to the horizon.

"There's Willa Cather's house," Rose Johnson cracked when she spied some farmstead out in the middle of nowhere. That morning, the girls had played a game of seeing who could spot grain silos first, but they had quickly tired of that and pulled out a deck of cards.

"Yesterday I saw Babe pull the pillows from behind the heads of some girls who were trying to nap," Lillian said. "She screamed at them to wake up."

"My god, what a brat," Evelyn Hall said, as she picked up a dealt card and placed it in her hand.

"And you know," Rose Johnson said, "she has her own sleeping compartment."

The rest of the athletes who comprised the 1932 U.S. Olympic team shared compartments.

"How'd she wangle that?" Lillian asked.

"I don't know," Evelyn Hall said. "But it's probably a good thing. Who'd want to sleep with her?"

In truth, there was something about Babe's presence that was an affront to them. If she was a girl, she was like no girl they had ever seen before. And realizing what they thought of her, Babe acted even more antagonistically.

"I heard she dumped ice water on Lidye and Louise in their compartment last night," Lillian said. "Didn't you hear them yelling?"

"Oh, is that what that was?" Rose said.

Lidye Pickett and Louise Stokes were two Negro members of the team who had both qualified for the relays back at the Nationals in Evanston. They were both considered nice, clean, modest girls, who usually kept to themselves. Who could possibly have a bone to pick with either of them?

"Really! Now that is awful," Evelyn said. Even though these white girls could hardly be considered radicals when it came to race, even to them Babe's actions toward Negroes, their own teammates for heaven's sakes, were beyond the pale.

Jean Shiley shook her head in disgust.

"I hear Mrs. Wood made her apologize to them, but still."

Jean thought a stronger measure should have been taken, but barring suspending Babe from the team, which wasn't going to happen, she didn't know what that would be. Well, at least she could be extra pleasant toward the Negro girls, in compensation for Babe's meanness.

By now Babe had grown tired of running through the Pullman cars.

Winded, she plunked down, legs sprawled out, next to her chaperone, Mrs. Wood, who had been contentedly reading the current issue of *McCall's.*

Babe had little interest in reading but sitting next to Mrs. Wood was where she felt she belonged on the train anyhow. Not with any of those girls.

Mrs. Wood looked up from *McCall's* and regarded her charge. She had some inkling of what Babe had been doing a few minutes ago because she had overheard a few girls complaining about Babe the day before.

"Bothering the other girls?" she asked. "That's not a good way to make friends."

"Aw Mrs. Woods, I'm bored," Babe said. "I gotta keep moving or my muscles will wilt."

"Your muscles aren't going to wilt on this short of a train ride. Why don't you play cards with the other girls?"

Babe looked idly at the Negro porter who was passing down the aisle, a serving tray balanced in his hand. That was what colored people should be doing, waiting on white people, not competing with them at the Olympics. At least that's what she had been told back in Beaumont. Not by her parents so much—who looked on blacks with befuddled incomprehension—as by just about everyone else in her neighborhood.

Babe dipped her head a bit and frowned. "Because they didn't ask me to play cards. Anyway, all those girls talk about is stupid stuff."

"They do?"

"Yeah, they're always talking about boys and clothes and stuff. I got no time for that nonsense." Babe folded her arms.

"Jean Smiley talks only about boys and clothes?"

Everyone knew Jean was a serious girl, a college girl.

But Babe did not reply. Instead, she pulled out a harmonica from her back pocket. She had bought the harmonica from a Beaumont Woolworth's back when she was a kid, with money she earned from picking the bad spots off figs at a fig packing plant. She blew a few bars from "Home on the Range."

Mrs. Wood frowned. "I'm glad you know how to play the harmonica so well but don't do it now. Some people are napping. And even if they weren't, not everyone in this car wants to hear your harmonica."

Honestly, Babe acted just like a child at times. One would have thought she had had no home training, but Mrs. Wood had met Babe's parents and thought highly of them as kind, hard-working immigrants who had made a good home for their children, so she knew that that wasn't the case.

Feeling abused, Babe put the harmonica away and sat staring out the window. Wasn't she allowed to do anything on this trip? And wasn't the scenery they were looking at "the Range"? If so, it didn't live up to its billing. She hadn't yet seen one crummy antelope.

Mrs. Wood regarded Babe's sullen profile. "Babe, there's more to life than athletics."

Babe honestly considered this. She turned to Mrs. Wood. "I wasn't born rich. I need to help my family by making a name for myself. That's all there is to it for me."

"I understand that. And helping your family is commendable. But promise me you'll try not to make enemies out of the rest of the girls. They're your teammates after all."

Babe frowned again. "Yeah, they're my *Olympic* teammates, but I'm not playing any team sports. They're not gonna help me. The only one who's gonna help me is me."

"But, Babe, don't you ever get lonely?"

Again, Babe regarded Mrs. Wood with skepticism. She genuinely liked her. But Mrs. Wood was a family friend of McCombs and his wife, a married lady who wore silk stockings and fancy hats with feathers in them and gloves and shoes that matched her outfit and who attended luncheons rather than simply ate lunch. There were some things Babe couldn't admit to her, like how tough she had had to be growing up on Doucette Street, like how lonely she *did* get and why. Best to make light of it. Feelings were silly anyway. Feelings got you into trouble, like what had happened between her and Enid. Not that that mattered in the long run. What mattered was how you performed.

"I'm too busy to get lonely, Mrs. Wood," Babe said. "You know I'm a busy bee; I can't stay still. Buzz buzz buzz."

"Well, at least stop running and hollering in the train for a while. And stop that buzzing. If one of the porters doesn't throw you off, I've a good mind to."

Babe laughed.

Mrs. Wood leaned over and picked up her massive taupe-colored handbag. From its depths, she pulled out a magazine.

"You might like this one," Mrs. Wood told Babe. "It's *Time*."

Babe read here and there in the magazine. Since it had a sports section, she thought it would be a fine thing to be written up in its pages. Or better yet be on the cover. She could see it now. "Babe Didrikson: America's Greatest Athlete." If this broad, Pauline Morton Sabin could do it, why not she?

Back a few cars, the girls had finished playing gin rummy. A late afternoon lassitude had set in, made even more soporific by the July heat, and conversation had largely ceased. Soon it would be time for supper in the dining car. There was that to look forward to.

12

"IS EVERYTHING IN this burg white?" Babe asked Mrs. Woods as she and the rest of the girls piled out of the bus that had taken them from the train station. Many of the houses and other buildings they passed on the way to their hotel had been white, stucco with red tile roofs in the Spanish colonial style. Now they stood gazing at the white archway that led to where the women's Olympic team would stay: the gleaming white Chapman Park Hotel on Wilshire Boulevard.

Three Negro porters came hustling out to unload the luggage.

"Guess not everything," Babe said as she regarded the porters, who chatted to each other as they retrieved the suitcases and trunks. "And these palm trees. We have palm trees in Texas, but I never seen this kind. Say, this place is ritzy."

She studied the sculpted flower beds of poppies, salvia, and daisies that led past the white hotel bungalows to the main building.

Babe had never seen a city like Los Angeles. The air seemed less heavy here, the light more intense, the shadows deeper. Unlike Beaumont and Dallas, creatures of the sultry South, the City of Angels seemed to preen in the sunshine like a movie star.

Reporters and photographers from Los Angeles press and radio outlets had been awaiting the team's arrival.

"Ah'm here to win every event I enter," Babe announced to them. Unfortunately for her and unlike at the Nationals, three events were the maximum any female Olympian was permitted to enter. It was a shame: Babe felt she could easily win at least five events, maybe six, given the opportunity.

"Some say you have the best coordination of any female athlete ever," one reporter said.

Babe grinned her crooked grin. There was something piratical about it.

"That's a powerful lot of language to use about one little Texas gal," she told the newsmen.

The gentlemen of the press loved Babe. While it was like pulling teeth to get most athletes to say anything other than the usual banalities, Babe was the opposite. In her folksiness, she reminded them of Will Rogers, another showman from the heartland.

"So, you don't foresee any major challenges at these Olympics?"

"There's always challenges," Babe replied. "But ah figure the Olympics will be a lot less taxing than the Nationals. You know, that's when ah had to compete in every single event, and ah won almost all of 'em."

After a few more questions, the reporters went off to file their stories. Babe turned to Mrs. Wood, who had patiently waited behind with her.

"So, when are we gonna see some movie stars?" Babe asked her. "I bet this place is practically crawlin' with movie stars." She gazed around her at the hotel grounds, as if expecting to spy a movie star behind every tree or bush.

"I've heard they can be found at the Zephyr Room," Mrs. Wood replied. "It's a lounge connected with this hotel. But we can't very well hunt them down in there. We've got to get ready for the Games."

"That's all right. I imagine they'll be plenty at the Olympics," agreed Babe agreed, as they walked to the hotel entrance. "Gary Cooper, Claudette Colbert, Clark Gable, you bet I'll get me some autographs. They'll get mine too, if they want it."

THE TEAM BUSES rolled down to Exposition Park and the Coliseum the next morning, and Babe got out and gaped for a minute. The stadium, which was not yet a decade old, dwarfed any other stadium she had ever seen, and she had seen a few. It had been built to be as grand, even grander than the Coliseum in Rome: a huge white oval with archways wide enough for chariots to go through.

Over the main entranceway, the words Los Angeles Memorial Coliseum were set in raised letters. Mrs. Wood told Babe it memorialized the veterans of the Great War. Below these words were the five interlocked circles of the Olympics. Above all that—you had to crane your neck and lean back and look up high—was a tower with a torch on top that jutted up into the clear California sky. Flags of the competing countries, flapping in the breeze, festooned the outer walls. Just looking at such magnificence, Babe could practically hear the trumpet fanfare that formally opened the games.

As Babe walked through the main archway with her teammates, she felt like one of the gladiators she had seen in the movies—*Ben Hur* or someone heroic like that. Though she would not be engaging in bloody combat with man nor beast, her challenges would be real enough.

She well knew that certain important people, high-ups like AAU president Avery Brundage, still doubted that women athletes should play any part in the Olympics. Women were the delicate sex, according to these men. Furthermore, they pointed out that the original Greek games did not permit women athletes, so why should they? Didn't matter if the first Olympics was held over two thousand years earlier, and women had come up in the world since then. Well, Babe would show all the naysayers that men couldn't hog all the glory. And she would make her family proud back in Beaumont.

PRIOR TO THE opening ceremonies, there was a meeting of all the competitors on the American team. During the meeting, they were reminded of the decorum required in representing their country.

"The eyes of the world will be upon you," a spokesman for Avery Brundage intoned.

After the speech, all the women were issued white jackets bearing the Olympic rings in an American crest, white skirts, white pumps, and silk stockings. Babe had never worn silk stockings before and regarded the pair in her hand with distaste. They felt slithery to her.

"Well, if I gotta, I gotta," she told herself.

Then, as she stood at attention in front of a crowd of tens of thousands during opening ceremonies, a male athlete holding aloft a flaming torch ran into the Coliseum to light the giant Olympic cauldron. As he did so, a stentorian voice proclaimed the Games officially open, and a flock of white doves rose into a cloudless California sky. Along with the other athletes, Babe followed the flight of the doves as they flew over the stadium and disappeared. Then Babe slipped out of her heels, which were pinching her feet.

COMPARED TO THE opening ceremonies, which seemed to drag on a bit, the actual events came as a relief to Babe. The first event was the javelin. On Babe's first toss, she threw the javelin 143 feet 4 inches, a new

Olympic and World record. This toss handily beat that of a larger German girl who had been the favorite. However, on her second toss, Babe's hand slipped off the javelin's cord handle, and she felt a sharp pain tear through her shoulder. Fortunately, the injury was nothing that would impede her in her track events.

Babe's second event was the 80-meter hurdles. She knew that the competition in this race would be keen. Evelyn Hall of Chicago had won the AAU outdoors title in 1930 and the indoors 40-meters title in 1931. Babe had narrowly beaten Hall in the AAU Nationals this past spring and knew she would have to run her absolute best to beat her again. At the halfway mark, Babe was ahead, but Evelyn gained ground during the last 10 meters. Babe flung her arms out at the finish line, indicating she thought she had finished first. It was a photo finish, impossible to judge with the naked eye. Even after reviewing the film over and over, the judges had a difficult time deciding who had won. But they finally awarded Babe the gold. She just looked so confident.

But Evelyn Hall believed she had won the event.

"It pays to play to the reporters," she bitterly concluded.

"Those judges are so dumb," Babe thought. "Just wave your arms around and they'll give it to you." Anyway, she felt she had probably won the event.

The third event was the high jump. Babe and Jean Shiley matched each other's jumps, one jump after the other. Finally, both Jean and Babe tied at 5 feet 5 ¼ inches, a new world record. But the judges awarded Jean a gold medal and Babe a silver because Babe's unorthodox jumping style, the Western roll, had never been used in Olympic competition.

The women on the US team crowded around Jean Shiley as the results were announced.

"Way to go, Jean!" they told her. "You really put that loudmouth in her place."

For her part, Jean breathed easier. Now she would have gold to take with her on the long journey back to Philadelphia.

The gentlemen of the press, however, felt differently about Babe winding up with silver.

"Babe, you got a raw deal," Grantland Rice assured her after the competition, having worked his way down from the press box to tell her that. "You used the same technique before in the AAU Nationals. They should have given you a gold too."

Hands on hips, frowning, Babe stared down at the ground. From the aggrieved look on her face, one would have thought she had finished dead last. In her book, finishing second was last.

"Well, they didn't, Granny."

Grantland put a hand on her shoulder. Hoping to cheer her up, he asked, "How about coming out and playing golf with me and the boys?"

Babe looked up at Grantland. It was funny how she got along with some men, older men, better than women.

"When?" Babe asked, squinting into the bright California sun.

"How about tomorrow?"

13

"YOU KNOW I haven't played but a little golf," Babe told Grantland Rice as they stood together at the first tee at Brentwood Country Club in West Los Angeles. Like most days in southern California, it was a beautiful day for golf, with a bright morning sky and fresh ocean breezes rolling in off the Pacific. Unlike the almost constant humidity of the deep South, where houses and lawns and trees seemed to meld and blur into one enervating mass, everything in Los Angeles appeared sharp and vivid: distinctly itself.

"Are you sure you haven't played much?" Grantland asked.

While Grantland looked dapper, decked out in a Scottish golfing outfit, complete with dark blue knickers, crisp white shirt, and a blue bow tie, Babe wore a yellow cotton top and a blue wrap-around skirt she had bought for the Olympics. She had had to run out and buy golf shoes yesterday evening.

"You told me you could drive the ball 250 yards."

"I can. That's the amazing thing about it all." Babe grinned. "I mean without really practicing the game." The morning sun glinted in her eyes, causing her to squint. Next time she would remember to bring a golf cap.

"I know a hustler when I see one," Grantland told himself. But from what he had seen at the Olympics a few days ago, Babe just might have enough talent to back up her boasts about golf.

Babe and Grantland's three competitors soon appeared: Westbrook Pegler, a rabble-rousing columnist for the *Chicago Tribune*, Braven Dyer of the *Los Angeles Times*, who religiously covered the USC Trojans, and a tall, swarthy fellow named Paul Gallico, who wrote for the *New York Daily News*. It was Gallico who most stood out to Babe since she had read some of his columns in the *Daily News*. Now she noticed him studying her through his round, black-rimmed glasses.

"Fellas, I've got a hunch this gal might be just as good at golf as she is in other sports," Grantland said as he introduced Babe to the other writers.

All three men greeted Babe affably, but inwardly Gallico was skeptical. He approved only of female participation in the so-called "beautiful sports"—which to him were riding, skating, archery, shooting . . . sports in which they didn't break a sweat and thus appear unladylike. Now he was looking down at Babe. She had no curves whatsoever, breasts like bitter, unripe plums, taut muscles, a too-prominent jaw, thin lips; a homespun manner that struck him as coarse. He couldn't see why his friend Grantland had taken such a shine to the girl.

"Would you look at that!" Grantland suddenly exclaimed.

Babe's opening tee shot had soared straight down the middle of the fairway and landed 240 yards away.

While Dyer and Pegler were mildly appreciative, Gallico was mute. He became somewhat relieved, however, as play continued and it became obvious that Babe was not a professional golfer. Though her drives went a long way, as long as most male golfers, her iron shots were often off-target, and her putting was inconsistent. Nonetheless, word of how good she was for a girl spread throughout the course and clubhouse. By the time the group reached the twelfth hole, a crowd of people had formed to watch the phenom.

On the seventeenth hole, Babe and Grantland pulled even with Gallico and the others. As Grantland and Babe both hit shots into the bunker, Gallico reached the green with his second shot. Smiling broadly, he thought he had the match won. Sizing up the situation, Babe and Grantland huddled, conferring in whispers. It was Babe who devised the plan.

"Hey, Paul," she said turning to Gallico, "race you to the green?"

"Sure, Babe. Here Granny, hold my glasses."

With his long legs, Paul Gallico was confident he could outrun her. But in only moderately good shape, he was in no condition to challenge a world-class athlete of either sex. The faster he ran, the faster Babe ran ahead of him, effortlessly, like one of those stuffed rabbit lures at dog races. Then when he was obviously out of gas, she slowed down, tauntingly keeping two feet in front of him.

As Gallico reached the green, his knees buckled. He collapsed onto the grass, sweating and panting. When he finally sat up, all four of his companions were looking down at him.

"Too much for you, eh Paul?" Grantland Rice observed.

"Looks like the little girl got your goat." Pegler chuckled.

Babe offered Paul a hand, but Paul did not take it. Frowning, he rolled over, got to his feet, bits of grass clinging to his clothing, took his glasses from Granny, and went on to four putt the hole. Babe and Grantland Rice won the hole and the match. The crowd that had gathered applauded Babe, and she waved to them in appreciation.

Afterward Grantland took her aside, put a hand on her shoulder.

"If you worked at it, you could be a championship golfer," he told her. He had already decided to write up the match in his next syndicated column, complete with Paul's collapse. It would make a most amusing column, a veritable David and Goliath story, with Babe playing the part of David.

As the four men headed back to the clubhouse, Babe made her good-byes and scurried toward the women's dressing area.

"Maybe Babe should join us in the men's locker room," Gallico blurted to Grantland.

Grantland stopped short, looked at Paul through narrowed eyes. "What do you mean?"

"I mean, she's more boy than girl."

"She's a great girl, Paul" he said, frowning. There was a warning in his tone.

Gallico said nothing. But he was already planning a little story he would himself write about Miss Babe Didrikson.

14

BABE WAVED TO the crowd that had come out to welcome her home to Beaumont as she perched on the top of the back seat of the fire captain's red Packard. She had to watch when the Packard stopped or made a turn. She didn't want to lose her balance and go pitching off the seat into the blanket of roses. That would not have been dignified. As the Beaumont High Marching Band played "The Washington Post" and other Sousa tunes, members of the current Royal Purples basketball team marched like praetorian guards at the side of the car. Lining the roadway, parents held up small children just so the kids could get a glimpse of the hometown girl who made good. Some held up hand-made signs saying things like "We Knew You Could Do It!" and "Beaumont's Babe!" and "Babe is the Best!"

"Well, stars and bars, there's Candace Dilford!" Babe exclaimed as she spotted her former classmate in the crowd. Accompanying Candace was a dark-haired man holding up a little girl with strawberry blonde hair. As Babe grinned and waved back at Candace and what she presumed was her husband and daughter, she reflected that her classmate must have gotten over the fact that Babe never let her wave her hair.

That noon, during the rooftop luncheon, Babe sat as the guest of honor at the head table. Facing the crowd was a large white banner that proclaimed in gold script "Babe Didrikson, World's Greatest Woman Athlete." Most of the people were Beaumont bigwigs and leaders of the Kiwanis Club whom Babe had never met, but Ole sat to her left, stoically uncomfortable in his blue serge suit, while to her right, Hannah smiled and waved a pretty fan that Babe had had Clark Gable autograph. Dora, her husband Tom, Ole Jr, Esther Nancy, Lillie and the rest sat at a table near the front of the room. None of the Didriksen siblings were used to being served by white-jacketed waiters, and though they were sitting under umbrellas, they all seemed to shrink into their store-bought new clothes in the August heat.

Speaker after speaker went up to the microphone and sang Babe's praises as well as those of Beaumont—a city they said was best exemplified by Babe's "can do" spirit. Next, Babe's former teammates from the Miss Royal Purples awarded her a silver cup engraved with the words: *We Knew Her When.* As culmination of the event, the mayor awarded Babe the Key to the City.

Then it was Babe's turn to come to the microphone. The sight of so many people, so many bigwigs, hanging on her every word daunted her in a way that competing in Olympic events hadn't. This wasn't a time for tall tales and boasts. Besides, everyone was hot as Hades.

"I'm tickled to be back home. Thank you," she said and sat back down.

"Well, that was nice and short," Ole told her afterward.

As Babe cut into her barbecued spareribs, she tried to imagine what the catty high school girls were thinking now. Would they be sorry they had treated her so poorly? She savored remembering the evening at the movie theater with Enid Adams, where Enid sprung her boyfriend Carter on her. She had only a vague recollection of putting the frog's leg in Enid's purse, but she could easily picture Enid and her crowd at the luncheon now, eating crow.

IN FACT, ENID Adams, now Mrs. Enid Elder, knew all about the parade and luncheon that had been planned in Babe's honor. Knowing about it was unavoidable as the newspapers had been full of her Olympic success and its aftermath. Even Carter had mentioned it.

"I see they're having a parade for that Babe Didrikson," he said a few days before. "Wish I could go, but I don't want to miss accounting class."

"But you barely knew her." The fact that Carter mentioned Babe struck Enid as disloyal, though she wasn't really sure why. It wasn't like he would ever be romantically interested in such a person. Who would be?

"I know, but now she's a big deal . . . an Olympic gold medalist and all . . ."

Carter could barely remember the evening at the movies that stood out so powerfully in Babe's imagination. But what if Babe Didrikson became an important figure in the Texas scene? Well, if he ran into Babe, he could always tell her he had attended the parade. It was a white lie, and who would know? He would read about the parade in the paper.

Unlike her husband, Enid had no wish to attend the parade. While it was taking place and her husband was attending class, she was attempting to spoon pureed carrots into the unwilling mouth of her seven-month-old, little Carter. She and Carter Sr. had gotten married right out of high school. Truth be told, they had had to get married and rather hastily, one of the damned rubbers having broken. But it wasn't a catastrophe: Carter could still attend Lamar College, maybe transferring to Baylor or Texas Tech later. His dad had agreed to pay for his education, and things would be all right.

Still, Enid did sometimes think about Babe, the boyish girl who had once put a frog's leg in her pocketbook. Enid felt certain that Babe had once been attracted to her. What if she had taken pity on Babe and had sex with her, the way she had with Carter, rather uncomfortably, in the back seat of his Chevy while they were still high school students? What could a girl do for you that a man couldn't? Enid was curious about sex between women. Evidently, from what she had secretly gleaned from library books, some women actually preferred sex with other women. But the Bible said it was wrong and evil, so she *would* never, *could* never take the risk of finding out.

Meanwhile, Carter was off attending college while she was home dipping diapers. It seemed like she and Carter saw so little of each other these days! Worse yet, he seemed to have (temporarily she hoped) lost interest in her romantically now that she was a mother.

"Dammit, Cartie. Eat these carrots."

The area around her son's mouth had become an orange mass dribbling lava-like down his chin. There was even a splotch of mashed carrot on his forehead where he had touched his face with a tiny fist. The spot of carrot stood out like a birth mark beneath one blond curl.

Gazing at her son in frustration, Enid suddenly saw everything quite clearly. She would have to give up on carrots and switch to something more pleasing to his taste, like apples.

15

BACK IN HIS apartment overlooking Washington Square in New York City, Paul Gallico had also been thinking about Babe. He didn't want to write a newspaper column forever; he had ambitions to become a bona fide fiction writer—someone on the order of Ernest Hemingway, only more urbane, better educated. He had met Hemingway not long ago at the bar in the Plaza Hotel. The author was all he had imagined—big, gruff, stoic, but gracious all the same as he put aside his martini for a moment to autograph Paul's first edition of *A Farewell to Arms*. Hadn't Hemingway started his career as a journalist, writing dispatches for the *Toronto Star*? And Hemingway didn't even have the benefit of a college education. If Hemingway could switch to fiction, so could he.

Now, as Paul sat before his trusty Underwood, he knew he had a first-rate idea for a short story, one which the magazines would certainly be interested in. The story would be about a female track and field star by the name of Honey Hadwell. Honey would be a tough talking, hard scrabble boy-girl from the wrong side of the tracks in Texas. The boys wouldn't know what to make of her; neither would the girls. More than one of them would refer to Honey as "it." One character, a handsome blond athlete from Poland named Mike Suss, would feign romantic interest in Honey because he wanted her to give him some pointers on how to throw a javelin. Honey would fall for Mike. But once she had given him the pointers, enabling him to easily win the men's javelin competition, he would jilt her. Honey would, in turn, win the women's javelin throw by imagining thrusting the javelin through Mike's betraying heart. Later, overcome by self-loathing, she would hit herself in the face, tear her hair, and bemoan her failure to land a boyfriend. After all, athletic success for a woman was poor compensation for being unattractive to men.

After Paul Gallico finished a rough draft of the story, he sat back in his chair and took a satisfying drag on his cherrywood pipe. Dusk was falling now over Washington Square and the streetlights were winking on. It had been a satisfying workday for Paul who now looked forward to a late dinner out with his wife. Once he completed the final draft, he would submit the story to *Vanity Fair*. He was friends with the fiction editor and felt sure they would publish it.

16

"C'MON YOU STUBBORN son of a gun!"

It was a sultry summer Sunday afternoon in Grand Rapids, Michigan, and Babe Didrikson, clad in a gray flannel baseball uniform, was sitting on a donkey, trying to get the reluctant beast to walk or even trot to first base. She was the headliner of a barnstorming baseball team called the House of David. Their gimmick was that all the players, all the men, wore Hebrew-type full-length beards. And as a stunt today, Babe was riding a donkey to get from base to base.

Babe was the star attraction. Barnstorming with the House of David wasn't glamorous, it wasn't dignified, but people would still fork over the "do-re-mi," as Babe often called money, to see the World's Greatest Female Athlete in the flesh.

It wasn't like Babe had much choice of athletic pursuits. There had been exhibitions she put on in a few theaters—running on a treadmill, throwing a few pitches, that kind of thing. There had been a few movie offers, all of which had failed to materialize. Except for barnstorming, there were few other options for female athletes to earn big bucks. Babe had tried tennis in hopes of becoming another Helen Wills Moody. But her shoulder still hurt from when she injured it while throwing the javelin during the Olympics, making serving excruciatingly.

At Grantland Rice's urging, Babe had practiced golf diligently a few months ago when staying in Los Angeles.

"You should get some lessons from Stan Kertes," Granny had said.

Kertes was an excellent young golf instructor at the Riviera Country Club who helped celebrities like Bing Crosby and Bob Hope with their games. Seeing Babe's raw talent, Stan had worked hard with her and watched as she practiced from morning to night, until her hands bled and had to be bandaged from hitting the ball.

But then Babe's money got low, so she had to stop practicing golf all day and find some sort of gainful employment. She needed the money more than ever now that her father Ole needed an operation to remove a tumor from his lung. So, Babe had signed a contract with the House of David. She was a little wary of dealing with Jews, having heard stories about their supposed penny-pinching ways and ruthlessness in business. But their owner, Judge A.T. Dewhirst, had been reassuring.

"Don't let our name fool you," Dewhirst had told Babe. "We're all God-fearing, Bible-reading Christians, although of a somewhat different stripe from your standard denominations."

Though she wasn't a Bible thumper herself, this was reassuring to Babe. So was the fact that the great Grover Cleveland Alexander had pitched with the team the year before. Though "Old Pete" was by now a washed up drunk, he still had drawing power.

Just as Babe and the donkey, who finally broke into a trot, reached the first base bag, at about the same time as the ball, a large woman in a hydrangea-print dress rose from her seat and shouted out to Babe from the first base stands.

"Hey, Babe, where are *your* whiskers?"

Babe, brushing aside a swarm of gnats that had gotten near her eyes, turned to look at the woman who had addressed her. There she was, standing mountainous against the other fans.

"Ah'm sittin' on 'em lady, same as you are," Babe shouted back.

The crowd gasped, then roared. No matter what you thought about Babe's boyish looks, you had to admit she had a quick mouth. A moment later, as if to punctuate the exchange between player and fan, the donkey made a deposit just north of the first base bag. Again, the crowd roared.

Looking down at the mound of steaming manure, Babe, for once, was struck speechless.

"Ah guess Ah'm a long way from the Coliseum," she told herself.

A FEW DAYS later, Babe spoke with her family, including brother Ole Jr., when she made a long-distance call home to Beaumont. After filling Babe in on the condition of their father, who was slowly recovering from his operation, Ole Jr. went on to other matters.

"A buddy of mine told me there's a story about you in this magazine, *Vanity Fair*," he said.

"That so?"

Her curiosity aroused, Babe plunked down thirty-five cents and bought a copy of *Vanity Fair* from the hotel newsstand. The story was written by none other than her old golfing buddy, Paul Gallico. What she read that night as she lay in bed made her sick to her stomach.

It was obvious that his story "Honey" was based on her. You would have had to be an idiot not to realize that. There was even a glossy photo of her on the facing page. Here this stoop-shouldered weakling who she had run roughshod over at golf, this four-eyed Gallico was claiming that she, or a raw-boned Texas girl uncomfortably like her, had fallen for some boy at the Olympic Games and then had been miserable when he tossed her aside. Miserable—she wondered where he had pulled that one out of. Babe prided herself on having not once flirted with any male athlete and had paid scant attention to the females, except to crush them in competition.

"That bastard is still mad at me for whipping him that day at Brentwood," she told herself. This thought was slight consolation.

As she lay in bed that night, unable to sleep, she wondered if people really did think of her as some "dried up little bitch" with "cold eyes" and a "pale slit for a mouth," as Gallico had described Honey. More horrifying yet, did some people think of her as a "lez"? That word had also been bandied about in the story. Even though she had heard such descriptions of herself on and off throughout her life, from classmates, from teammates, from so-called fans, they were only whisperings, while *Vanity Fair* was a national magazine. How many people would read this story and take it as the god's honest truth?

And she wasn't a "lez," was she? True, she had had a crush on Enid Adams, but that didn't mean anything. Lots of girls had special friends, didn't they? Whatever was the case, as she lay sleepless and the hours ticked by, she reluctantly concluded that she would have to change her act, maybe fancy herself up just a little bit. She was making good money playing for the House of David this summer, enough to pay for her father's operation. But barnstorming on the back of a donkey wasn't really a proper long-term occupation for her. When the barnstorming season ended, which was soon, she decided she would return to Dallas, work again for the ECC at her old, modest salary of three hundred dollars a month—she knew McCombs would be glad to have her back—and use all her free time to practice the more ladylike sport of golf.

17

"COME ON, BABY, baby, baby," Babe muttered. The twentieth of twenty putts glided along the plush gray carpet in McCombs' office and went toward a makeshift hole, actually a piece of white paper cut into a circle and taped to the carpet.

"Yes!" It was lunch hour at Employers Casualty Company back in Dallas, and Babe was doing what she did during virtually all of her off-hours—practicing golf.

McCombs sat back in his padded chair and took a puff on his cigar.

"Well, Babe, I do think you are going to give those blue bloods their comeuppance," he said.

Though as a company man he had a healthy respect for the powers that be, he knew that a certain faction of the Texas women's golf association had tried to prevent Babe from entering the Amateur Championship. This faction had even gone so far as to question her membership in the Beaumont Country Club, as a player had to be a country club member to participate. They had been forced to accept her application only after she was found to be, surprisingly, a dues-paying member. McCombs had paid for her membership.

"I sure hope so, Colonel," Babe said. "After what them rich dames put me through with that country club membership."

Babe had been putting herself through a rigorous routine. From Monday through Friday, she got up with the chickens, headed to a driving range in her beat-up jalopy, and hit drives for three hours before work. Then when work let out, she drove out to the Dallas Country Club and took a one-hour lesson from its resident pro, George Aulbach. After that, she'd hit balls until sundown, until her hands blistered and bled. She'd tape her hands and there'd be blood on the tape. But with each swing of the golf club, she'd feel herself getting closer to her goal: that ideal state where she knew she was unbeatable. If she could truly do what she thought she could, it would be well worth the bloody and stinging hands. Glory would rain down on her, she knew it.

Another putt and another ball "into" the white paper. This was getting too easy. If only the McComb's office were bigger, say the size of a green.

"Ah, Colonel, do you mind if I play a bit more?" Babe asked.

"Actually, I'm heading out to lunch now myself, Babe, so the office is yours."

With that, McCombs rose, took his jacket from a stand, placed his fedora on his balding head and went out, shutting the door behind him.

With that, Babe walked over to the Colonel's desk and hit a long putt from that angle.

"That a baby," she cackled as the ball went into the "cup" once more.

She had already eaten her lunch, a peanut butter and jelly sandwich she had brought from home.

18

FORT WORTH NATIVE Bertha Bowen had always been the unaffected, fun-loving type. Even after she married R.L, a wealthy power company executive, she did not put on airs. Those in her social set could be such bores sometimes. As if they had a pedigree that set them apart from the rank and file. When it came right down to it, Bertha was honest enough to admit that they, just about all Texans, were nouveau riche when compared to the famous old families of the East—the Lodges and the Biddles and the Roosevelts, for instance. But don't mention FDR around these parts unless you meant to vilify the man.

Now Bertha and her husband were attending a cocktail party in Houston, preliminary to the opening of the 1935 Women's Texas Amateur Championship. Bertha, who sat on the board of the group that managed women's golf in Texas, was holding a gimlet and listening to one of Texas's best lady golfers, Peggy Chandler, hold forth. Peggy was a tall, slender brunette with porcelain features and impeccable taste in clothing and coiffure. She too came from money, had married even more money, and was always announced on the circuit as Mrs. Dan Chandler, never Peggy Chandler.

"We really don't need any truck driver's daughters in our tournament," Peggy was saying, martini glass in one impeccably manicured hand. A diamond big enough to put your eye out blazed on her ring finger. Her husband Dan stood by her side, content for the moment, to let his beautiful and accomplished wife do the talking.

Bertha Bowen knew exactly who Peggy was talking about. She also knew that Peggy was one of those who had attempted to deny Babe entrance to the tournament.

"I believe Babe Didrikson's father is a cabinet maker, not a truck driver," Bertha said. "If that's who you're talking about." But her cheery manner served to offset the distinct breath of challenge in her words.

Truth be told, Bertha had met Babe recently at the Fort Worth Women's Invitational, which was Babe's first golf tournament, and they had hit it off. It seemed that whatever Babe liked to do, she and R.L. also liked: golf, billiards, fishing. The Bowens, who had lost their infant son Bobby in 1930, were delighted to share their life with an energetic young person, so they invited Babe to stay with them for a few weeks. Unlike those who cringed at the idea of Babe joining the women's amateur golf circuit, Bertha felt the opposite. After listening to the young woman's salty tales of growing up in Beaumont and of barnstorming with the House of David, she felt if anyone could breathe a breath of fresh air into the stale swank of women's golf in Texas, Babe could.

There was an awkward silence as Peggy Chandler studied Bertha the way a boxer studies an opponent for flaws in technique. The woman was undeniably well-bred, forthright, and good-hearted. Peggy couldn't help respecting Bertha, even if she did think her misguided, like some of the other wealthy Texans who had a soft spot for that bleeding heart, FDR.

"Oh, Bertha, always out for the underdog," Peggy said, as if pointing out a character flaw. She really couldn't say something truly cutting to Bertha, as she and R.L., who was off near the bar jawboning another fellow, were fully the social equals of the Chandlers.

"Why not?" Bertha replied. "I believe in talent, wherever it comes from."

"Do you know Babe?"

"I met her at the Women's Invitational."

"Then you know how she comports herself." With these words, Peggy knew she risked being accused of snobbery, but she didn't care. She truly believed in the refined style of living—some might call it aristocratic—that wealth and social status made possible. Wasn't that what society, especially Southern society, was all about?

"How do *you* think Babe comports herself?" Bertha asked Peggy.

"She's crass, like some sort of fish wife."

Bertha sipped her gimlet and smiled.

"Comports." She repeated the word as if underling its pretentiousness. It was funny how people could interpret behavior so differently. The free-spirited ways that Peggy thought of as crass had charmed Bertha. Unlike most of the women in her social circle, she didn't give a fig for convention. Not much before and not at all after her baby son Bobby died. Such things as social status took on a whole new meaning, or rather lack of meaning, after she witnessed the boy turning blue and struggling to breathe in his tiny hospital bed. "Defective heart," they called it. "Not fully formed."

All that the doctors could do for him had been done. No avail. He died less than a week after he was born. Their only child. From that heart-wrenching experience, Bertha Bowen had come to the distinct and certain realization that suffering was for everyone, from the top of society on down. If some people hadn't realized that sad fact yet, they most certainly would.

"I have a story about Babe," Bertha announced. "When reporters asked Babe how she managed to hit the ball so far, she turned to them and said, 'Ah just loosen my girdle and let it fly.' Isn't that clever?"

"Yes, that is kind of cute," Peggy agreed. "Cute" was one of her favorite terms, often used to refer to babies, small dogs, and those in her social circle who thought they had fashion sense but hadn't.

"Oh, Babe is a little rough around the edges. Lord knows she hasn't had the social advantages we've had. But she's young yet. And oh, that drive of hers. Two-hundred-and-fifty yards, on average." Bertha looked heavenward in rapture, knowing full well this expression would tick Peggy off.

What could Peggy say? She didn't enjoy being reminded of Babe's awesome drive, and the tournament was set to begin tomorrow. But long drives or no, she was confident that she could beat the boy-girl upstart, the carpenter's daughter from the wrong side of the tracks in Beaumont. Although Peggy took great pains to appear poised and polished, beneath her Playtex girdle, she was as fierce a competitor as anyone in the game. A real killer.

19

"ISN'T IT FUNNY the way all these society dames play under their husbands' names?" Babe mused as she stood looking out over the River Oaks Country Club course.

And here she was, just good ole Mildred Ella "Babe" Didrikson from Doucette Street in Beaumont, playing at the fancy River Oaks in Houston. Babe thought back to Paul Gallico's story. She knew that others were saying similar things about her; that she was too tough, not ladylike enough to be a proper "lady" athlete, and she was tired of hearing these things. It would be nice to have the protection of a man, to fit in that way. In truth, a man, a boyfriend, would be a shield for her.

The River Oaks course was wet from showers early that Saturday morning in April 1935, making the green expanses look crystalline as the sun burned off the dew. Droplets of rain dripped from tree branches, and rainwater pooled in low places, but Babe knew it would get steamy soon. She and this Mrs. Dan Chandler broad would play eighteen holes in the morning and eighteen in the afternoon. Fair enough; it would be a true test of each golfers' stamina as well as her skill.

Before they began, they posed for a photograph. Peggy Chandler looked as glamorous as ever in the photo, not a hair out of place, elegant in a blue short-sleeve top and crisp white skirt. The lines of her body and clothing flowed together as cleanly as those of a model out of *Vogue*. You could tell she was used to posing for photographers. Babe didn't look nearly so well-put-together, with her hair frizzy from the damp weather, her striped shirt a bit wrinkled, and her socks sagging like flags on a breezeless day.

Babe knew she wasn't nearly as stylish as Peggy. Still, she didn't appreciate the way Peggy took her arm for the photo, proprietarily, the way you would take the arm of a child who needed guidance. It was if Peggy knew all sorts of worldly things that Babe didn't. But there was nothing Babe could do about Peggy's condescension except tee off.

Babe started off fast, making an eagle on the first hole while Peggy bogeyed. Babe's lead held up throughout much of the morning.

"This gal ain't so great," Babe told herself.

But at the fourteenth hole, Babe began to lose her touch. Her long drives headed for bunkers, and her putts fell short or long. Peggy won six consecutive holes. By lunch Peggy was one hole ahead and breathing a little easier. At lunch she told herself, "Babe ain't the only one who can loosen her girdle and let it fly."

But that afternoon, as the Texas sun beat down onto the heads of the golfers, sapping their stamina, Babe came roaring back. Through sheer strength and skill, she managed to correct for her errant drives, and her putting became authoritative. She traded winning a couple of holes with Peggy and then she won the next two holes, tying the match.

Then Babe hit an errant shot that splashed into a tire rut outside the golf course on the back end of the green. Peggy hit her third ball a few feet from the cup; a short putt from winning the hole.

Now Babe would have to use all her powers of concentration. Here she was in a muddy rut, not even on the golf course with Peggy. How humiliating was that?

"Keep your head, girl," she told herself.

Grabbing a sand wedge given to her by none other than Stan Kertes, she followed her instructors' advice to keep nearly all her weight on her left foot. She adjusted her grip and focused on the small white orb before her, now a pearl precious beyond measure. Then she swung.

The ball leaped out of the muddy water and headed resolutely toward the cup. As it glided along the soft, still sparkling grass, there was a hushed silence. It rolled close, closer to the cup and dropped in with a plop. No paper "cup" this time. All the practice had paid off. As the gallery roared and swarmed Babe, one fan was so overcome with excitement that he accidentally knocking her into the puddle she had swung from.

"Watch it buddy!" Babe told the young man, but she was not angry, not now. Uttering a string of apologies, the young man abashedly helped her up. Babe had made an eagle three and was now one stroke ahead.

Bertha Bowen watched the whole thing from the gallery, Babe matching Peggy on the seventeenth hole and then winning the eighteenth.

"Yee-haw, that's my girl!" Bertha hollered, then guiltily, gleefully, cupped a hand over her mouth. Hollering her lungs out on a golf course was not something a lady usually did.

Stunned by the outcome, Peggy managed a forced smile and shook Babe's hand in congratulation. However, once inside the "nineteenth hole," her friends were hissing over their high balls.

"Can you believe that," a well-bred Dallas matron, the wife of a banker, was saying. "That low-class kid."

"I hear she's a lesbian," another woman said out loud.

"Lesbian? What's that?" a stout woman wearing a granite gray dress asked.

The woman who had made the pronouncement whispered something to her; the stout woman gaped.

"Now now," Peggy said. "Babe won fair and square."

Peggy felt comforted to have the support of her friends at such a low moment. As far as they all were concerned, Babe was a usurper. And Peggy believed as much as anyone that Babe did convey the wrong image of women athletes. Many people—even the better people—still looked upon women athletes as less than ladylike, Peggy knew, and a person like Babe was certainly not helping matters. She was beyond untutored; she was positively boyish—more male than female and with not a lick of style about her. There must be a way to keep her from ruining women's golf in Texas. They would simply have to find it.

20

TWO WEEKS AFTER Babe's win at the Texas Women's Amateur Championship, the United States Golfing Association sent a registered letter to her Dallas apartment. What she read made her weak at the knees: she had been banned from competing in the 1935 national championship. Her application to play in the Women's Southern Amateur had also been rejected. The reason? The Amateur Status Committee had ruled that since Babe had played professional baseball, basketball, and billiards, she could not compete as an amateur in golf.

Babe reread the letter with tears in her eyes, unwilling to believe its reasoning. True, she had taken money barnstorming and playing exhibition basketball and billiards, but that was only to scratch out a living and help her folks. She had never, not once, played professional golf. Actually, at this time there was scarcely a women's professional golf circuit in which to play. And the same entity that had cleared her to play in the Texas tournament was now telling her she couldn't play in any more amateur tournaments. It was all very confusing. More than confusing, it was infuriating.

"Those rich bitches," Babe said.

Peggy Chandler didn't fool her. Babe knew that behind her slick smile and friendly words, she despised her. Well, her parents might be poor, and she didn't dress the right way nor talk the right way, but she knew she had more talent than all those broads put together. Talent was the most important thing, wasn't it?

"Fuck them all," she said.

Bertha Bowen was sitting in the living room of her Fort Worth home playing solitaire when the phone rang.

It was Babe. Her voice quavered and broke as she told Bertha the contents of the registered letter.

"What I don't get is, BB, why did they clear me to play in the Texas Amateur at all?"

"It's because they didn't think you were going to win. You shocked them all."

Bertha knew Peggy and Dan were good friends with Joe Dey, the USGA's executive director. Obviously, Peggy, cheered on by her friends, had worked behind the scenes to get Babe barred. Bertha, too, knew people at the USGA. From comments she had heard, she knew they didn't want a girl like Babe playing against them. They were the self-styled Texas elite, most of them born to wealth. Their world would be turned upside down if a poor, scrappy nobody like Babe competed against them and won.

"We'll hire a lawyer to present your case," Bertha told Babe. In the meantime, she advised Babe to let matters unfold calmly. "Don't push it too hard. You don't want to seem like a troublemaker."

"Can I at least tell the press what happened?"

"Yes, you can do that," Bertha advised. "But don't cast aspersions on the USGA."

Babe didn't know what "aspersions" meant and said so.

"It means to badmouth."

"I'll try not to, but darn, BB, those people really get my goat."

"I know, I know. They get mine too."

Babe wondered about that. Here Bertha was rich and a perfect lady, yet she was so different from Peggy Chandler and the others, who were trying to cut her off at the knees. What made some people so good-hearted and others mean-spirited? Well, don't look a gift horse in the mouth. She was grateful for Bertha's kindness.

Babe wasted no time in contacting Tiny Scurlock, Grantland Rice, and other gentlemen of the press who happened to be her friends. She knew she already had their sympathy. Unlike the Mrs. So and So lady golfers, who were as dull as dishwater to interview, Babe, with her salty way of talking, realized she was a reporter's dream. After all, they had deadlines to meet and papers to sell. They were working stiffs, just like her.

After her conversation with Babe, Bertha called her lawyer. Together they agreed to launch a formal request for clarification of the USGA's ruling. Pending the result of that, they might take further action. That phone call taken care of, Bertha looked around the room, thinking. Her gaze fell on a framed Kodak photograph sitting on an end table, next to R.L.'s favorite chair. The photograph was of Babe, herself, and R.L. sitting on the front porch of the Bowen's Colorado cabin.

Bertha rose, picked up the photograph, and studied it. There was Babe wearing shorts and a sleeveless top, barefoot, sun bronzed and grinning—her chestnut hair no longer than a boy's. Thinking back,

Bertha remembered the day the photo was taken as one they had gone trout fishing. Bertha pondered the photograph. A young woman looking like Huckleberry Finn was all well and good when you were on vacation, or if you wanted to remain an outsider all your life, but not if you wanted to compete and thrive against the country club ladies of organized golf.

What Babe needed, Bertha thought, was a good shopping trip.

A week later, Bertha Bowen and Babe Didrikson went on a shopping expedition at Neiman Marcus in downtown Dallas. Babe had been to department stores before, but Neiman was a horse of a different color. It was where the wives of oil millionaires and the cream of Dallas society shopped for fashions otherwise available only in Paris, or so the store claimed. Great white pillars, marble counters, gleaming displays behind glass, impeccably dressed mannequins who seemed to be looking down their thin noses at the gross, sentient world. This was a place you could buy a mink coat, for gosh sake! Even the salesgirls, who couldn't be making all that much money, looked rich and haughty. Babe felt intimidated, but Bertha was her fairy godmother, only she was waving a charge plate instead of a wand.

Babe swore she would pay her back for her largesse, and Bertha had agreed, though she really had no intention of ever asking Babe to do so. She had money to burn.

"First of all," Bertha said, "let's get you some proper undergarments."

Babe blushed. By now she wore a bra, but it was a pathetic old thing; the elastic was shot. Even the dressing rooms were classy at Neiman Marcus, with deep plush carpeting and plenty of places for people to sit down while waiting. Babe looked at her scantily clothed self in a cubicle mirror. Though she was proud of her tautly muscular body and didn't really feel the need to embellish it, she obediently tried on the silk bras, slips, and even a garter belt that Bertha selected. She balked at trying on a girdle but did so at Bertha's urging. When she tried it on, it constricted her middle like a snake. When she told Bertha, who was sitting on a plush chair just outside the dressing room, just how the girdle felt, Bertha relented.

"Anyway, you have no stomach to speak of," she told Babe.

Next came the outerwear.

"How about three or four nice ensembles? You really need some outfits for the course."

Babe couldn't resist looking at the price tag on one of the skirts, a simple-looking tweed.

"This thing costs more than my weekly pay."

"Don't worry." Bertha smiled.

"Goddang, she must be loaded," Babe thought.

Next came a tailored linen suit and gloves, even a satin evening gown.

"I ain't never gonna wear this thing, so don't waste your money," Babe told Bertha after she emerged from the dressing room wearing the peach-colored gown. She was almost ashamed to come out of her cubicle wearing it. To her eyes, she looked as odd in the gown as her younger brother Bubba would have.

"Looks lovely. You'll see, it'll come in handy after you win more tournaments," Bertha assured her. "There will be a lot of celebrating to do."

Following Bertha's instructions, a smiling, terrier-like salesgirl whisked the gown away to add to the pile they had already accumulated.

Next, they stopped at a makeup counter and let the girl there apply foundation, powder, red lipstick, rouge, mascara, the works. Babe knew the pretty, blond cosmetics girl would have looked down her nose at her if she hadn't been with Bertha, whom she knew by name as Mrs. Bowen. But now as the girl dabbed on the makeup, she practically glowed with friendliness.

When the cosmetics girl was finished, the face that gazed out of the mirror at Babe looked brazen. Unnatural, like a mask or a painting of somebody else. But she did kind of like the way the red lipstick accented her lips. She knew she had very thin lips. "Snake lips," some of the kids used to call her back in school.

She turned to Bertha.

"This ain't really me, is it?" she asked.

"You look fine," Bertha told her.

Babe still looked dubious. The hurdles you had to jump. All this to play a little golf.

As if reading her mind, Bertha added, "Don't worry. Think of it as war paint, like the Indians used to put on before they went into battle. You can still sock 'em on the course. And when you're at home, you can leave off all this stuff."

That evening, Babe laid out her new purchases on her bed and gazed at them. Maybe she was a glutton for punishment, but she hadn't been able to resist reading Paul Gallico's column after she had won the Women's Texas Amateur. She half hoped her brilliant win against Peggy Chandler might earn his praise. She hoped wrong. The bastard had complimented Peggy more on her wardrobe than he had praised Babe on her win. In fact, he *hadn't* praised her on her win at all. He had claimed the reason for Babe's tenacity during the tournament was that she was just getting back at Peggy for dressing so much more stylishly than her.

Now Babe held a chic bottle green sweater to her breast and gazed in the full-length mirror on her closet door. All dolled up with clothes and makeup from Neiman Marcus. Now what could Gallico say about her?

21

AS BABE AND Bertha Bowen were shopping for clothes at Neiman Marcus, a powerfully built young man with slick dark hair stood dripping sweat onto his opponent, who lay prone on the canvas in a hot and smokey wrestling arena in Spokane, Washington. This was the first part of the match, anyhow, the part where arch-villain George Zaharias, dominated his opponent, launching himself against the ropes and boomeranging back, shoulder first against him, sending him flat on his back. Then, when George's opponent, in this case a blond-haired young Turk named Gentlemen Joe Marshall, lay as seemingly helpless as an upturned turtle, George kicked him in his stomach and stomped on his face. Of course, he pulled his blows. Wanted to make it look real but didn't want to kill the guy.

But the turning point of the match soon came. After being subjected to punishment that would have seemingly killed a lesser man, Gentleman Joe rose phoenix-like, as it were, from the ashes of almost certain defeat.

Now Joe had George Zaharias in a bear hug. A few moments later, he held George over his head and was tossing him to the canvas as if dumping a bale of hay.

George bounced on the canvas, sending sweat flying into the crowd nearest the ring. Every part of his body hurt. But it was all part of the game for the "Crying Greek from Cripple Creek," as George was known in the sporting news.

He had been born Theodore Vetoyanis, of Greek immigrant parents in Pueblo, Colorado. He too had grown up on a farm, which his parents didn't own but helped work. Times were hard. Sometimes all they had to eat was Greek bread dipped in olive oil. George and his father left off farm work and worked in the steel mill. Then George dropped out of high school and traveled around a bit by himself. In Chicago, he discovered professional wrestling when he noticed a poster for a bout between the great Polish wrestler, Stanislaus Zbyzsko, and Joe Stecher. Entranced by the professional grapplers, he took his grandfather's surname as his wrestling moniker, Zaharias having a zing to it that Vetoyanis didn't. Greeks were known for wrestling—in fact they had practically invented the sport—so it didn't hurt to have a Greek-sounding last name even in America. Z-Z-Zaharias!

As the match continued, George staggered to his feet, only to have his opponent kick him in the chest, knocking him once again to the canvas. The next time he rose, he grabbed Gentleman Joe by his thick right arm and swung him into the ropes. Joe bounced off the ropes and shoulder-slammed George once again onto his back. The back falls were rough. The skin stung from landing on the canvas so hard.

As George lay on his back gazing up into the overhead lights through a smokey haze, he reminded himself how much money he was making to take this punishment. It was a very good living: sometimes fifteen thousand dollars for a night in a larger city on the circuit, say Milwaukee or Chicago. Spokane wasn't that big a payday, but hey, it was handsome, nonetheless. No more bread with olive oil. Instead it was steak, steak, steak. Red meat for a red-blooded man.

Joe and George had been at it for a while, back and forth with their whirling and grabbing and slamming. When George got tossed again, he knew it was time for the waterworks. He rose to one knee, raised his hands in supplication, begging for mercy. Real tears tumbled down his thick face. George was a very good actor, a Barrymore in trunks, and this was part of his act: first play the arrogant, glowering villain and then the abject coward. The crying part wasn't hard: just think back to life on the farm.

The crowd rose to its feet, hooting and hollering, shaking its arms amidst the smoke and smell of liquor. The crowd loved professional wrestling. It was poetry. It was ritual: Good defeating Evil. So what if the outcome was pre-ordained by the promoters? The audience knew it, they must have, and didn't care. It felt good to cheer for the virtuous, like them, in these troubled times, even if the outcome was fakery, more akin to opera than legitimate sports.

Not that George and others like him weren't fine athletes. You had to be in this game. George could bench press nearly four hundred pounds and was agile for a big man—light on his feet. What's more, he loved the action of it. The booing didn't bother him in the least. He knew it wasn't personal. It was show business.

By this time, Gentleman Jim had George pinned against the canvas, the ref was counting him out, the crowd was roaring, and that was it for the night. Almost. Now George was no more or less lustful than the average man, but who could resist pretty girls when they threw themselves at him? And though Ma wouldn't approve, there was a particular girl he liked back in Denver: Miriam, who had flashy red hair. And it was genuine. During the day, Miriam worked as a clerk in a downtown Walgreens. The poor kid didn't make much more than enough to pay the rent. George wasn't planning to marry her, but at least he could show her some excitement.

When he was in Denver, he and Miriam would go out to a watering hole after a match. Although George was not yet a heavy drinker, he was a talker and a listener and a smoker and loved to be in on the latest sporting news. He would sit at a table with Miriam by his side, smoking a stogie and shooting the breeze with his wrestling buddies, who had their own girls at their sides. Sometimes there'd be hangers on, wrestling fans lapping up every bit of reflected glory they could. To George, it was all far better than the farm, far better than the mills where he had worked as a teenager, far better than the hat-cleaning business in Oklahoma City where he once worked for an uncle who had expected him to work behind a counter all day taking dirty clothes from strangers.

So what if he woke up the next day bruised and sore all over? At two-hundred-and-thirty pounds of solid muscle and still in his twenties, he could take a lot of punishment. He would swallow a few aspirin and feel pretty good. Besides, with his ring proceeds, he had already bought his parents a new house. He was smart and knew he couldn't do it forever, even now the knees ached, so he was branching out into promoting and other businesses. A fast talker as well as a wrestler, he would take new wrestlers under his wing, strong young hicks from the dust-busted farms and dead-end towns throughout the Midwest and West, groom them, inspire them with visions of success, and hopefully mold some of them into marquee names, with him taking a sizeable part of the action, of course.

George also bought a dry-cleaning store in Los Angeles. He was busy. He got around. Maybe he would get married someday and settle down, have kids like his mama wanted. Not yet. Waiting for him tonight at his dressing room in Spokane was another girl: Dolores. Dolores was a blonde but not a genuine one.

22

"SQUIRE," BABE DIDRIKSON said. "Did you hide a bottle of Scotch in those weeds?"

The gallery roared. Only Babe had the brass to rib the great Gene Sarazen for one of his few errant drives.

Gene grinned and pointed his club at Babe.

"You're sharp as a needle, Babe," he said.

Actually, it tickled him the way she addressed him as "Squire," as if he were some British aristocrat wearing a cutaway and riding breeches. The word "squire" amused him all the more since he had been born Eugenio Saracini, the son of poor Sicilian immigrants in humble Harrison, New York and had first entered the golf world by caddying at a local club.

Babe couldn't beat Gene Sarazen but sometimes she outdrove him, for he was a short man, an inch or two shorter than she. But long drives weren't the point. Squire was her tutor and mentor in the finest points of golf, universally respected and a living exemplar of what and what not to do on the course. She would study every move he made and learn the finesse part; she wouldn't necessarily emulate Sarazen's refined manner on or off the course.

Babe had needed something to do. Despite the best efforts of Bertha Bowen's lawyer, the USGA told Babe that she had to wait three years before she could again compete as an amateur golfer. Because she needed money, she wasn't about to officially reapply for reinstatement yet. She earned a tidy sum—a hundred and fifty dollars per round playing these exhibition rounds with Sarazen. But there was more to it than even mentoring and money. This was where she developed her rapport with the gallery, making them into her fans by the force of her personality.

When Sarazen made a sweet recovery out of the weeds, launching the ball onto the green, Babe turned to the gallery and said, "That's my squire. That's why he makes all that do-re-me."

The two were barnstorming together, with Mrs. Sarazen acting as chaperone. Not that Gene's wife had anything to fear from Babe, the insiders knew that. But it looked better to the public that way, Babe still being a single gal.

Babe had other ways of enthralling the gallery than poking fun at Sarazen. Like a good teacher she'd had back in Beaumont—Mrs. Scurlock—she'd ask the crowd questions, and they'd respond. Participate. Like when she hit a particularly impressive drive.

"Don't you men wish you could hit a shot like that?" she'd ask.

The women would laugh, and the men would laugh, too, a little reluctantly.

Babe also entertained them with trick shots. She'd lay down a row of golf clubs at intervals and then pop the ball over the clubs to land in the hole. Or she'd put her foot in front of the ball and putt it over her foot, plop! into the hole.

Babe never felt so comfortable as when she was on a golf course. And now with her permanent wave, makeup, designer clothes, and bright red nail polish, she looked every inch the lady golfer. It seemed that the nasty remarks about her were finally dying down.

Even Paul Gallico had taken note when he attended one of her exhibitions, Babe made sure of that. She had wasted no time calling him over after the match, hitching her skirt a few inches and showing him a bit of her lacy underthings. She even opened her pocketbook and let him see her compact, lipstick, dainty change purse, and other accouterments of femininity. She wanted him to know she had gone whole hog.

"Yep, I got everything," she told him.

"Ah ha," Paul said, nodding. "I can see you did."

After exchanging a few more words, Babe watched grimly as tall, stoop-shouldered Paul picked his way along the flagstone path.

"Put that in your pipe and smoke it," she said to herself.

The next day Paul Gallico wrote in his column: "I hardly knew Babe Didrikson when I saw her. Hair frizzed and she had a neat little wave in it, parted and prettily combed, a touch of rouge on her cheeks and red on her lips . . . The tomboy had suddenly grown up."

Babe read the column with satisfaction.

But the tour with Gene Sarazen was drawing to a close. With the money Babe had earned, she returned to Los Angeles, rented one half of a duplex, and practiced again with Stan Kertes, the resident pro at the Riviera Country Club. Her parents and Lillie had decided to come out to live with her for a while, and Babe welcomed their company. Now in his early sixties, Ole Didriksen was no longer working as a carpenter, having never fully recovered from the lung operation that Babe had paid for. Oh, the doctors had extracted a tumor, but Ole never seemed to regain his strength. Lillie could get a job and help out. In the meantime, younger brother Bubba, who now preferred to be called Arthur, would live in the house on Doucette.

Stan Kertes was a nice, trim young fellow with neatly parted hair who radiated the cheerful, non-discriminating optimism of a new father, which he in fact was. Furthermore, he was known to be discreet among the celebrities whom he taught golf. That is, he wouldn't go blabbing to the press about anything that happened at Riviera.

Babe admired Stan too, more than most men. She thought that if she *were* to someday fall for some guy, it would probably be someone like Stan . . . nice, polite, quiet, with a high forehead that gave him a thoughtful look, sort of like Douglas Fairbanks, Jr. Sometimes they'd have lunch together in the Riviera dining room and talk shop. It was a swank place that was frequented by the Hollywood elite. A year ago, Babe would have felt out of place in it. Now, under Bertha Bowen's and Gene Sarazen's tutelage, she was starting to feel more at ease among the country club set.

There was a waitress at the Riviera who usually waited on Babe and Stan. According to the name tag pinned to her uniform her name was Kathy. Just Kathy. Kathy was a young woman of about twenty-three, with a wholesome face—heart-shaped, tanned but with skin smooth as cream, widely spaced brown eyes—*dark* brown eyes that along with her dark brown hair suggested she might be part Mexican—and a cute, upturned nose . . . full lips, but not full enough to signal lasciviousness, just a little makeup, hair wrapped in a neat bun. It took a few lunches at the Riviera for Babe to realize that Kathy was paying special attention to her, smiling at her, standing closer to her than was really necessary.

Kathy's attention startled Babe at first. While she was barnstorming with her House of David comrades, she had eaten meals with the fellows in restaurants throughout the country—from roadside cafes and greasy spoons to hotel dining rooms. From that experience, she came to realize that, despite her prior Olympic celebrity, most waiters and waitresses paid far more attention to the hairy House of David crew even though Babe paid her part of the bill. And her fellow ballplayers were good athletes but not nearly on her level of accomplishment.

It was always the same: she and the boys would go into a restaurant and she and the boys would crowd into a booth or around a table. Then the boys would joke with the waiters or waitresses. Of course, there were cracks about their long, flowing beards.

"You know what they say about men with long beards," one ballplayer, a man named Roy Simmons, hinted one evening to a waitress. "That that ain't all that's l-l-long on them."

The waitress guffawed while one of the other fellows, a genuinely pious man named Kelvin Burdock, tried to hush up Roy.

"Shut up, there's a lady present," Kelvin said.

"Who's that? Babe?" Roy said. "She don't mind. Do you, Babe?"

"Naw, I don't mind," Babe said.

Despite their religious vows of celibacy, Babe's House of David teammates sometimes went home with waitresses and female fans. It was interesting the way the boys managed it—sometimes after a game, sometimes when they'd all go out to a nearby roadhouse. Her teammates would get to talking, discrete conversations with various girls and then wander off somewhere with them, while she went back to her single bed hotel room. None of her House of David comrades ever propositioned her, not that she wanted any of them to. She told herself they weren't her type.

But this Riviera waitress Kathy was different. She was cheerfully polite to Stan, but with her warm, dark, chocolatey brown eyes, she seemed to positively dote on Babe, as if she were some exotic gift that she hadn't expected to receive.

One time during lunch, Babe noticed Stan staring at Kathy then abruptly draw his gaze away. Even though he was happily married, he too must realize that Kathy was very pretty. Babe thought the waitress must get come-ons all the time from the men in show business who golfed and dined here. Yeah, they'd ply her with lines like "you should be in pictures," "come in for a screen test," and so on. By now even Babe had heard about the casting couch. She hoped Kathy never took them up on their offers. She didn't seem the type.

"Hello, Miss Didrikson, hi, Mr. Kertes," Kathy said. "Good to see you again. What can I get you?"

"Call me Babe," Babe told her. "Everybody does."

"Babe then." Kathy smiled.

When Kathy took Babe's order, she stood so close to her that Babe thought she could feel her body heat through her starchy waitress's uniform. Maybe it was her imagination. Maybe it was unintentional. It couldn't be. Didn't Stan notice? He seemed not to. He was studying his menu, abstractedly rubbing his chin.

"I'll have the tuna salad with Italian dressing," Babe told Kathy.

Though there were much fancier items on the menu, French food with names Babe couldn't pronounce, the money she made playing exhibition rounds with the squire had to last a while. She was supporting her parents and Lillie, who were now living with her in a modest two-bedroom duplex they rented in Echo Park.

After Kathy took their orders, she turned on her hip and disappeared through the swinging door of the kitchen. Babe couldn't help but watch her, her fine figure beneath her waitress uniform, disappearing.

"Heck," Babe thought wonderingly. "She's more feminine than me."

When Kathy came out to serve them their meal, she once again hovered over Babe. As she did, Babe felt a charge go through her such as she hadn't felt since that day in the locker room with Enid Adams. Then, as they were eating, Kathy returned twice to fill their water glasses and to see if they needed anything else. She was wearing perfume . . . a delicate citrusy scent.

She and Stan usually split the bill. But Babe made sure to give Kathy a generous tip, not wanting her to think she was a cheapskate.

That night back at the duplex when she was in bed, Babe thought about Kathy. An almost unwanted thought came to her mind and a feeling she hadn't felt since she was back in high school. Maybe Kathy actually was one of those women Babe had only heard about—women who loved other women, lesbians.

"Lezzies," she had heard people call them. What a silly word. It reminded her of what they used to call old Fords, Tin Lizzies. But from what she had heard, lesbians were freakish characters, not people anyone in polite society would want to associate with. *Bulldaggers* was another word Babe had heard used to describe them. She had heard this word during the Olympics when people, sportswriters, were talking about some of the women athletes from other countries, like Germany and Poland. These were big, muscular women, mannish. Babe thought lesbians must be strange like that, not really women. But here Kathy was so soft, so feminine. Prettier, Babe knew, than she was. Therefore, if anyone was strange, it must be Babe herself.

As Babe lay in bed, she imagined drawing Kathy to her, kissing her welcoming lips, embracing her, the two melting together in apocalyptic passion. But what would everyone think? Her aged parents were sleeping in the next bedroom, and Lillie was snoring three feet away from her in her twin bed.

Babe and Stan Kertes had lunch at the Riviera Country Club a week later. Again, Kathy waited on them, seemingly with genuine pleasure. What a pretty face she had. At least as pretty, to Babe's mind, as some of the movie stars and starlets who hung around here. And all the prettier because she was so unaffected. Upon request, she had already given the waitress her autograph, had scrawled it on Kathy's waitress pad. Kathy had told her she had followed her in the '32 Olympics.

For his part, Stan noticed that Babe sometimes blushed in the waitress's presence and that there seemed to be an attraction between the two. But he tried his best to ignore it, the way he ignored the scurrilous gossip that the celebrities he taught golf sometimes exchanged: who was screwing who, which actress was a real ball breaker or a dyke or a nympho, which one was a neurotic or a hop head or a cunt or a rummy or a nitwit, or which actor was a faggot or a drunk or a dope fiend or a cradle robber. Par for the course, so to speak. All the celebrities knew Stan was discrete; that is, he wouldn't rush off and peddle dirt to a tattle sheet.

So Stan tried not to think much about the obvious attraction between Babe and Kathy, the waitress. Anyway, who was he to pass judgment on people? At Riviera, he was just a hired hand.

Back at home, as Babe lay in bed night after night in a kind of feverish expectation, she thought about writing a note to Kathy and leaving it somewhere where she could find it. But she couldn't very well leave it with the check that Kathy presented to them—Stan would surely spot it and wonder what was going on. Still, Babe thought about doing something. It would feel so good to be alone with Kathy, to hold her in her arms. Then she looked across at Lillie, oblivious, sleeping like a log.

Babe thought about what the note would say.

"Dear Kathy, I like you. Let's go out together." Sincerely, Babe.

The thought was ridiculous. Anyway, what if she were totally wrong about Kathy. What if she was just imagining things?

The next time Babe and Stan had lunch together at the Riviera, there was something different about Kathy, a kind of tenseness. Then, after having taken their orders, as she was standing across the room near the swinging doors to the kitchen, she gave Babe a look that was unmistakably intent, desirous, focused solely on her.

Babe blushed and looked down at her Caesar salad. What could she do? March up to the girl and declare her love? In the Riviera Country Club?

So she did nothing and after finishing her lunch, left for home.

The next time Kathy waited on Stan and Babe, she was no more than formally polite toward Babe, and she did not stand nearly as close to her. Babe tried kidding with her, belatedly realizing that Kathy had interpreted Babe's lack of response to her overture as rejection.

"Why the long face, kiddo?" Babe said. "Your two favorite customers have arrived."

"Sure, Babe," Kathy said.

Babe was dismayed by this new coolness, but what could she do? If she did something, that meant she was a "lezzie." And she wasn't that horrible word, was she?

A few weeks later, a different waitress waited on Babe and Stan, a Jean Harlow wannabe with a too-large mouth named Susan. Babe figured that Susan, who waited on her in a cursory manner, was here to curry attention from the Hollywood elite. Babe was nothing to her.

When Babe mustered up the courage to ask the maître d' Rudolfo about Kathy, he told her that Kathy had quit and moved back to Fresno to be closer to her mother.

"Her mama's sick," Rudolfo explained.

Stan noticed Babe's crestfallen mood as the two ate lunch.

"That Kathy was a nice kid, wasn't she?" Stan asked gently.

Babe looked at Stan. How much had he guessed? Not much, she hoped. She didn't want him to think there was something wrong with her.

"Yeah," she said. "She was real nice."

Sometimes Babe read reports in the *Los Angeles Times* of the LAPD raiding bars where male and female homosexuals—deviants or moral degenerates, they were called—hung out. The police would haul these moral degenerates off to the police station in paddy wagons and book them. Their names would be printed in the paper, so everyone would know how truly depraved they were. That would be the worst thing of all to Babe, the publicity. So the best thing to do was to forget all about Kathy the waitress. And just play golf.

23

EVEN THOUGH BABE had been disqualified from taking part in amateur tournaments, there were still a few tournaments she could enter, ones that were open to professionals and amateurs alike. All you had to do was enter.

Almost on a whim, Babe entered the Los Angeles Open in January 1937. It was a men's tournament, but since there was nothing in the rules preventing women from entering, Babe took the plunge. She knew she wouldn't win, but she wanted to test herself against some of the best male golfers of the day. Besides, it would be great publicity if she played well. She already knew she could outdrive some of these fellows, if not actually outplay them.

At the opening of the tournament at Griffith Park's Wilson course, Babe was disappointed to learn she had been teamed with a professor of religion and minister from Occidental College named C. Pardee Erdman, as well as a professional wrestler, George Zaharias.

"Damn, a wrestler," Babe said to herself. Probably some pug ugly fellow with a shaved head, beetle brow, and cauliflower ears. Couldn't they have at least teamed her with a real golfer? But this was Hollywood, she reminded herself, where the fake was real, and people lapped it up.

The day was bright and clear, if a bit cooler than usual with a brisk breeze rushing in from the Pacific: a great day for golf. Babe wore the green cardigan sweater she had bought at Neiman Marcus and a camel's hair skirt that reached midway down her calf. She thought of how pleased Bertha Bowen would be to see her wearing the outfit. Maybe she should get someone to take a photo of her in it and send it to BB: proof positive of her transformation.

For his part, George Zaharias was disappointed about being teamed with Babe. Was that what they thought of his golfing ability? He didn't want to be teamed with a girl, any girl, but what the heck; he had only entered this tournament on a lark after finally breaking 80. It was his wrestling buddies who had dared him to. He knew he didn't stand a chance of winning—he wasn't that much of a chump. But it was good publicity for his wrestling career. He had heard something about this Babe Didrikson being a champion at track and field but that was only girls' sports. He hoped she wasn't an ugly, muscly dame, like some of those girl athletes were.

From the clubhouse, caddy trailing her and C. Pardee Erdman by her side, Babe strode over to the first tee. As they approached, they noticed a massive figure already standing there. Hearing soft footsteps behind him on the yielding grass, the figure turned around to greet his partners.

Introductions were made. Babe, who had paid scant attention to Erdman, looked upon George Zaharias for the first time.

Far from the pug she had imagined, he was young and quite handsome, with penetrating, even wary brown eyes. He had broad cheeks, a firm mouth, strong jaw, and the sun shone off his straight black hair like patent leather. True, his ears were a bit damaged, but who noticed ears in such a fine overall package? He was powerfully built, with the neck and shoulders of a bull, a powerful torso that led down to a trim waist.

For his part, George smiled at Babe, a little awkwardly, a little confused. He prided himself on being a shrewd judge of people, male or female, but he hadn't known any lady athletes before. He decided right away Babe was pretty, with her deep hazel eyes and cute, crooked smile, stylishly cut chestnut hair. And it was clear that this girl was no barroom floozy, no wrestling hanger-on; she radiated fitness and purity.

"They tell me you're the greatest girl athlete there is," he said to Babe in a gruff voice. The words sounded like an accusation.

"Well, I don't know about that," Babe said, looking down at her golf shoes, unusually shy in this big, good-looking man's presence. Then she looked up and grinned that lop-sided grin. "You can judge for yourself when we play."

Reporters and photographers, who had been alerted to the unusual threesome, were on hand to record it, jockeying for position at the first tee.

"Hey, George, how about putting a wrestling move in Babe?" one of them suggested.

With Babe's consent, George obliged, putting his great right arm around her neck: a gentle headlock. Then Babe put a headlock on George. He had to kneel for her to do so.

The cameras were snapping, the reporters were scribbling. George and Babe warmed to each other with the press as middleman. Playing for publicity was a game, something they both understood.

It didn't take long for Babe to also realize that this Zaharias fellow was a good golfer. At least he could drive the ball a mile, if his short game was still a little rough. Watching him move those massive shoulders as he swung was like watching Babe Ruth turn on a fastball. The ball soared high and long in the cool California breeze before bouncing to rest, sometimes near the green, sometimes not, but still impressive, for an amateur.

And it didn't take long for George to realize that Babe was an excellent golfer, not just for a woman but for anyone. With a promoter's eye, he studied the way she set herself for each shot, the steely grip, the look of total, unbreakable concentration, and then the release: the rhythmical flow of her body as she swung. Whap! And the way the ball flew. He had never seen a woman and few men, hit the ball with such authority. And her chip shots and putts were very good indeed—all the practice with Kertes had paid off. Yet she was no Brunhilde with bulging muscles, just a twig compared to him.

Babe strode ahead of her partners, down the fairway, her light brown skirt catching the dappled sunlight. As she did, she felt eyes on her. Surely not those of C. Pardee Erdman, the married minister. She turned and said to George over her shoulder, coquettishly. "Are you looking at me?"

George nodded. He had a nice smile, strong white teeth. "I like what I see."

Babe liked what she saw in George. As they trod the course together, she realized from the way he tossed off the names of the cities he had seen and the people he had met that he had led a life similar to hers—up from poverty, self-made, risk taking.

"When I was in Chicago," he told her. "When I was in 'Frisco, Seattle, St. Louis . . ."

She didn't bother to tell him much about her own barnstorming days. "Let him do most of the talking." She had gathered that much advice from the women around her.

For his part, George found Babe intriguing. For one thing, he found her ability to concentrate to a pinpoint degree fascinating. She clearly was nothing like the other women—the hoochie-coochie girls of his acquaintance. They were marshmallows compared to Babe. While women like that were fine in bed, the fact was you couldn't spend your life in bed.

As George and Babe walked along together through the bucolic course, George sensed that Babe had never been with a man. Just something about her, a shyness bordering on skittishness, an aloneness. She was a clean kid. She already knew plenty about golf, but he imagined he could teach her other things as well.

"Lookin' forward to seeing you tomorrow," George told Babe after the round. They were set to play another round in the tournament the next day.

"Same here," Babe said.

As she drove home through the Los Angeles traffic, she realized that she hadn't felt this happy in quite a while, especially after the fiasco with Kathy. Yet she decided not to tell her parents and Lillie about this wrestler, George Zaharias. What if the whole thing blew up in her face?

The next day, between George's errant shots and Babe's unusual lack of focus, they didn't come close to making the tournament cut. George scored one point better than Babe, an 80. Not bad but not great either. Babe was disappointed in her play, but it seemed there were to be benefits to the tournament, nonetheless.

"You two seem to be getting along well together," C. Pardee Erdman commented at one point. He wore glasses but he wasn't blind.

George nodded agreement. "Reverend, if this keeps up, you may have to marry us soon."

Babe blushed.

"How about goin' out for dinner and dancing tomorrow night?" George asked Babe on the way to the clubhouse.

She said yes. Now she would tell her folks.

"Yeah, I was born and raised in Pueblo, Colorado," George was telling Babe's folks. He had stopped by the duplex to pick up Babe. "Dad and I did some farming; then we worked in the mines. Guess doin' all that grunt work made me strong enough to be a wrestler."

It was easy for Babe's parents to see that fame had not spoiled George, that he was cut from the same cloth they were. And they were thrilled that Babe was finally going out with someone. Before George, she had never dated a man, though her brothers had vainly tried to fix her up with a few of their buddies.

For her part, as she was dressing for the night out with George, Babe said a prayer of gratitude to Bertha Bowen for taking her shopping. She had some clothes suitable for dinner and dancing.

"Well, well, well," George said, gazing at her in admiration. He already knew she had a fine, spare figure, lean as a whippet. But now she looked curvier in a pale blue sequined gown with a matching jacket and tiny shoulder bag.

"Pretty dress," he said.

"What did you think I was gonna wear? A golf outfit?"

"I didn't know if you lady golfers ever dressed up."

George sure was handsome in his pinstriped suit, his thick dark hair brushed back, his broad shoulders taking up the entire door frame. Babe could have never imagined someone who looked like him would be attracted to someone who looked like her. But maybe she didn't look so bad, after all.

As they left the house, George put on his gray fedora and slanted it at a rakish angle.

He held the passenger door of his shiny blue Caddie open for her.

"Thank you, sir. Where are we going?" Babe asked.

George looked at Babe from behind the wheel. He winked. "You'll see."

AS THE SATURDAY evening traffic in Los Angeles flowed along, George took the turn-off for Culver City. After a few minutes' drive on Washington Avenue, they pulled up at a large, half-timbered structure that resembled something out of the Elizabethan Age. At first Babe thought the building odd, but then she remembered this was Los Angeles—full of buildings that resembled something else: men's derby's, Chinese pagodas, Egyptian palaces, the Garden of Allah, pineapples, donuts, anything you could imagine.

Overhead was a huge metal sign that proclaimed, "Sebastian's Cotton Club." Babe turned to George with a quizzical look.

"I thought the Cotton Club was in New York," she said. She had seen it in some newsreel or other, she didn't remember where. It was where a lot of swells went.

A uniformed Negro valet came out to hold Babe's door open for her and to take George's keys as they alighted from the car.

"They have one out here, too," George said. "And tonight they got Fats Waller and his orchestra."

"Wow, Fats Waller!" Babe looked up at the bold letters on the giant marquee over the front entrance.

"I bet you don't even know who Fats Waller is."

A Negro attendant in maroon livery held the door for them.

"Yes I do. No I don't," Babe admitted. "At least I heard of him."

"You'll see," George said.

Inside, the ceiling was a multicolored fabric that draped down and billowed, tent-like, over the room. Rows of tables flanked either side of an enormous parquet dance floor. White tablecloths of course, and fancy place settings with fresh flowers. On either side of the stage were bucolic images of trees and a river. Was the river supposed to be the Mississippi? Babe didn't know.

George ordered a giant Caesar salad, the largest steak on the menu, baked potatoes, and a bottle of champagne.

"What's the champagne for?" Babe asked. "We didn't win the tournament."

George smiled and shook his head.

"Who needs to win some old golf tournament?" he asked. "Bein' here with you is winning enough for me."

Babe was charmed. It was the kind of remark she heard in the movies, not something she ever thought anyone would say to her.

"Aw, you're sweet!"

George grinned. In truth, despite his conquests among the ladies who hung around professional wrestling, he did not consider himself a ladies' man. The women he was used to bedding were low-hanging fruit. You could give them any old line, and they'd jump at it like bass. And, quite frankly, those were the types of broads, not Bryn Mawr grads, who hung around professional wrestlers.

But Babe was different. George didn't want to get cocky with her. She was like a deer. One false move and she'd be bounding off into the woods.

George plowed right into the food. It seemed like he polished off the salad in two bites and then wolfed down his entrée.

"My, you do have a big appetite," Babe commented. "Guess that's to keep all those muscles working."

She hoped she wasn't being too forward, but George just smiled and said, "How's them crab cakes?"

The floor show began. All the dancers were colored girls of various hues, beautiful girls with long legs, wearing scanty costumes, smiling and shuffling and shimmying around the stage in time to the music. The orchestra was colored, too. Babe had never seen so many Negro people together at one time.

"But they're all colored," she told George. A few years earlier she would have called them niggers but had been cautioned by Bertha Bowen that white people of good character no longer used that crude term.

George, who had by now devoured his entrée and ordered three slices of chocolate cake, two for himself and one for Babe, regarded Babe with amusement.

"The coloreds make the best entertainers," he assured her. "Louie Armstrong, the Duke, Fats, Lionel, all those guys. When you go to the Cotton Club, you know you're getting topnotch entertainment."

It didn't strike him as odd that while all the entertainers were black, all the patrons were white. Though he considered himself more enlightened than many of his friends on matters of race—Greeks sometimes being criticized for their relatively dark complexions—there were limits to what his imagination could envision for the Negroes.

Babe noticed the patrons were all white but said nothing. This scene was new to her. She was far more familiar with country music, catching the Grand Old Opry on WSM whenever she could. But she didn't dare tell George that. He would probably laugh and call her a hillbilly.

Derby-hatted, cigar smoking Fats Waller came out to cheers, sat down in front of the piano and played a set, including his signature song, "Aint' Misbehavin." As he sang, he grinned and mugged. All was right with the world when Fats played. He launched into "Honeysuckle Rose" while a pretty light-skinned colored girl sat on his piano, looking at him adoringly. More girls shimmied in the background.

As Fats played to his "honeysuckle Rose," George fixed his dark eyes on Babe with such intensity that she looked down at her plate, blushing. Having achieved what he wanted—to convey his romantic interest—George gazed back at the stage.

Babe sipped a little more champagne. She noticed that George had consumed much more than she had, but he didn't look drunk. Big men could drink a lot without showing it, she told herself. But whatever George did, she must be sure to maintain her self-control. That's what they said the woman had to do, anyhow. Because often men couldn't.

"I'm gonna go say hello to Fats when he takes a break," George announced to her.

"You know him?"

"Sure, I know a lot of these big-name guys," George said. "They watch me in the ring, and I watch 'em on stage. Wanna come and meet Fats?"

The thought shocked her. What would she say to a colored man?

"Naw, you go. I'll sit here and hold the fort."

"Okay, I'll be back in a few minutes."

Babe watched as George threaded his way among the sea of tables and then sidled along the perimeter of the dance floor. She saw him talking to a uniformed attendant, slip him a bill, and then disappear behind the stage.

It was hard for Babe to comprehend being on a friendly basis with colored people. She had always looked down on the colored kids in Beaumont, who dressed even shabbier than she had and lived in poorer houses. People had said it was the coloreds' own fault they were so poor. That they were lazy and foolish and drank too much and got into knife fights. That was why white people didn't want to live around them or go to school with them or hire them. And here George was friends with a big colored entertainer.

Babe thought back guiltily to the time she had thrown ice water on the two colored girls, members of her own Olympic team, on the train ride out to Los Angeles. Those girls hadn't been lazy or foolish or drunk. They couldn't have been Olympians if they had been. It was the first time in a long time that Babe thought back on that incident. George would probably think her mean for doing that to them. Well, she had been a kid then. Maybe she had been mean back then. But she wasn't anymore.

George returned from visiting Fats.

"Well, how was he?" Babe asked.

"He's fine," George said, his face lit up with pleasure. "You know, he's a topnotch piano player. Someone said he could play classical music, Beethoven and all that, if he wanted. But that's not where the money is."

This was even more confusing to Babe. A Negro playing Beethoven? Even she knew who Beethoven was. Her mama used to listen to that kind of thing on the radio. Sometimes.

After dinner, she and George danced. At first, she felt nervous when he held her in his arms and pressed her to his chest. She felt uncomfortably engulfed. She had never danced with a grown man before, only with her siblings when they were goofing around at home. But she liked the smell of George's cologne, brisk and manly. Wasn't that funny? He was wearing cologne and she wasn't. She had some Chanel stuff back at home but had forgotten to put it on. Dancing with a man was darn awkward at first, but then George made a joke about it.

"Don't worry, I only stomp on people in the ring," he told her.

But he was surprisingly light on his feet. As Fats and his band played and they moved along with the other couples, it felt good to Babe to have George holding her in his arms. She felt protected by him, his massive body, his worldliness. What's more, she felt the eyes of others on the dance floor admiring him. No one would mess with George Zaharias. With a swagger worthy of a Hollywood gangster, he fit right in with this celebrity-crazed Los Angeles crowd. From what he had told her about his wrestling career, he was an actor himself—the "Crying Greek from Cripple Creek." It amused Babe to imagine big George sobbing, and she began to relax in his arms.

"If they could see me now," Babe told herself. Then, from out of nowhere, rose the painful memory of Kathy back at the Riviera Golf Club. But that whole business was best swept away. It wasn't right, two women together, Kathy should have known that. This thing with George, this handsome hunk of a man who seemed to genuinely like her, this was right.

While Babe was thinking of what she hadn't done with Kathy, George was thinking what he might do with Babe. As he led her around the dance floor, he was already planning it out: he would wine and dine Babe, then he would marry her, if she would have him, and manage her career. They would be an unbeatable combination: his business sense and her athletic talent. Why not? To become involved in the swanky sport of championship golf would be a big step up for George. Besides, it wasn't like he didn't have real feelings for Babe. She was a sweet, cute, funny kid who looked up to him and who brought out the protective side of his nature. And she was clean, too, virginal he would bet on it. Back in Colorado, Ma would certainly approve.

24

ONE DAY ABOUT a year later in St. Louis, George told Babe, "We're gonna get married this week or the deal's off."

What could Babe say to that? Frowning darkly and his brow knit, George sure didn't look like he was kidding. They would have gotten married earlier, but their various commitments took them in different places. When George was free, Babe was appearing at a golf exhibition in Dubuque. When Babe was free, George was wrestling in Salt Lake City or else taking care of some business venture in Los Angeles or Denver. He now owned a cigar store in Denver.

"Okay," Babe said. "Let's go."

Yet as Babe contemplated her imminent wedding, she was still a bit doubtful about the whole thing, even though she was certain she was in love with George. She wasn't sure why she was doubtful. It was certainly different being around George, who was definitely the boss. Babe hadn't had a boss in a long time, ever since she quit Colonel McCombs and Employers Casualty Company for good. And looking back, that whole gig had been small potatoes . . . she, the famous athlete, having to type to survive.

Now George was telling her he would make her into the biggest female golf star in the world. They were having dinner in a small restaurant on a side street in downtown St. Louis. They both liked down-home cooking even if the place's ambience wasn't exactly stellar. Good meatloaf and mashed potatoes compensated for a lot.

Earlier, Babe had explained to George about the amateur golf thing. She was tired of playing exhibitions and wanted to get her amateur status back so she could play in more tournaments. The way things stood, they were adding women's amateur tournaments all the time, but you could still count the number of women's professional tournaments on the fingers of one hand.

"Golf is a racket like boxin' or wrestlin'," George told her as he sat back in his booth seat. He took up the whole seat, especially with his legs spread. "If you're tired of doing exhibitions, you gotta get your amateur status back."

"Before they'll let me do that, I can't make any money at all off golf for three years," Babe explained, stirring some sugar into her coffee. "How am I gonna support myself?"

"Dummy," George said. "Don't you know you got a rich fiancé?"

"You'd support me if I went amateur?"

"Of course I would. You're the greatest, kid. And eventually you're gonna be making money, I'm sure. With a marquee name like you, I bet women's golf will be a big thing."

Babe was not opposed to George managing her career. He seemed to know what he was doing, having made pots of money himself.

"My body's wearin' down," he added. "Especially my knees and shoulders, they ache like crazy sometimes. I give it another couple years before I go into promotin' full time."

George was thirty years old.

Babe didn't doubt the toll wrestling took on his body. She had watched him wrestle a couple of times and found it exciting—her George in the ring!—but unsettling. Especially when his opponent, some monstrous guy, got George in a bear hug and she thought his back was going to crack. Or when an opponent stood on a turnbuckle and dove with his knee onto George, who was lying prone on the mat. Or when an opponent picked George up, held him over his head for one photogenic moment, and then dropped him to the canvas. You could see both man and canvas bounce after such a throw. That had to hurt, even if the match's outcome, as George had explained to her, was already decided.

When she asked George why professional wrestling was so fake, he told her.

"The public won't sit still long enough for real wrestling. To them it's boring."

Babe guessed this was true, having been to a couple of her brother Louis's wrestling matches at Beaumont High School. The boys weren't flashy, to say the least. But the boys worked hard at it, and you knew the outcome wasn't rigged.

"Waiter! More coffee please," George shouted. "Anyway, I got a lot of irons in the fire now," he continued. "I know how to promote fights. And I always got my eye on more business deals."

He had recently bought part ownership in a men's clothing store in Beverly Hills. He owned a few apartment complexes in LA and one in Denver, along with the cigar store. He was often on the go.

"Sounds great to me, honey," Babe said.

LEO "THE LIP" Durocher, of the St. Louis Cardinals, was George's best man. The two men were both talkers, hustlers. Some considered them both obnoxious, Leo for his savage bench-jockeying and George for his "Crying Greek" routine, which they felt was becoming stale.

"So you're the little lady that finally roped George," Leo told Babe, whom he had not met before.

"Yep, I roped him," Babe said. "And he's gonna stay roped."

Babe was sad that her family couldn't be there, especially her parents and Lillie, but what the heck. The ceremony was held in the living room of one of George's St. Louis-based wrestling promoter friends. It seemed George knew everyone in the sporting world. Press releases had gone out, and reporters and photographers from the St. Louis papers were there to publicize the event.

After the reception at a ritzy St. Louis hotel came their wedding night at the same hotel. They were both nervous. But the champagne they had both consumed at the reception helped to take the edge off things.

After putting on a sheer pink nightgown in the bathroom, Babe lay in bed. She watched George pull off his starched shirt and dress pants in front of her. She had already seen him nearly naked in the ring. Of course, he was beautiful. A Greek god.

He sat on the bed to pull off his boxer shorts. He snapped off the bedside light, lay on his side on the bed beside her and gently kissed her, then a deeper kiss. As he kissed her, he rubbed one hand up and down her torso, and then caressed her breast.

"Don't be nervous," he told her.

"Not with you."

She put her arms around his shoulders and drew him to her. She could feel his chest, a little prickly because he shaved his chest for the ring, pressing against her breasts, and the feeling aroused her. He slid off her silk panties and pulled up her nightgown. Babe felt a little pain and then George entered her. She liked the feeling of fullness he gave her. But then it felt strange to have George on top of her, pushing and breathing heavily like that. Back and forth, back and forth like a steam shovel. She hadn't expected the pushing and heavy breathing. There was a rhythm to it that she didn't feel a part of but that seemed to excite him. But she was pleased, nonetheless. That a man would want her enough to do all that. She was like other women, after all.

"It will get better," George assured her before he drifted off to sleep.

She was surprised by his comment. She thought it had gone fine. What did she know? He knew she hadn't come, but that was to be expected. He was right; she had been a virgin; you could tell. He would have been shocked if she had launched right into it like one of his girlfriends, practically breaking the bed in her lust. Babe coming like a house afire, that would have disturbed him. Thank God it hadn't happened. He wanted to bring her along gently, like a prize filly. His alone.

25

BABE AND GEORGE were sharing a blanket on the beach in Honolulu. Babe kneeled behind George as she applied suntan lotion to his bare white back, which to her seemed the size of a tabletop. Sailing from Long Beach, California, on a Matson liner, the SS *Lurline*, they were now officially on their Hawaiian honeymoon. Last night they had eaten at a genuine Hawaiian luau, complete with roasted pig, tiki torches, languorous Hawaiian music and hula dancers. When one of the hula dancers got a little too close to George with her undulating hips, Babe had playfully placed her hand over his eyes. He had laughed. They both sipped tall, tropical drinks and gotten more than a little tipsy, which helped the sex immensely. It had all been perfect.

"You sure are white," Babe commented as she lathered coconut oil onto George's muscular torso.

"Don't get much of a tan under arena lights," he said, gazing out at the broad blue Pacific. He looked a little hung over, his skin around his eyes a little puffy. In deference to her, he had put out his cigar in a trash basket near the entrance to the beach. Around them, but not too close, other couples and families sat or lay on beach blankets under umbrellas that shielded them from the sun, which was now high overhead. Little children sprinted around laughing or else made sandcastles, while teens threw around a multi-colored beach ball. Some raced into the surf and jumped the waves while others went farther out, swimming or floating in the azure water.

"Don't put any lotion on me," Babe told George. "I'm goin' in the water right now. Want to come?"

"Na, I look like a whale in the water."

"Okay."

Babe jumped up, ran into the water, and swam for about fifteen minutes, out past where the greenish blue waves were breaking. She was an excellent swimmer, as she was an excellent overall athlete. As she relaxed and cavorted in the water, George sat on the beach, wearing his sunglasses and reading the *Honolulu Star-Bulletin*; more specifically the sports pages. Even in the middle of the Pacific, you could get day-late box scores and important stuff like that.

From her vantage point in the water, Babe looked back to see George, now rather small on the beach, reading. She knew he wasn't crazy about the water and had never learned to swim. But they would go out partying again tonight in Honolulu. George loved Chinese food, raved about San Francisco's Chinatown, so they would go to the one in Honolulu. Babe had noticed there were plenty of Orientals around here. After that, they'd find a nightclub. That should make him happy.

A rogue wave came up unexpectedly when Babe was floating on her back, sending her sprawling and gasping, getting saltwater in her nose and mouth. She swam back to the beach. When she got out of the water and began to towel herself off, George glanced up from the newspaper and told her what he had planned.

"Honey, listen," he said. "Tomorrow we're doing an exhibition at the Oahu Country Club. So you might wanna get your clubs out and practice a few swings when we get back to the room."

Babe was aghast. "What do you mean, an exhibition? This is our honeymoon. All I wanna do is swim, lay on the beach, and relax." She sat down on the beach blanket with a thud.

"I wanna relax too, sweetheart," George said, leaning into her and wrapping one massive arm around her shoulders. Under ordinary circumstances, Babe liked the feel of George's arm around her. Now it just felt heavy.

"But this deal is too good to pass up," George added.

Squinting in the sun, Babe turned to look at George. He had put on sunglasses and his eyes were impenetrable behind them. Her own sunglasses were back at the bungalow they had rented not far from the beach.

"That's why you didn't want me to apply for reinstatement," she accused him. "You had this whole thing figured out."

He shrugged, removing his arm from around her shoulders. Roughly three yards away a tanned little boy in red trunks shoveled sand into a yellow pail.

"We might as well make some money while we're spending it," George replied. "And we'll make big bucks for this exhibition."

Babe narrowed her eyes. "How big is big?"

The little boy, who looked to be about six, paused in his shoveling to listen to their adult conversation.

George named a handsome sum—three hundred dollars for the day.

"Well, that is a lot," Babe had to admit.

Still, the thought of her working on their honeymoon rubbed her the wrong way. As did George not even bothering to consult her about whether she wanted to do this exhibition. But this was married life, she guessed. The man was the boss. Maybe she should be grateful to George for taking such an interest in her career and making these decisions. Before she met him, she was on her own.

"It'll be a good haul," George said.

"Where is this club?" Babe sighed.

"Only a few miles from here." He turned around and pointed behind him. "Up in those hills."

"How we gonna get there?" It seemed to Babe that she had been on the road most of her life, and she didn't relish riding on some stuffy tourist bus.

"I rented a limo. Only the best for my baby."

George pulled her closer to him and kissed her on the lips. His big body felt smothering on this hot day.

"Money sound good to you?" he asked.

"George, please, people are watching."

In truth, only the little boy was watching, but upon seeing George kiss Babe, he frowned and went back to shoveling sand.

"Oh hell, Babe, we're married. And it's not like we're doin' anything serious."

Babe looked around. The kids were still playing, the parents were still sitting or lying about. The pretty single girls were still gabbing with each other and eyeing the young fellows who eyed them back, just as they had at Beaumont High. The sun was still high overhead, casting negligible shadows on the pearly sand.

"Well, I guess you're right. It's just I barely had time to get my bathing suit wet and now I have to go play golf."

"But you told me you love to play golf. Besides, playing this exhibition is a great way to get your name in front of the public."

That was a hard one to argue with. Babe did love golf and she did love publicity. Here in Hawaii, way out in the Pacific, she guessed these benighted people barely knew who she was. She looked back up at the hills behind them, where George had pointed. The hills seemed bushier, thicker, darker than hills on the mainland, as if the vegetation had grown devouring in this tropical paradise. Then she looked back at George. He had put on a pleading face, eyebrows raised, rubbery lips pursed like a little kid begging for a cookie. Not for nothing was "The Crying Greek" known as one of the best actors in professional wrestling.

"Please honey, please, please," he begged.

"Okay, it's fine."

Babe kissed George back. She still had the taste of salt in her throat.

26

THE EXHIBITION AT Oahu went well. The cream of Hawaiian society was thrilled by how hard and how far Babe could drive the ball. The three-hundred-dollar smackers went straight into George's wallet since it had already been mutually decided that he would manage money for them both. That way Babe could be free to concentrate on what she did best: swing a golf club. The deal seemed okay to Babe. Wasn't that what most couples did? Well, not exactly. In most cases the man was the breadwinner, while the woman stayed put at home. But it was true that George was earning most of the money that they lived on.

After a week's honeymoon in Hawaii, it was on to Australia on the *SS. Mariposa*. In Australia and New Zealand, George had scheduled a grueling string of exhibitions both for himself and for Babe. He would put on wrestling exhibitions; she would put on golf exhibitions.

Babe didn't object to these exhibitions the way she had in Hawaii. She guessed she had done enough lying on the beach; she didn't want to get soft. Besides, she could tell George was getting antsy. He didn't seem to be able to relax and just do nothing like she could. At dinner he'd drink too much and smoke too much. Get sloppy. One night he accidentally overturned his glass reaching for something else on the table. He tried sopping up the bourbon with his napkin. When the waiter came, he discretely cleaned up the mess. George didn't bat an eyelash.

"We might as well earn as much money as we can while we're on our honeymoon," George told her.

In Sydney, George began giving wrestling exhibitions against the local favorites—and soon had the bruises to prove it. After a long day, he and Babe would have dinner and then relax on the bed in their hotel room. The windows would be open, allowing whatever breeze there was to waft through the room. Often, she'd give George a massage, kneading his thick muscles in her strong hands.

Straddling him as he lay on his stomach, Babe could see firsthand the toll wrestling took on George's body—black and blue marks, the yellowish greenish marks of older bruises, reddish rope burns . . . a pallet of colors. George told her his right shoulder was always sore; sometimes he flinched when she tried to massage it, so she very gently rubbed lineament into it with her fingertips.

"You know, honey, you still thinking of retiring?" Babe asked him. The lineament smelled strong.

"Every day," George said. "But I don't wanna do it for year or so yet. Still got some money to squeeze out of this old body."

George and she were the same. Both came up the hard way, always thinking about money.

Then it was her turn for a massage. They traded places on the bed. Babe took off her nightgown and lay on her belly.

"You got some strong muscles, girl," George told her as he was kneading her back and shoulders. He meant it as a compliment. He had had enough of soft women, lazy women who expected him to earn their keep. Babe was strong, like him—a go-getter—yet vulnerable too. After one of George's expert massages, powerful yet gentle, Babe felt all the tension go out of her body, to be replaced by lassitude.

George kissed her neck and shoulders. Then he pulled down her silk panties, fondled her and entered her from behind. This position was new to Babe, but she liked it. She didn't feel so smothered by George. She was getting used to sex. It was like an ocean, the rhythm of it. This time, for the first time, she came in response to George's rhythmic strokes.

Afterward, she was a little embarrassed. It seemed animalistic, like something dogs did.

"So you like it that way." George smiled, well pleased with himself.

"Yeah," she had to admit. She had liked the way George's full weight wasn't pressing her down as he kneeled behind her, rocking into her. As they lay back in bed, Babe wondered about his life prior to meeting her. He was so skilled, so knowledgeable.

"You know so much about everything," she said. "How'd you get so good at this?"

"Whattaya mean 'this'? Fucking?"

"Yeah," she said, giving him a playful slap on his belly.

He looked at her, brown eyes narrowed, not exactly sure how much he should tell. Women were sensitive sometimes. Things were going good with him and Babe, romantically speaking; he didn't want to throw her into a tizzy.

"A coupla girls threw themselves at me. What was I supposed to do, turn 'em down?"

"No, I guess not." Oddly, the thought of George being with other women did not particularly displease Babe. With his gladiator physique, he was a very desirable man, after all.

"Anyway, I don't plan on doing that anymore," George assured her. "Besides, they were floozies. Couldn't hold a candle to you."

"You better say that."

After George fell asleep. Babe lay awake thinking. What would George think if she had told him about Kathy, the waitress back at the Riviera? The girl had practically thrown herself at Babe, and Babe had turned her down. What would have happened if she hadn't? Would she and Kathy have had the same passionate sex that she and George had just had? Of course, it wouldn't be the same because they were both women. But Babe could imagine passionate embraces, nonetheless. And hands, delicate hands, and softness that made her swoon to think about. Anyhow, George would be horrified if she told him about Kathy. Wouldn't he? So she didn't plan to.

AFTER THEY DOCKED in Australia, Babe was impressed by the beautiful courses: those in Sydney, Melbourne, and other big cities. But some in the parched red outback were difficult to get to because of the terrible roads, and less than impressive when they got there—brownish greens, unkempt fairways, seedy clubhouses that were little more than ramshackle huts.

But everywhere they went, their hosts were warm and friendly, their accents charming. And the crowds were all that Babe and George could ask for. More than once, Babe looked back at the gallery behind her to find the rolling course completely obscured by people.

George nudged her. "Didn't I tell you this trip would be worth it?"

He was with her on the last exhibition she was putting on, at the Royal Wellington course in New Zealand. New Zealand was always green, as lush as the outback was parched. She had just completed her final round and was heading back to the clubhouse. George had taken out a cigar and was blowing smoke up into the clear blue sky of the southern hemisphere. Soon the stars would be out, the constellations totally different from what they were used to seeing.

"Yep, you did," Babe had to agree. She was exhausted by the pace they had kept throughout the past month. But fame was what they both wanted, wasn't it? And fame took work.

27

AFTER ALL THE touring, it felt good to Babe to finally climb aboard the *SS. Monterey* and sail for home. The *Monterey* was a beautiful ship, sleek as a knife, white, and fast, with the latest amenities, like air-conditioned common rooms. Yet somehow, the voyage home seemed longer than the voyage out had been, even considering that they weren't stopping in Hawaii this time.

One night, Babe and George decided to go to the ship's main theater and listen to Helen Weston sing. Though not famous herself, she had recorded with some well-known bands, and Babe was looking forward to hearing her. She got George dressed up in his white smoking jacket and black tie. She thought he looked handsome, but he said he didn't like wearing the jacket or tie, that he preferred one of the bright Hawaiian shirts he had bought.

"This stuff is starchy," he said. "It feels too tight."

"Just for this evening?" Babe asked. "You look so handsome in it."

"Okay."

In the theater, they sat down at their little round table and ordered drinks—bourbon for George and a gin and tonic for Babe. She wasn't about to drink beer in this kind of place; drinking beer seemed low class. A hidden voice announced the headliner. The spotlight went on. The audience applauded. Helen Weston was a sultry blond who wore a black gown and a white stole around her bare shoulders. The stole glowed like snow in the spotlight. If you squinted, she looked a little like Barbara Stanwyck. She sang some of the latest songs off the hit parade, songs like "Over the Rainbow," "Moon Love," and "Stairway to the Stars." Midway through her first set, George rose from his seat.

"I'll be back," he told Babe.

Babe thought he was going to the men's room, but fifteen minutes, a half an hour, and he still wasn't back. Babe looked around. She was the only woman sitting alone at a table. Everyone else seemed to be enjoying the show.

Between sets, Babe got up and found George in the smoking lounge, puffing on a cigar, drinking, and playing poker with some men he had apparently befriended on ship. His jacket was slung over his chair and his collar was open. The smoke was heavy in the room, practically choking.

One of the card players, a gray-haired man with a neatly trimmed moustache, looked up as Babe entered the room.

"Looks like the little lady is here," he commented drily. He didn't recognize Babe as a famous athlete.

George looked up. Babe noticed his tie, now rumpled, lying beside a full ashtray on the table next to him.

Hi, honey." He grinned, not at all abashed, and waved at Babe. "Found me a little action."

He laid a card on the table and took a sip from his glass. Probably bourbon. From the jolly way he acted, it seemed like abruptly rising and leaving his wife alone to watch a show was the most normal thing imaginable. Not willing to cause a scene in front of George's newfound buddies, Babe said, "See you later" and walked back through the ship's narrow corridors to the show.

But she was fit to be tied. Anyhow, no goddammed wrestler was going to dampen her enjoyment. Helen Weston was a fine singer, maybe not as good as Kate Smith but pretty darned good. So Babe sat down alone and listened to her.

The next morning, George was still snoring when Babe woke up. After getting dressed, she went down to the ship's dining room and had breakfast: sausage, eggs over easy, toast, and orange juice. When she returned to the cabin, George was awake. He had ordered room service, and a metal breakfast tray was parked on the bed beside him.

"George, why did you leave me alone last night?" Babe asked.

He looked like hell—unshaven, hair tousled, bags under his red-rimmed, bloodshot eyes.

"Did I?" he asked.

"Of course you did! We were listening to Helen Weston, remember?"

"Oh, yeah. Sorry about that." George bit into a piece of toast. "But there's one thing you gotta know about me, Babe." He chewed thoughtfully. "I can't sit still for too long. I gotta be doing somethin' all the time. Nothin' personal. I've always been that way, even when I was a kid."

Babe didn't know if George was telling the truth or not. He probably was. Ever since she had known him, he had been on the go: this city, that city in his blue Caddy. She traveled a lot, too, but she didn't like it all that much. She had to. And last night's gambling? Well, she had known before she married him that he liked to gamble. Fortunately, he was too cheap to wager large amounts of money.

"Well, at least next time let me know where you're going and how long you'll be away."

"Okay," George said. He gulped some black coffee.

The next day, Babe swam in the ship's pool and struck up a pleasant conversation with two other swimmers.

"It's kind of funny that a ship should have a swimming pool," Babe said to an older couple from Huntington Beach, California, the MacPhersons. "You know, water on water." She wasn't crazy about the pool's sulfurous smell.

"Well, we can't very well take a swim in the ocean,' Mr. MacPherson commented cheerfully. "We're a thousand miles from land."

"You got that right," Babe said.

The ship also had a gym, which Babe told George about. While Babe ran on the treadmill, George lifted weights. He was impressive doing that; in fact, he put on a show for the other passengers, bench pressing over four hundred pounds. He told her he had to keep in shape or he would get fat. She didn't doubt it. She had heard that long ocean cruises put pounds on you, and it appeared to her that George had already gained ten or fifteen pounds around the middle on this honeymoon.

At night, after dinner in the ship's dining room, Babe said she wanted to go again to the floor show. There would be a different singer performing. Chastened by the night before, George agreed.

"Do I have to wear my monkey suit?"

"No, just wear a sport jacket." Babe had noticed a number of men in sport coats the night before and didn't want to seem unreasonable.

This night the headliner was a male singer by the name of Clive Cummings, who wore a black tuxedo. Clive was blond, almost prettily so. When he sang a slow number accompanied by the ship's orchestra, George and Babe danced a little, then sat down.

"I think that guy is queer," George told Babe after listening to Clive for a while.

"Really? How do you know?" Babe asked.

George made his left wrist go limp to demonstrate.

Babe watched Clive's wrists caressing the microphone. Maybe he was a little swishy at that. She had known a boy in high school everyone said was queer. His name was Teddy Appleton. He was delicate and enunciated clearly. A lot of kids made fun of him, but Babe didn't. She just kept her distance. They had nothing in common anyway: Teddy sang in the glee club and acted in school plays, while Babe played sports. She later learned that Teddy had moved to New York City to become an actor. That was the last she heard of him.

After a few songs, George fidgeted so much that Babe finally gave him leave to go play poker. It was okay. He had tried. Besides, while they were dancing, she had noticed the nice older couple, the MacPhersons, she had met earlier while swimming.

"Now that all of my children are out of the house, it's time to enjoy life," Sarah had told Babe by the ship's swimming pool. "You don't have any kids yet, but when you do, you'll know what I mean."

"I guess," Babe said. She didn't want kids right now. Neither did George. They had started using protection when they had sex.

After George went to play poker, Babe rose and walked over to the MacPhersons' table. She didn't mince words.

"George wanted to go play cards," she said. "Mind if I join you?"

Of course, they said yes. Babe had told them who she was at the pool, and they were only too happy to be hobnobbing with a famous athlete. Maybe she could get them some free tickets to a golfing event.

Babe hung around a lot with the MacPhersons for the rest of the voyage. They were a sweet couple, good company, even if Sarah did talk a little too much about her grandchildren, who now numbered eight with one on the way.

28

WHEN GEORGE AND Babe landed at the cruise terminal in Long Beach, a gang of reporters and photographers were there to greet them; George had made sure of that by wiring his contacts in the press of their arrival date. The news appeared in the *Los Angeles Times*, accompanied by a photo of the beaming newlyweds, arms around each other.

"You sure know how to work things," Babe said.

"I learned the hard way," George said. "I seen great wrestlers no one knows about because no one promoted their careers."

George laid his hand on Babe's back as he accompanied her down the gangplank. "But you don't have to worry about that with me, Babe. I'll see to it that the whole world knows about you."

Later, when they were back in the duplex they had rented in Los Angeles, George contacted C. Pardee Erdman, their golfing buddy from the day they met. George hadn't forgotten that Erdman was on the board of the West Coast United States Golf Association. It was Erdman who advised them about the procedure for Babe seeking reinstatement as an amateur golfer. After Babe officially reapplied, Erdman told her and George that she would have to wait three years, during which she could earn no money from playing exhibition golf or any other appearances.

"That's a hell of a long time to wait," Babe mused. She had known all this before, but now it was official: no more golf for money.

"Yeah, but at least you don't have to worry about nothing," George said. He was sitting in a massive brown armchair he had purchased at Bullocks on Wilshire. "'Cause my businesses are doing good." He had recently bought another rental property on La Brea. Not all of his investments had panned out, but a lot of them had. The depression was finally easing.

"You're so generous, honey." She was grateful, especially since he was now not just supporting her but helping out her family here and there. Somehow, the rest of the Didriksens couldn't seem to get off the ground financially the way she had.

Now Babe's big problem was staving off boredom. Since the shoulder injury she had suffered during the Olympics had long since healed, she took up tennis in a big way. With her contacts at various country clubs around the city, she even beat some of Hollywood's top celebrity tennis players, stars like Peter Lorre and John Garfield. She thought about going on the women's amateur tennis tour. However, she stopped when she learned she could never be an amateur tennis player since she had taken money for playing other sports. Tennis was even stricter than golf in that regard.

Through it all Babe kept her golf game sharp by practicing four times a week. Riviera brought back bad memories, so she resumed her game at Brentwood Country Club. But after she shot a 64 there, she decided the course was too tame for her.

"What about Hillcrest?" she asked George. They were sitting around listening to Glenn Miller on the radio one evening in their duplex. "It's on Pico right across from Fox Studios."

"That's the Jewish club," George told her.

"So?" Babe said. "I just want to practice there, not join the religion."

Babe's attitude toward Jews had changed since her childhood days in Beaumont. Before she had thought of Jews as Christ killers because that's what all the kids in the neighborhood said. The kids also said that Jews were cheap, always pinching pennies. Babe's parents, who weren't religious but who also pinched pennies, hadn't said much on the subject other than to warn Babe never to take out a loan from a Jew.

"They charge too much interest," Ole had said. "That's usury."

Now through exposure to the broader world, Babe saw Jews as people with an inordinate talent for business. She knew they practically ran the movie industry.

"I don't know if they'll let you in," George said. "They only take Jews as members."

"Don't you know any big-shot Jews who'll help me get in?"

As it turned out, George did, a boxing promoter by the name of Artie Jacobson, who happened to be a Hillcrest member. Artie was a good guy who liked to boast about being friends with Bugsy Siegel. George enjoyed his stories about Bugsy, who it seemed, had actually "rubbed out" someone. George gave Artie a call.

"Are you kidding? They'd love to have Babe practice there," Artie replied. "I'll escort you two myself."

Babe was impressed by Hillcrest. You would never imagine from the club's understated entrance that such a beautiful course lay within the city limits. The restaurant, clubhouse, tennis courts, swimming pool were all first-rate.

"I thought Jews were cheap," she whispered to George as they trailed behind Artie, who was giving them a tour.

"They're not," George whispered back. "They're just tough in business."

"Maybe I'll see Groucho here," Babe said. She loved the Marx Brothers movies.

After a month of practicing at Hillcrest, Babe was eating in the club restaurant when a thoughtful-looking man with receding hair and wearing a neatly trimmed moustache and wire-rimmed glasses, walked in with a fellow she did not recognize and sat down at a nearby table. It was himself, Groucho, minus his movie makeup. She hesitated a moment, rose, introduced herself, and he shook her hand.

"Babe Didrikson? I've heard of you, you're related to Babe Ruth. No? But you've got the same first name. Anyhow, don't tell me that the skies opened, a tablet came down, and you've converted to our faith?"

"Ha, ha, no I haven't, Groucho. But you fellows have the best course in L.A., so how could I resist?"

When they finally played, Groucho told her, "I told you I was a glutton for punishment."

She had beaten him by fifteen strokes.

"My pleasure," Babe said.

Groucho was a funny fellow, but she longed for the day when she would have real competition.

29

"YESTERDAY, DECEMBER 7, 1941, a date which will live in infamy . . ."

George and Babe were sitting in their living room, listening to the president's address on their RCA radio. George was sitting in his easy chair, smoking another cigar. Babe had her legs curled up under her as she sat on the couch.

"Those yellow sons of bitches," George said. "I'm gonna enlist."

Babe looked skeptical but said nothing. She was worried about her brothers joining up. It would be the patriotic thing to do, but she didn't want to lose any of them.

As it turned out, the recruiters took one look at George lumbering through the door and rolled their eyes. Although they humored him and gave him a physical, there wasn't much need for overweight men with varicose veins and bad knees in any branch of the armed forces.

"I thought at least they might let me teach the guys hand to hand combat," George remarked to Babe a week later.

They were again sitting in their living room, listening to the news. Things sounded dire. The Japanese had destroyed most of the Pacific fleet and now the country was gearing up for war with Hitler, too. Babe's younger brother Arthur had already enlisted in the Navy. Ole Jr and Louis had wanted to enlist, but they were already in their mid-thirties, family men with kids. So they contented themselves with building warships at the Beaumont shipyard.

Babe wasn't surprised that the military had rejected George. His belly hung like a potato sack over his belt. His once bullish neck had become flabby. He had had to buy lots of new clothes, larger clothes. And now he was drinking another beer before dinner, gulping it down, then wiping the froth from his mouth with a beefy hand. Beer put the weight on.

They both decided that Babe would do charity golf exhibitions with various celebrities. And George would arrange and promote charity wrestling bouts. The money raised would help the war effort.

"Bing is the one I want to play against," Babe told George. "He might even give me a run for my money." Bing Crosby was known as the best celebrity golfer in Hollywood.

"He'd go for it," George considered. "He's too old to enlist."

AT SAN GABRIEL Country Club, Babe and Patty Berg, one of the best woman golfers in the country, played a charity round against Bing Crosby and Bob Hope. Even though they couldn't be described as close friends, Babe got along with Patty all right. She was a stocky freckle-faced spark plug of a woman who could also hit the ball a long way. Even though she came from a wealthy family, she didn't put on airs—just played consistently excellent golf. George had seen to it that the press was there.

After posing together for the cameras, the group started to play.

Bing Crosby was rather quiet, aloof, and played golf with finesse, his pale blue eyes focused on making the best possible shot, but Bob Hope clowned around a lot. After he made one drive that landed in the trees, he turned around and cracked to the gallery.

"It's great to be playing here today. The only trouble is, Babe swings like a man, and I swing like a girl."

As they played, Babe noticed Hope repeatedly smiling at a young woman at the front of the gallery. The young woman was hard to miss even by Los Angeles standards, where a lot of young women—aspirants to stardom—were good looking. She was a stunning brunette who wore a short-sleeved lime green sweater that emphasized her endowments. She looked to be about twenty.

Babe walked back to the gallery rope while waiting her turn. George was there watching the competition.

"Who's that girl Hope keeps smiling at?" she whispered to George, who was munching a bag of salted peanuts.

"Who?"

Babe pointed the girl out, and George spotted her. His eyes widened. "Probably his girlfriend. She's a knockout, ain't she?"

"I thought Hope was married."

George snorted. "He is but he's a bed hopper. A lot of these stars are. The wives don't seem to mind as long as hubby brings home the bacon."

Babe frowned. How do you like that? These Hollywood fellows thought they could get away with anything.

"Well, I'd mind, and you better not try anything like that," Babe warned, giving George a playful chuck under his chin.

Even though she now realized that George left something to be desired as a husband, he was still hers, and she wanted to keep it that way.

WHEN SHE AND George got back home that night, she got a call from her sister Lillie in Beaumont. Lillie and Babe's parents had moved back home from Los Angeles shortly before Babe and George were married. Since Babe was now a married "lady," it no longer seemed necessary to live with her.

"Are you sitting down?" Lillie asked.

"Spill it," Babe said.

"It's Papa. He died this morning," Lillie told Babe.

The news didn't come as a surprise. Ole Didriksen had been ill with lung cancer for several months. Actually, he had had an operation to remove a tumor that proved malignant over a year ago. The doctors soft-pedaled Pop's condition, telling the family they had gotten all of the tumor, but you could tell by the way Pop seemed shrunken into himself the last time Babe saw him that the cancer must have spread. The sturdy carpenter, proud of his workmanship, now a feeble old man who spoke in a wheezing whisper. And his once powerful arms, capable of pounding nails into the hardest wood there was . . . well, the muscle had been eaten away by cancer the way termites eat through wood.

After she hung up the phone, Babe told George she was taking the next flight to Houston. From there she would rent a car and drive to Beaumont.

"Do you want to go?"

"I'd like to but I can't," George said. "I gotta travel to Denver. We got some big charity matches coming up."

Babe understood. It was George's way of contributing to the war effort. And being with her family would give her time out of George's shadow without getting lonely.

30

BABE WAS SITTING alone with her mother in the kitchen on 850 Doucette Street. It was the evening after the funeral, and the other siblings had departed to their respective homes. Everyone was cried out. What remained for Babe was a feeling that was both empty and serene—all the dutiful things—the church service, the burial, the repast afterwards—had been done. What was left were the memories.

Babe looked around. The Didriksen kitchen had changed since her childhood, Babe had seen to that. She had bought her mother a sleek, white electric stove and a refrigerator complete with freezer to replace the old wooden ice box. It had cost a pretty penny and it was probably the first of its kind on the block, but Babe had gladly shelled out the money when she was still doing paid exhibitions. Even the kitchen table and chairs were new: the tabletop was white Formica, while the chairs were red with white piping. In contrast, the kitchen cabinets were the same ones Pop had constructed over thirty years ago. These cabinets showed their age: stained by cooking steam, and the hinges creaked when you opened them. Now that Pop was gone, Babe thought she might ask Mama if she wanted new ones. No, not right now she wouldn't. They had just buried the man, the excellent cabinet maker.

"It sure is nice to have ice cubes," Mama commented as she sipped at her drink.

"You shouldn't be drinking that soda pop," Babe said. "I thought Dr. Tatum said it ain't good for your diabetes."

"It ain't. But I love soda pop."

Babe sighed. Who was she to take away one of her mother's few indulgences?

Babe was drinking beer from a bottle—Lone Star. It tasted great ice cold. Hannah Didriksen didn't begrudge her daughter the cold beer. The heat in Beaumont hadn't changed any. Unlike Los Angeles, still humid as a sauna.

As Hannah sat with one hand on the table before her, she picked at a stray bread crumb, her arthritic fingers swollen at the joints. Although

Babe had bought her a new automatic washer several years earlier, the kind without a wringer, years of washing clothes the old way had taken their toll.

"Now that Pop's gone, will you be all right living alone?" Babe asked.

"Sure, Lillie is down the street, and the boys stop by."

She meant Ole Jr. and Louis. Left unmentioned was the fact that Babe's younger brother, Arthur, was in basic training in San Diego. That he would soon be onboard ship in the Pacific was a constant worry, better left unspoken.

"They better," Babe said. But she felt a twinge of guilt because she was living so far away. She rose and looked inside the refrigerator. There was plenty of food, including frozen meat, enough to last her mother two weeks. She had told Babe her appetite wasn't that good anymore. Babe worried about that.

She sat down. "Remember when I let that mutt eat the stew meat?"

Hannah smiled. "I sure gave you some whacks for that."

"I deserved it. I was a pistol, wasn't I Ma?"

"You were a good girl, *min Bebe*. You just had a lot of what do they call it? Spunk."

"Still do," Babe replied. "And when I get my amateur status back, I'm gonna show a lot of those girls what for."

Hannah smiled wanly. Babe had never lacked confidence. "How's George?"

Babe sat back in her chair, one arm slung on her lap. "Ah, he's the same. Busy or he would have come with me. Now he's talkin' about us moving to Denver. He says it would put him closer to where he does most of his promoting."

"Denver? That's in the mountains, isn't it?"

"Yep. They call it the Mile High City. Air is thinner there."

"Do you want to move there?"

"It's a nice city. Been through it a few times with George. I wouldn't mind."

They had nice golf courses around Denver, even if you could play on them only part of the year.

Hannah looked intently at Babe. "Does George treat you good?"

Babe had to think about that one. The wooden wall clock, brought from the old country, ticked off the seconds. It was dark by now, and flies and moths buzzed and plunked raggedly against the screens, playing a discordant tune.

"Yes, I guess so," she finally said. "There's times when I don't like what he does, like he's always bringing his buddies home for me to feed without warning, but I guess I shouldn't complain."

"Men are men." Hannah sighed. She thought about the times Ole had done things that irked her. For example, she never had liked the smell of pipe smoke. But she had put up with it for over forty years because he didn't drink much, he worked hard, and he didn't see other women.

Then she cast Babe a suspicious look. Babe had already told her that George spent lots of time on the road. A promoter was like a traveling salesman, wasn't he?

"George isn't fooling around, is he?"

Babe, who had taken up smoking in Los Angeles, pulled a Pall Mall from her purse and lit it with a book of matches that read Brentwood Country Club. Her mother did not castigate Babe for this habit. Lots of movie stars smoked.

"George with other women? Nah. At least I don't think so. Who'd want him?"

Hannah was surprised by Babe's rather cynical remark.

"George is a good man," she firmly announced, well aware that George was supporting Babe and contributing money to the Didriksen family. Although all Babe's brothers now had jobs and her sisters were married to men who worked, it seemed the money they earned wasn't enough. Or maybe it was just that when they saw Babe married to a "rich" man, their outlook changed. They wanted more. More for private schooling, nicer cars, new appliances, additions to their homes. Etcetera.

"Yeah, George is a good man. I can't kick."

She and George were alike in a lot of ways, always hustling, always looking out for the main chance, working the angles. If he wasn't very sensitive, well, as her mother said, men were men. If she sometimes longed for a gentler touch, well, that wasn't something she could tell anybody.

"That reminds me," Babe said. "I played against two celebrities recently."

She went to the living room, retrieved her purse, and returned to the kitchen. She handed a golf scorecard to her mother. Bing Crosby's and Bob Hope's autographs were on it. She wouldn't have bothered getting Hope's autograph, the lout, but she thought her mother would like it.

"My Babe with Bing Crosby and Bob Hope!" Hannah exclaimed. "They didn't beat you playin' golf, did he?"

Babe blew a smoke ring.

"Nah, those duffers, are you kidding? Me and Patty Berg beat their pants off." She didn't tell her mother that Patty had outscored her by one point. It was for charity, anyway. It didn't really count.

Before she left for Los Angeles, Babe reminded her mother to call her if she needed anything.

"I will," Hannah replied.

31

THE TUDOR-STYLE house in Denver was a far roomier place than Babe had ever lived in before. Though it was still only a rental, she decorated it and furnished it with care. Bertha Bowen with her Neiman Marcus taste had schooled her on what brands to look for in home furnishings.

George didn't care much about such things. Just so long as there was food in the refrigerator, liquor in the bar, an ashtray within reach, his easy chair, and a desk to spread out his business stuff, he was happy.

Since it would soon be the dead of winter, Babe decided she had to do something or go stir crazy. Taking to heart a suggestion from Bertha, she began volunteering to work with the city's poor kids. There were plenty of them—orphaned kids, kids with patchwork clothes, kids with rickets or suffering the after-effects of polio, kids worse off than she had ever been as a kid.

She'd drive down to the YMCA and teach them to swim. The fact that all the kids were white barely registered with Babe. After all, she had grown up in the segregated South. Someone told her there was a black YMCA in the Five Points section of the city, but she didn't dare go there. There'd be black men there, and a white woman around black men? Of course not.

Anyhow, it was fun teaching the kids to swim. They'd cluster around Babe, and she'd get them quieted down in the shallow section of the pool. They called her Miss Babe. Then she'd demonstrate a stroke in the lukewarm, chlorinated water. There were always a couple of kids who were desperately afraid of the water. One of them was a tow-headed little boy whose right leg was stunted due to polio. His name was Johnnie. She'd be extra gentle with Johnnie and the rest of the timid kids, ease them into it, hold their bodies parallel with the water and then release them. Seeing Johnnie finally learn to swim reminded her of the time she had caught a bass in a lake outside of Beaumont and then released it. She felt she had accomplished something.

Teaching the kids at the YMCA made Babe think about having kids of her own. But did she really want to take care of a child full-time when she had so much athletic talent? She had to admit to herself that she didn't, not right now anyhow. Neither did George. With his constant coming and going, he'd be a lousy father. So Babe continued using a diaphragm when she and George had sex. The "bottle cap," she called it. So far, no accidents.

ON JANUARY 21, 1943, a letter arrived in the mail addressed to Mrs. Mildred D. Zaharias. After she read the letter, she gave a hoot and a holler.

"What the hell happened?" George, who was sitting at his desk in his office, just off the living room, shouted.

""Hallelujah, I've just been reinstated!" Babe shouted back. "Let me grab my clubs, I'm on my way."

George went into the living room and read the letter for himself. He was already envisioning Babe's future as a top amateur and then, maybe, as a professional again. With the ranks of women golfers swelling, George pictured a time when a ladies' professional golf tour would be financially successful. All you needed were a dozen or so strong players and a few players with *charisma*, a word he had heard at Hillcrest. His wife, Babe, certainly had that.

32

YOUNG PEGGY KIRK was sitting on a wooden bench, pulling on a pair of new golf shoes, feeling happy to simply be taking part in the Women's Western Open at Highland Country Club when the locker room door burst open and a voice with a Southern drawl shouted, "The Babe's here! Who's gonna finish second?"

The woman closest to Peggy, a golfer named Mabel Lindsay, rolled her eyes.

"She does that all the time," Mabel told Peggy, not bothering to lower her voice.

"Loudmouth as always," Patty Berg commented, who was standing on Peggy's left. Patty took Babe in stride by now. Sure, she was a showboat, but she got publicity for the women's game.

Babe tossed out greetings to her competitors, most of whom she knew by now, if only casually. But she stopped in front of Peggy.

"And who are you?" she asked, her hazel eyes landing on the inexperienced golfer like a hawk on a squirrel.

Because Peggy had been an avid sports fan since she was a girl, she knew all about Babe's Olympic triumphs and her exhibition rounds with the great Gene Sarazen and others. Who didn't know about Babe Didrikson? Now the legend was standing before her in the flesh. That raw fact almost gave her goose pimples.

Peggy swallowed her nervousness and introduced herself. As they shook hands, Babe sized Peggy up. She looked like a real nice kid, apple-cheeked, even-featured, with the strong shoulders and hands befitting a competitive golfer. Tall, too, a couple of inches taller than Babe. Of course, she wasn't about to tell her all that good stuff. Let the kid wonder.

"Where'd ya play?" Babe asked.

"Mostly just in Ohio so far," Peggy replied. "I won the Ohio Amateurs two years running."

"Well, that's nice," Babe said. "But this is the big time, Sis."

Overhearing their conversation, Patty Berg stepped in. "Now don't pick on Peggy. She's just out of college and smart as a whip."

"Oh, a college kid, eh," Babe said. "I eat them for lunch."

Peggy didn't know how seriously to take Babe, but Patty again stepped forward.

"Don't let Babe bully you. Her bark is worse than her bite."

"Whattaya mean by that?" Babe replied. "My bite is real baad." With that, she grimaced like the big bad wolf, showing two rows of clean, white teeth. But then she grinned, that appealingly crooked grin, as cavalier as a pirate.

"You're too much," Patty said.

Babe was still smiling. Though she didn't think Patty was quite the golfer she was, she respected her. That was the thing in women's golf. When push came to shove, the players at least tried to curb whatever animosities arose because they were all pulling for the same thing—the success of the women's tour.

"Anyway, it's nice to meet you, Peggy," Babe said. "I didn't mean to make fun of your experience."

"Yes, you did," Patty Berg replied.

As if in defiance of Patty, Babe told Peggy Kirk, "Listen, if you're still around on Friday, let's go out to dinner."

"If *she's* still around . . ." Patty said. "What if *you're* not around?"

"Don't worry, kiddo, I'll be around," Babe told her, slapping Patty rather heavily on the back.

Peggy Kirk agreed to dinner. The great Babe Didrikson!

Later that day, Babe won her first round. It had been a challenge, playing with the best in women's amateur golf, but she had risen to the occasion once again. Now it was late afternoon, and she was lying on the bed in her hotel suite, listening to news on the radio. The news couldn't be better out of Europe: Hitler had killed himself a few days earlier and the Germans had surrendered. The war with Japan was still going on, but so far Bubba was safe on his carrier in the Pacific. Babe was thinking sadly of some boys from Beaumont High who Lillie told her had been killed in the war when the phone rang. It was George, calling from Denver.

"I've got some real bad news, hon," he told her in his gruff voice. There was a pause as he gave her a moment to prepare herself. "Lillie called me. Your mom had a heart attack. She's in the hospital."

"How bad is it?" Babe sat down on the bed.

"She's . . . um . . . not expected to pull through."

Babe thought of her mother lying at death's door, alone in some crummy hospital room.

"I'm going home," she said.

"Listen," George said. "Lillie told me your mom said she wants you to finish the tournament."

"Mama said that?"

"Yes."

Babe wasn't sure if George was telling the truth. He always thought first about her career. Maybe he was just telling her that to keep her going. He sure as hell wasn't going to travel to Beaumont to see her dying mother. He didn't like hospitals.

"You're not kiddin' me?"

"No, I'm not," George said, a little offended by Babe's question. Did she really think he would lie to her at a time like this? Just because he sometimes made business plans without consulting her? He had a mother too, for god's sake, whom he visited from time to time.

"I'm gonna call Lillie," Babe told him.

"Okay, do that. She'll tell you the latest."

"I will."

"Sorry, honey," George added. "Your mama is a great lady."

Babe appreciated that. When push came to shove, her husband had a good heart.

When Babe spoke to Lillie, who had answered the call at the hospital nursing station nearest to her mother, she affirmed that Mama Didriksen did want Babe to finish the tournament.

"Besides, you know you can't get a flight out of there," Lillie said.

That was true. Due to wartime travel restrictions, Babe doubted she could get a plane or train ride out of Indianapolis. The public came a distant second to troop transport.

"Tell Mama I send her all my love," Babe told her sister.

"I will. I'm here almost all the time. And Esther Nancy and Ole and Louis have been here with their wives."

That consoled Babe a little. On the radio the Andrews sisters were singing "The Boogie Woogie Bugle Boy of Company B."

The next day, the people who managed the tournament told a few veteran golfers about Babe's mother. They spread the word to the rest. A few felt it served Babe right for being so cocky, though most didn't feel that way. Everyone had a mother.

Babe played well in the quarterfinals, despite everything. As she stood on the serene course waiting for her turn, she could envision her mother's labored breathing and suffering face. Mama usually wore her long, white hair up in a bun, but now it must be streaming out over the pillow. She hoped her mother was alert enough to understand what Babe had told Lillie to tell her.

When people came over to congratulate Babe on winning the semifinal, it was all she could do to thank them.

That night Esther Nancy called to tell her that Mama Didriksen was dead.

"They tried to save her, but her heart just gave out."

"I'm coming home," Babe said.

"She wanted you to win the match," Esther Nancy said.

"Did she really say that?"

"Yes, she did. We asked her, and that's what she said. She was still alert, and she knew how much golf means to you."

Esther Nancy's remark stung. Did her mother really think she was some kind of golfing machine? Didn't she know how much she loved her? Suddenly winning didn't mean much to Babe. She called up the airlines and the train service but couldn't get a flight or a train out of Indianapolis for several days.

The next day Peggy Kirk came up to Babe in the locker room before the match. She wasn't sure she should say something to Babe—whom she barely knew, but she decided she would.

"I heard about your mother. I'm so sorry."

"Thank you, Peggy," Babe said. Her eyes were red-rimmed, and she looked as if she was about to cry again. "I want to get home, but I can't get a flight or train. So I'm gonna win this thing for my mama."

Peggy was surprised that Babe took the time to explain her situation to her, a nobody on the tour. She thought it was nice of her.

Peggy Kirk and her friend Marge Rowe had dinner that Friday night in Babe's suite, the way they had planned to before Mrs. Didriksen's death. Peggy had thought that Babe might cancel having guests for dinner, but no, she said she'd appreciate their company.

"I don't have much of an appetite, but I'll order room service," she told them. "You two order anything you want. My treat."

Aside from a few remarks concerning the tournament, the three women, balancing their trays on their laps, ate in silence. No one felt like making small talk. After dinner Babe surprised both Peggy and Marge by taking out her harmonica and playing tunes that fit her mood. Listening to mournful country tunes like "Down in the Valley" and "My Old Virginia Home" and "Dark is the Color of My True Love's Eyes," Peggy thought, "She's good at everything she does."

"What was it like winning the Olympics?" she suddenly asked Babe.

Babe looked up with a vague expression, as if she had suddenly remembered that Peggy and Marge were there. Her harmonica now rested on her lap.

"Aw, you don't wanna hear about that stuff," she said. "I just ran a few races and won. I threw the javelin and won. My sport now is golf."

In truth, Babe didn't like thinking back on her track and field days. She had been so foolish then. Running wild on the train out to Los Angeles, messing with people's sleep and then having people saying she wasn't a girl, she was really a boy. She didn't even like to look at photos of herself from that time.

"Who is that freakish thing?" she'd ask herself whenever she'd stumble across a photo of her younger self, all raw-boned with short, boyish hair, tough jaw, no lipstick to offset her thin lips, not a speck of style.

"Yeah, best to forget those old times," Babe continued. "I meet nice people like you gals playing golf."

The next day Babe managed to hold on to her lead despite a late charge by Dorothy Germain. The gallery had been on her side throughout the tournament. Something about her made her a pleasure to watch, as if there was an energy within her, a sense of limitless possibility that others, no matter how talented, didn't have.

Babe knew she had it. And in better times, she loved getting the gallery involved in her play.

"Now ah wonder if ah should do this," she'd tell them, exaggerating her East Texas accent while selecting a club. "Nah, ah think ah'll try the 7 iron" and so on. But today there were no cheery comments to the gallery from Babe. She didn't have the heart.

As Babe held aloft the tournament trophy, she told herself, "I got it for you, Mama." Even to Babe it seemed like a corny thing to think, like something out of the movies—"win one for the Gipper" and all that slop. But in Babe's case it was true.

33

EVERYONE EXCEPT BABE had already seen Mama Didriksen laid out at the funeral parlor.

Esther Nancy told her they'd wait for her in the outer room and shut the door, leaving Babe alone with Mama. It was a top-of-the line casket, made of solid mahogany with handsome brass handles and a satin lining—Babe had seen to that over a telephone call with the funeral director. But Mama looked doll-like in the casket, waxen, nothing like the vigorous woman who had played such a great part in all their lives. Babe hadn't shed a tear for a few days, the effort of making travel arrangements keeping her mind occupied. But now she let go and sobbed. Even with George sitting outside the door, she had never felt lonelier.

The funeral, held at a local Lutheran church, was a subdued affair. Babe was too choked up to speak. But she noticed the attendees and appreciated that Tiny and Ruth Scurlock were sitting in a pew. Although she and Tiny had kept in touch by mail, she hadn't seen him in the flesh for a couple of years. During the luncheon afterward, Tiny, Ruth, and Babe sat together and reminisced about the old days. George, who had met Tiny at a golf tournament in Los Angeles, looked on.

"I remember when I first set eyes on you, Babe," Tiny recalled. "You were nothing but a kid then."

"That was at a game against Port Neches." Babe remembered because of the nice write-up Tiny had given her after the game, the first she had ever received in the *Beaumont Journal*.

"Yes," Tiny said. "I could tell you had that killer instinct."

"I wasn't much of a student, was I?" Babe asked Ruth.

Ruth, who had switched to teaching English at Lamar College, tried to be diplomatic. "I could tell you had other things on your mind. But you came up with some good ideas."

"I should've studied harder," Babe said, frowning. "Now when I meet these college girls on the tour, I wish I had." She was thinking of girls like

Peggy Kirk and Betty Jameson, whip smart and so much better educated than she.

"You've got lots of life experience," Tiny volunteered.

Babe shrugged.

"At least I read magazines."

After the funeral and burial, the family sat in the old familiar living room on Doucette Street and reminisced. There was plenty to eat and drink. Neighbors had brought tons of food—casseroles, cold cuts, a sliced ham, fresh fruit, various cakes and pies, cookies, orange Jello with bananas, so much that the Didriksen siblings would have to take some of the food home with them to keep it from spoiling.

The family had also brought home some of the funeral flower arrangements, so the little living room was cramped with the smell of bouquets, beer, perfume, and cigar and cigarette smoke. Babe's brothers and sisters were all there, minus Arthur, who had returned to the States safely but was still on the West Coast being mustered out of the Navy. Now they were telling Babe how proud Mama had been of her even to the last. They had told her of Babe's success during the Western Women's Tournament, though of course she had passed before the final rounds.

"The Didriksens are a tough lot," Ole Jr. said. He looked a lot like his dad, with the same pugnacious jaw and prominent nose but with the rounder face of his mother. He too smoked a pipe. He had been working as a welder at the shipyard since high school and would probably stay there the rest of his working life. By now he was a foreman.

Babe's sisters told stories of the old days when Mama and Papa were alive. Babe was sitting in what had been Ole Sr.'s armchair, smoking a Pall Mall and sipping a bottle of Lone Star.

"You remember when you jumped off that roof on a dare and hurt your leg?" Lillie asked Babe. Although Babe had jumped into a pile of sand near the half-built house, there had been a jagged piece of wood in the pile, which punctured her right leg.

"Sure do," Babe said. "And I still got the scar to prove it."

She pulled up her skirt a couple of inches to show them the white scar on her otherwise sun-tanned calf. Maybe it was coincidence, maybe providence but Esther Nancy looked over and noted that the scar resembled a golf driver.

"The Lord works in mysterious ways," she commented. How she got religion, no one could say since neither of the Didriksen parents was particularly religious. Neither was Esther Nancy's husband, Jack, a bald, taciturn man who was sitting placidly, chewing *Skoal* on the couch beside her. Every now and then Jack would stir, sitting up straight and leaning forward, giving people the impression that he was about to say something important. But all he did was spit snuff into a cup on the coffee table. In a way, it was disappointing.

"And then you jumped from that same roof the next day and broke three ribs," Lillie added.

"I was a hellcat," Babe admitted, taking another gulp of beer.

George was sitting in another armchair with his feet up on a brown ottoman. Babe could tell he was getting antsy at this family stuff by the way he chain-smoked cigars. Well, it was okay. They were flying back to Denver together the next day.

"That reminds me," Lillie said.

She rose and went into Mama's bedroom and returned with two large scrapbooks. She handed both to Babe, who set them on her lap.

"These things smell musty," Babe said, "like they been around a while."

"Mama kept them for years," she told Babe. "On a shelf in her bedroom closet."

Babe's eyes watered all over again. She didn't want to look at old newspaper clippings right now.

"Well, thanks, Lillie. I'll take them back to Denver with me."

But the others wanted to leaf through the scrapbooks, so Babe let them. They began at the front of the first scrapbook.

"Gosh, Babe," Louis commented. "You sure looked different playing for Employers Casualty."

Babe frowned. "That was before I discovered Elizabeth Arden. Now you can't keep me out of the department stores."

Everyone laughed.

"They got some good stores in Denver," George commented. "I know that from the bills."

"Now, honey, I don't spend that much, do I?"

"Na, but you don't spend that little, neither," George replied. Actually, it was a point of pride with him to be able to pay Babe's bills, and he wanted everyone to know it.

After her brothers and sisters looked through the older scrapbook, George said, "Here let me see that."

Babe said nothing as George perused the clippings. The folio-sized scrapbook looked small in his big wrestler's hands.

He looked up at Babe and squinted. "You sure did look different back then."

"Not as dolled up, huh?"

"Not as grown up," George replied. He wasn't a man who placed a great store on feminine beauty. He had had so-called beautiful, or at least very pretty women whom he didn't respect. He respected Babe, and she attracted him. She had a cute face, pretty eyes, lovely hair, and a beautiful figure. She was a fighter, like him.

George got to his feet and handed the scrapbook back to Babe, who placed it beside her on the chair.

Lillie and her family were already preparing to move into the family homestead, so it wouldn't stay vacant for long. She and her husband O.B. had two kids by now, a boy and a girl. Both under four, they darted around the living room like ferrets. Lillie grabbed Martin before he overturned a red and white flower arrangement sitting on a lamp table.

Ole Jr.'s, Louis's, and Esther Nancy's kids were already in their teens or close to it. They were patiently sitting out on the front steps or standing beside them, talking about their own concerns while waiting for the grownups to tire of each other's company. One of the kids, Jackie, had lit up a punk to help keep the mosquitos away.

Lillie stood up.

"Let's get you two to bed," she announced to her kids.

Lillie and her husband, O.B. Grimes, rose to go.

Babe was relieved. The kids, with their constant movement, were getting on her nerves.

Finally, the conversation wound down.

"When are you two leaving again?" Ole Jr. asked.

"Tomorrow," George said.

"We'll miss you all," Babe added. And meant it.

34

"I'M GONNA INVITE that sportswriter Bill Musgrave to the house for some publicity, whattaya think?" George asked Babe one evening as they were eating a meatloaf Babe had made. Having recently seen clippings from Babe's tomboy past, George wanted to put to rest any idea people still had of her being a "muscle moll" with all the charm of a lawn jockey. His Babe was now plenty feminine, he thought. It was true that after the first few years of marriage, she didn't seem to relish sex the way he did. But what decent woman did?

"Okay, but let me clean the house first," Babe said.

It bothered her the way George always slathered her meatloaves with ketchup, as if to drown the taste, but said nothing. It was funny the way little things about your partner got to you when you were married. As usual, George was having a Schlitz with his meal. For some reason he didn't like Coors, the signature Colorado brand.

Babe hoped this beer and the ones he had drunk that afternoon weren't the start of a binge. She had been married to George long enough to know that he got all soppy and sentimental when he drank too much. Either that or belligerent if you crossed him. Either way, it wasn't pretty.

"Who does Bill Musgrave write for?" Babe asked as she watched George take another long draught of Schlitz.

"*Sporting Times*," George said. "I think we can get some good publicity by showin' off this place and us in it."

"Sounds good to me," Babe said. "Want some bread with that butter?"

George had just put a huge slab of butter on his bread, but he ignored her smart comment.

"I'll give him a call then."

After they ate, Babe washed and dried the dishes, while George went into his study. An hour later, while Babe was lying on the couch listening to Jack Benny on the radio, he came out.

"Deal's all set," he said. "Bill's coming out next Thursday. He said *Sporting Times* will definitely publish the piece. He's bringin' a photographer, too."

"Shit," Babe said. "That doesn't leave me much time to get this house in order."

A week later, the writer Bill Musgrave and a photographer showed up at the Zaharias's front door. Both Babe and George greeted them. Babe had bought the doormat with the large Z emblazoned across it, sort of like the mark of Zorro. Before entering the house, the photographer—a young fellow named Fred Quinn—took photos of Babe standing in front of her prized rosebushes. She was wearing a silk beige dress, pearls, and heels.

Then the Zahariases showed the visitors around the house, including the master bedroom.

"That's some bed," Bill Musgrave said.

"We had it made special," Babe explained. "Sheets and blankets too. George is a big guy, and when he sleeps, he moves around a lot, so now we have room for both of us."

Indeed, the bed was eight feet by eight feet, custom built and so large you could sleep in it and barely notice there was someone else with you.

Bill Musgrave and Fred Quinn also noted Babe's bureau, which was laden with cosmetics, fancy bottles of perfume, hairbrushes, lotions, and cremes. Babe dared anyone to look at all that gear and say she wasn't feminine.

They also toured the study, which doubled as a trophy room. Babe had spent a lot of time getting this room straightened up. There had been a mountain of cigar stubs in the souvenir abalone shell George used as an ashtray, and the remains of various items on and around George's desk: apple cores, peanut shells, papers, empty match books, candy wrappers— Baby Ruth bars were his favorite—even a couple of squashed Schlitz cans. The wastebasket to the right of the desk had been overflowing. They were lucky they didn't have mice with all the crumbs.

"This is mostly Babe's stuff," George said, pointing to one large display case, which Babe had used Windex to make shine. It housed a collection of the trophies Babe had won in golf.

"Yep, and I plan to add to it soon," Babe said. She told her visitors about some of the tournaments she was going to enter the next year.

"That's a lot of tournaments," Bill said. "You're going to be busy. Does George help you with any of the housework?"

Babe was about to reply that he didn't.

"Sure, sometimes," George said.

"What's something you help her with?"

George thought. "Dishes."

"Ha! That would make a good photo," Bill said. "The mighty wrestler doing the dishes. Can we get a photo of that?"

"Sure. Why not?"

While they were in the kitchen, George obliged by putting on one of Babe's flowery aprons, knowing the sight would tickle readers.

"Tie this thing, honey," George said to Babe. The drawstrings barely fit around his middle.

After she did so, George lifted a dish out of the drying rack and pretended to dry it with a towel. Fred Quinn got the shot.

Bill asked George if Babe was a good cook.

"She's a helluva fine cook," George exclaimed. That, at least, was the god's honest truth.

"What's your favorite dish to cook?" Bill asked, turning to Babe.

"Beef burgundy," Babe said. "Takes a long time, but it's worth it. I bake cakes too, though I found out you have to adjust the baking time in Denver because of the thin air."

Bill found it hard to accept the idea of Babe being so flexible in her interests.

"Do you really like cooking?" he asked.

"Sure, but even if I didn't, I'd do it for George." She wrapped her arm around his. "I'd do anything for George. If he asked me to, I'd even give up golf."

"Aw, that's sweet, honey." George gave her a peck on her cheek.

After the men left, George asked Babe how she thought the visit went.

"Fine," she said. "But I can't believe you said you did the dishes."

"It could happen." George shrugged. "You never know."

Meanwhile, on the drive back to the airport, Fred Quinn asked Bill Musgrave if he thought George really helped Babe with the dishes.

"Are you kidding?" Bill replied. "He doesn't lift a finger."

35

"IT'S CRAZY THE stuff people lap up," Babe told herself as she was looking over Bill Musgrave's article in *Sporting Times*. It irked her just a bit to see her life with George presented in such a rosy manner. But then again, she thought of the bad press she had gotten from the likes of Paul Gallico, and George's unwillingness to help with any housework seemed a small price to pay. Besides, he was the one paying the bills.

The roses in her garden were all gone by now, the grass withered and the trees bare, save for the evergreens. It was a frosty November evening in Denver, with rain turning to sleet that crackled against the windowpanes. So cold, not at all like Southeast Texas, where it rarely got below 50 degrees. As Babe stared at the grass on her front lawn, which was becoming stiff with sleet, she got an idea and picked up the living room phone.

"I need a partner for the four-ball tournament that's coming up in Hollywood, Florida," she announced to Peggy Kirk. Four-ball was played with two teams of two players. Each player played her own ball, and the winner was determined by the score of the lowest team member.

"Well, I don't know," Peggy said. "I guess I could do it."

"Come on," Babe said. "You might as well win a tournament."

Peggy had to laugh at the cold truthfulness of Babe's remark. "Okay, but I hope I don't hold you back."

"Don't worry about it. I can beat any two of them by myself."

In truth, Peggy was the only golfer Babe *could* ask to be her partner. The rest were either put off by her cockiness or stars in their own right, like Patty Berg and Betty Jameson.

For her part, Peggy Kirk, who was not yet a star and might not ever become a star, had taken psychology courses at Hollins College. From these courses, she had learned that people often overcompensated for their insecurities by boasting. That insight seemed to apply to Babe.

IT WAS GOOD to be with the girls down in sunny Florida. George had approved of Babe's taking part in the tournament—anything to burnish her reputation—though he stayed behind in Denver. The blue skies in Florida, so wide you could practically imagine the curve of the earth beneath them, the balmy breezes, the placid water nearby all served to remove memories of the harsh northern winter. Even better, Babe, who had been lonely without quite realizing it, was beginning to think of Peggy Kirk as a younger sister. Peggy was also delighted to be partnering with Babe but nervous as hell. Insecure or not, Babe was one of the best women golfers in the country, if not the world. With Babe's fame on her mind, Peggy did dreadfully at first, scoring a 7 on the first hole.

Seeing Peggy struggle, Babe was unusually forbearing. Studying her partner as she hit her errant shots, she concluded that Peggy was putting too much pressure on herself.

"Listen, Peg, just think about playing for par," Babe told her. After that, Peggy did much better and shot a 74 for the round.

Maybe Babe was rusty from the layoff in Denver, maybe it was just one of those things. But she was off her game, and neither she nor Peggy Kirk won the tournament. Babe felt bad about that, both for her own and for Peggy's sake. Here, she had practically promised the kid a tournament victory and she had been the one to flop.

"Sorry I let you down, kid," Babe said. "Sorry" wasn't a word she was used to uttering, and it stuck in her throat.

"You have nothing to apologize for," Peggy said. "It was an honor to play with you."

Babe was touched by this generous response. But the loss still rankled. That evening in her hotel room, she had a few beers to take the sting off.

No matter. Based on her outstanding overall play for the year, the Associated Press named Babe Didrikson Zaharias Female Athlete of the Year.

After Babe flew back to Denver—she wouldn't drive with snow blanketing the Midwest—George suggested they celebrate her award by going out to the Silver Inn. Knowing that George was partial to the world-famous sugar steaks the Inn offered, Babe agreed. But then she looked out the living room window. It had snowed steadily in the morning, and then on and off throughout the day. Though the roads had been recently plowed, there was a new coating of snow on them.

"Are you sure we should drive in this?" Babe asked.

"I'll go slow," George told her as he opened the driver side door of his Cadillac. He no longer bothered to open her door.

Despite the icy roads and flurrying snow, George did drive slowly, and they made it to the restaurant without incident.

It was toasty in the place, which was not crowded, with a fire blazing in the fireplace. Both Babe and George liked the exposed beam walls and ceiling, blocky wooden furniture, and old portraits and utilitarian objects such as snowshoes and a miner's pick and shovel mounted on the walls. The floors were hard wood, too. It was like eating a meal in a very well-appointed log cabin.

George lit up a cigar. He had continued to put on weight, so much that he had to sit out a bit from the table. He was telling Babe about his promotional activities. He had signed a new wrestler he thought promising, a Croatian kid out of Boulder named Eddie Novak, whose dad had been blown apart in a mine explosion.

"I'd love for Eddie to be a success," George said. "And not just for the money."

Babe admired the fact that George had successfully promoted the careers of several wrestlers who would otherwise be in dire straits. And she'd rather hear George telling her about them than about the problems he had with some laundromat he had bought in San Diego. How much fun was it to hear about messed-up coin slots in washing machines?

During a lull in the conversation, Babe told George a bit about some of the girls she played golf with.

"Peggy Kirk is a real nice kid," she told him. "She's smart as a whip, went to Hollins College. That's a girls' school in Virginia."

But George's eyes went glassy when she told him a few details of their recent partnership. So she stopped. It was funny how men were. They could talk all day and night about stuff, some of it blindingly boring, and you were expected to listen. But the minute you started talking about stuff important to you, they paid no attention. It was like it was poison to them.

While they were eating, George got gravy on the front of his open-necked white shirt but seemed oblivious to the fact. He was drinking Jim Beam. The waiter had to come back several times to refill his glass. Lately he had gotten into the strange habit of wiping his mouth not in his napkin but on the tablecloth itself. Babe cringed, looked around, hoping none of the other patrons noticed. They seemed like a well-heeled lot.

"George," Babe said when he did it again. "That's uncouth."

"Uncouth?" George repeated. "Where'd you pick up that word? Bryn Mawr?"

He glared at her, and she knew better than to say anything more about his dining habits. Instead, the conversation switched to the upcoming tournaments Babe would play in. With the war over, there were twenty women's amateur tournaments that year. Babe would be on the road a lot, a fact she viewed with ambivalence. On the one hand, it was nice to have George along with her—with his gregarious manner he could be good company. On the other hand, he often got on her nerves, like tonight when he rambled on too much about business.

"I don't go in for all that self-esteem talk," George had once told her. That was true enough. But just having him on tour was worth it to Babe.

After watching George consume several more tumblers of Jim Beam, Babe volunteered to drive home, but George wouldn't hear of it.

"I'm not drunk," he said, though he reeked of liquor. Babe felt nervous getting in the car with him, but once again he did drive slowly. Still, Babe's knuckles were white from digging into the seat cushion by the time they got home.

26

LOUISE SUGGS AND Babe Didrikson Zaharias were both Southerners but were opposites in most respects. While Louise's father had money and owned a golf course, Babe's father had been a cabinetmaker and barely made enough money to support his large family. Louise was a short, stocky woman whose square face seemed to accentuate her quiet stolidity and who preferred to let her golf game do the talking. Babe, on the other hand, with her jutting chin and beaky nose, was known as a braggart. Then there was the undeniable fact that while Louise paid scant attention to the gallery, Babe had the uncanny ability to cozy up to the fans, enlisting them on her side.

When they had first met, Babe had ignored her young opponent's outstretched hand and asked, "So, you ready to finish second?" Nothing since then had made Louise Suggs like Babe any better.

Thus, it was particularly satisfying to Louise when she soundly beat Babe at the Western Women's Amateur that year. But she knew that this loss would only make Babe more eager to beat her the next time.

After winning two more tournaments, Babe lost another tournament in August. But after that, she entered the U.S. Women's Amateur, held in Tulsa, Oklahoma. It was considered the most prestigious of all women's tournaments—the equivalent of a women's golf championship. The course—Southern Hills Country Club—was a long one, which Babe liked since it catered to her ability to drive the ball farther than anyone else. If you couldn't drive them long on this course, you might as well pack it up.

"I've wanted to win this tournament for thirteen years," Babe told the press. "Ever since I took up golf seriously. It would be a terrible thing to go through an entire golf career without ever winning the National."

She needn't have worried. She trounced her nearest competitor, Clara Callender Sherman, by a margin of 11 and 9. It was the second widest margin in the history of the championship.

She also won the last tournament of the season, the Women's Texas Open, defeating Betty Hicks. As a result of her winning, she was again voted the AP Female Athlete of the Year.

She was tired, though. After winning in Texas, she started the long road trip back to Denver, a seven-hundred-mile journey up through the desolate high plains of the Texas panhandle. There, she'd sometimes spy a jackrabbit racing through the brush along the road, his mottled coat blending in with his stark surroundings. Sometimes she spotted coyotes and antelope, roadrunners. These creatures were her fleeting companions on the long journey north and west.

She drove on into northern New Mexico and finally into Colorado, and then home. Once George helped Babe unpack, she flopped down on their sofa, putting her feet up.

"I want to take the winter and spring off," she told George.

"Why?"

"It's not the golf so much," Babe told him, "it's living out of a suitcase. All those hotel rooms kinda blur into each other."

She knew she would get cabin fever in Denver, but at least she would be in her own home. She could sleep late if she wanted to. Maybe she would volunteer at the Y again. Maybe she would learn to ski. That's what the upper crust did in Colorado during the winter. That's what her mother, Hannah, had done back in Norway. Yes, the thought of gliding across the snow on skis was appealing, and she told George so. She didn't doubt she'd become an excellent skier if she worked hard at it.

"People break their legs skiing," George told her as he put down his newspaper.

"I wouldn't break my leg."

"You could," George warned. "Anyhow, you got somethin' going with this streak. You want to continue it. No better thing for an athletic career than a streak. Look at Joe DiMaggio hitting in fifty-six straight games. More than the batting titles, that streak made him a legend. Besides, there's some soft tournaments in Florida this winter."

"Whattaya mean streak?" Babe asked. "I lost in Spokane before I won the National."

"Ah, the press will forget that little one in Spokane. It's really *like* you won three straight."

"I don't know," Babe said, shaking her head. She knew she could bullshit the press to a certain extent but getting them to ignore the loss in Spokane seemed a bit much. And the thought of going out on tour again wearied her. George wasn't the type to spring for plane tickets except when he absolutely had to.

She lit up a Pall Mall. "It's easy for you to say go out on tour. You never joined me once this past year."

George looked at her. Well versed in the gripes of professional athletes, he wasn't entirely unsympathetic to her feelings. "Aw, honey, I promise to go this time."

But when the time came for Babe to depart for Florida, George bowed out, saying that he had to stay in Denver to promote some important boxing and wrestling matches.

"You're some fibber," Babe told him as she was packing her suitcases. Packing was tedious when you were on the road for months, and she practically threw a golf skirt into one suitcase, which was battered from use.

"Well, I gotta provide for us, don't I? I got business to attend to," George said. That's what he always said. "And anyway, I'll try and meet up with you on the tour."

"Great. Now lug these suitcases out to the car for me."

So Babe began the two thousand mile drive to Florida alone. True, George had let her trade in her older Buick for a Cadillac with all the latest features, but still. Colorado, Missouri, Kentucky, Tennessee, the hills and valleys and towns and cities rolled by—on through the piney woods of Georgia until she finally arrived in Florida. Let's see, how many hotel or motel rooms was that? How many meals eaten alone? Tallying them up only depressed her.

However, there was one small benefit: more and more of the waiters and waitresses she encountered along the way knew who she was. And if they didn't, if she could see them wondering about her, a lone woman out on the road like some sort of traveling salesman, she'd simply announce she was Babe Didrikson Zaharias, and she was on the way to play in a big golf tournament. They'd look pleased then, sometimes astonished, to be waiting on a celebrity and hover over her, ply her with more coffee, fill her water glass more often, lemon meringue pie on the house, ask for her autograph. Of course, Babe would give them one.

And she'd always leave a big tip.

27

IN FLORIDA BABE won five successive tournaments. They weren't majors but they counted. After narrowly winning the Palm Beach Championship, her sixth in a row, she again teamed up with Peggy Kirk at the Women's International Four Ball in Hollywood, Florida.

Babe was quite pleased to see Peggy Kirk, though she tried not to get mushy about it. She respected Peggy as the opposite of George: refined, educated, modest. Besides, Babe knew Peggy would never be as much of a competitive threat to her as Louise Suggs or Patty Berg or a few of the others, so she could relax in the younger woman's presence, that is, as much as she ever relaxed.

"This warm weather is nice," Babe told Peggy. "That cold weather in Denver is enough to freeze cat piss."

Peggy laughed, appreciating Babe's earthiness. The country club scene could be so pretentious.

As they sat together at lunch, Babe lit a Pall Mall. She didn't tell Peggy that she hadn't wanted to come back to Florida this time of year, even if the weather was warm, that she was sick of traveling, but Peggy guessed that something was up by her subdued demeanor.

"How's George?" Peggy asked.

"He's George," Babe replied.

She had been looking with distaste at a painting on the wall near them, a British fox-hunting scene. That was something Babe would never do, follow a pack of yapping hounds to kill a fox. She liked wild animals, what she had seen of them on her car journeys, and she disliked packs on principle, except for ones she could control, like the gallery or a pack of reporters.

Peggy had never met George, but she had seen newsreel footage of him and heard some scuttlebutt about him from the other golfers. The impression she had of him was that he fit the image of a professional wrestler: big, dominating, rather coarse. The rumor was that he drank too much. She wondered how Babe put up with that, but she knew better than to meddle.

"Well, Peg, are you ready for tomorrow?" Babe asked. Now there was a playful look in her hazel eyes. She was thinking about the future, not the past.

"As ready as I'll ever be," Peggy smiled.

"That's good. I'm sure Louise and all them will be gunning for me . . . for us."

This time Babe didn't boast about how she didn't really need Peggy to play well, that she could beat the opposing teams all by herself. She needed Peggy to play damn well but didn't tell her that; she figured Peggy already knew.

Although Babe confided in no one, she was feeling the pressure of her streak. She was smoking more than she usually did and sleeping fitfully. She hadn't yet gotten her period this month, but it was often irregular. With her luck she'd get the curse out on the course. She thought of George's reaction if she lost. Back in icy Denver he would be hot. Especially if she lost because of a dumb error.

"Now I know how DiMaggio felt," she told herself.

Babe and Peggy's opponents in the final were Louise Suggs and a tall, thin, cheerfully gregarious newcomer named Jean Hopkins. Before the round that morning, Louise saw Babe sizing up Jean in the locker room, noticed her look of cold appraisal, like a hawk about to dive on a mouse. When Louise stepped over and introduced Jean to Babe, Babe gave her a cursory hello and did not extend her hand. There was the same cold look in her eye.

"For crying out loud," Louise thought. "You don't have to be hostile about it." Then when Babe was out of earshot, Louise told Jean, "Don't let her intimidate you. That's what she's trying to do. She does it to everyone."

"I won't," Jean said.

As the tournament unfolded, Louise and Jean played exceptionally well, with the older, more experienced golfer proving a calming influence on her eager young teammate. The match was close and lasted deep into the afternoon. But with the long shadows of dusk descending as the players played the thirty-fifth hole, they felt like they were teeing off in a tunnel. There was a commotion up ahead; someone claimed that someone from the gallery had run out and moved a ball, but no one could be sure. Shortly thereafter, the officials huddled and called the game on account of darkness, announcing there would be an eighteen-hole playoff the next day.

Louise stood for a moment, hands on hips, at the tee for the thirty-sixth hole. What did it matter if they could barely see their shots? They could walk up and find them, like Easter eggs. Then again, maybe it was Fate that the game was being called.

The next day, Babe and Peggy won the playoff, 4 and 2. Of course, Louise and Babe and Peggy and Jean shook hands and made nice when the trophies were awarded. Babe was all smiles now—no hint of the coldness she had exhibited earlier. It was just as well, Louise thought. The gentlemen of the press would be quick to report any cattiness among them.

For her part Babe was jubilant that she hadn't let Peggy down. Nudging her partner playfully on the shoulder, she asked, "So how does it feel to win a tournament?"

"It feels great, Babe," Peggy told her. "You know it's not something I'm used to."

"You never get used to it."

As they walked together on the path to the clubhouse, Peggy invited Babe to join her and a friend for dinner.

"Warren Bell is an old high school friend of mine," Peggy explained. "He drove down from Ohio."

That Peggy had a man friend was news to Babe, and she felt a little twist in her stomach.

Peggy sensed Babe's discomfiture. Babe had probably taken it for granted that she and Peggy would have dinner together again this evening.

"Warren would love to meet you," Peggy quickly added. "He's followed your career."

"Are you sure I won't be a third wheel?"

"Oh no, Warren will be very disappointed if you don't join us," Peggy said. "He thinks of you as quote the great Babe Didrikson Zaharias unquote."

Babe smiled, her dismay subsiding into something like acceptance, and curiosity about this fellow who had so impressed Peggy.

"When you put it like that, how can I refuse?"

"SO PEG HAS a boyfriend." Babe mulled over this news as she was dressing for dinner in her hotel room. Of course, Peg did; she was a pretty girl with a sweet personality. Still, Babe couldn't help feeling a bit disappointed. Somehow, she had hoped that Peggy would remain immune to all that boy-girl stuff. Love might take away from her golf game.

At dinner that night, Babe met Peggy's friend, Warren Bell. The young man was tall, blond, and strikingly handsome in his tan sport coat—the very picture of the All-American boy, but he didn't seem dumb or full of himself. Babe knew that type. Nothing much on their minds but hair.

"Warren's an athlete, too," Peggy explained. "He's playing basketball with the Fort Wayne Pistons in the NBA. They call him 'Bullet Bell.'"

"Actually, I'm hardly a bullet, but I thought I'd give pro ball a shot before I go into business," Warren explained.

This broke the ice: he didn't seem at all inclined to boast about himself. Instead, he asked Babe questions about her career, when it was that she knew she wanted to be a golfer, what it was like to tour with Gene Sarazen, what it was like to win her first major, questions like that, which she readily answered.

Babe regarded the two of them across the dinner table. If you had to get married, she reasoned, it would be good to marry someone like Warren, an educated fellow with good manners. Someone who would stay tall and thin, not some wrestler whose muscles sagged and turned to fat soon after he hung up his trunks.

After saying good-bye to Peggy and Warren, Babe went back to her empty hotel room and called George.

"Hey, we won," she told him.

"That's seven in a row," George said. "Louise folded, right? She's too sensitive for her own good."

"She gave us a good game." Babe was never going to underestimate Louise Suggs. Rather than detail the particulars of the tournament, she told George about having dinner with Peggy Kirk and her boyfriend.

"It would've been nice if you could've joined us."

"I wish I could've," George said.

There was a pause, as Babe considered the fact that George might have felt out of place around a nice, college-educated kid like Warren Bell. He might have drunk too much and said something embarrassing, like the time he tried to give Stan Kertes a free deed to an apartment. Still, ole George could turn on the charm around new people. Warren might have liked listening to his wrestling stories. A lot of people seemed to.

"So when you coming down?" Babe asked.

"Aw, honey, I'm trying," George said. "I'll get down there just as soon as I can."

"When will that be?"

"Soon."

38

IT WASN'T UNTIL after Babe's tenth straight victory that George joined her on the tour. It was during the North and South Women's Amateur in historic Pinehurst, North Carolina. It promised to be a tough tournament, far tougher than the "soft" ones in Florida, with Louise Suggs again out for blood.

It was true: Louise arrived at Pinehurst locked and loaded. She had mulled over their last head-to-head competition and concluded that Babe had to be taken down a peg. To add to her resentment, she had heard from Peggy Kirk that George Zaharias was planning to show up. That slob. Louise detested the way Babe and George always cuddled for the press. There was something phony about it. Put on.

Louise wasn't married. Though she was a pretty brunette, there was no one she was seeing. It was difficult to see someone when you were touring. And Louise guessed that a lot of fellows were intimidated by successful women athletes like her. It wasn't like men would approach the women golfers with romance on their minds, like she had heard some women approached the male golfers. As a result, she had few people on her side except her mother and father, who had taught her golf when she was twelve and who occasionally made it to her tournaments. She was friends with some of the other women golfers, but they were still competitors.

Louise stood out on the practice tee early, driving shots into the clear, North Carolina distance. Some of her drives went as far as Babe's.

GEORGE HAD CALLED Babe from Denver and told her to book a suite at Pinehurst, so she knew he was coming. In fact, he was in the room, lying on the bed with his shirt tails out and shoes off, reading the *Charlotte Observer* when she got there.

"Honey!" he said when she came in the door.

"Hi, George."

Shambling to his feet, he kissed and embraced her, but she was stiff in his arms. Months had gone by since she had seen him, and she hadn't forgiven him for not showing up sooner.

Babe kissed him back. A peck.

"Is this all the greeting I get?" he asked.

"I'm still mad at you for not showing up sooner."

"Well, I'm here now, ain't I? That's what counts."

He made another attempt to embrace her, and she relaxed a little. His was a warm, familiar presence, a teddy bear in his better moments.

"Feel like getting some dinner?" George asked.

That was fine with Babe. How long could she stand here being hugged by George? The only alternative to dinner was lying down with him, and she sure didn't feel like doing that.

During the last day of the tournament, just as Babe had anticipated, Louise Suggs was proving her toughest opponent. Still, Babe was matching her, shot for shot. She was ahead by one and thought she might eke out a victory to continue her streak when she lost her concentration, just for a moment. Her tee shot flew off course and landed at the base of a pine tree, the tall kind they had at Pinehurst, where the branches didn't begin until way up on the trunk.

"Hell's bells, what'd I do?" she muttered.

Realizing that a straight shot was impossible, Babe decided to hit the ball against the tree and hope it would carom off onto the green, sort of like in billiards. But as she reached down to move a clump of pine straw from around the ball, her hand accidentally moved it. She had to declare a penalty on herself and wound up with a five for the hole. Louise tied the game by scoring a four. The match was tied at the end of regulation play. Now they would play until someone won a hole.

George stood in the gallery, smoking his perennial cigar. Babe knew he was there, but she didn't look at him. She was in this one alone. She and Louise tied on the next hole, but then Babe sunk a beautiful long putt to win the final hole and the tournament.

Naturally, Louise was disappointed. She had really wanted this one and had played her absolute best. But you had to hand it to Babe; she had the proverbial ice water in her veins. Now Louise noticed Babe reapply her lipstick for the cameras.

"The perfect lady," she thought.

Babe invited George to stand with her as she was awarded the first-place trophy. They exchanged a loving kiss, with Babe wrapping her arms around George's fat neck.

"Couldn't have done it without my man!" Babe exclaimed to the crowd of reporters and fans.

"Her man," Louise snickered. After posing for a few obligatory photos with Babe, each of them smiling, Louise turned on her heel and walked back to her hotel room.

THAT EVENING, OVER dinner, George started talking about the next tournament Babe should enter. There was always a next tournament.

"You really gotta go over to Scotland to play the British Women's Amateur," he told her.

"Scotland," Babe said. "Well, at least I won't have to drive over there."

She knew it was the home of the most prestigious tournament in women's golf besides the US Women's Amateur. She also knew that no American woman had ever won it. Some had tried, but they all had folded in the clutch, as if under a curse.

"Yeah, Gullane in Scotland, that's the big one this year," George added.

"Enough of Scotland. Let me just enjoy this win for a few days, and I'll think about that later."

They were enjoying a lobster dinner with champagne. Melted butter was dripping down George's chin. Sometimes Babe thought George was simply trying to annoy her with his sloppy eating, paying her back for something. No one could be that much of a slob. If so, he was succeeding. She knew he'd get mad at her if she told him to wipe his chin, so she held her peace. It took a few long minutes before he finally wiped the butter from his face. At Pinehurst he didn't dare use the tablecloth.

"Okay," George said. "But don't forget what I said."

Later, Babe thought more about entering the British Women's. They had driven back to their house in Denver, and it was nice to have company. George was right: she *had to* enter it if she wanted to prove she was the world's greatest woman golfer. But the thought of the ocean voyage and a foreign country daunted her, even if they did speak English over there.

"Will you go with me?" Babe asked George. They were sitting in the living room. As usual, George was reading the newspaper and sipping a beer while Babe was listening to Jack Benny on the radio.

"Sure, if I can get away for that long," George said.

"Don't give me that bull. That means you're not going."

"It's not like I'm playing around. I gotta work! Entering these amateur tournaments don't come cheap you know. Pinehurst cost me plenty."

Babe had to admit this was true. Tournament fees and travel added up. It was strange but you had to be practically rich to be an amateur. She knew that some of the other women struggled financially to stay on tour. They didn't have a rich husband like she had. She was lucky in that regard, she guessed.

"Okay, okay," Babe conceded.

In the end she purchased a single ticket for the transatlantic crossing on the *Queen Elizabeth*. Rather than having the placid waters of the Pacific Ocean to gaze at, as she had on her honeymoon with George, she stood alone on the promenade deck and looked out at the cold, swirling waters of the North Atlantic.

39

NOW BABE WAS standing, driver in hand, on Gullane #1, the oldest course of three at the nearly hundred-year-old Scottish club. The course was set on the Firth of Forth, along Scotland's craggy eastern coast, with cliffs jutting up off narrow beaches. Tall grasses, whipped back and forth by a brisk wind, bordered the fairways. Unlike Pinehurst or the balmy, postcard perfect courses in Florida and California, trees were few and far between at Gullane, and one could see for miles out over the land and water. Standing in this harsh, remote place, Babe imagined herself the last person left in the world.

Even though it was June, the weather in Scotland had turned colder than she had anticipated. Colder and windier, with the wind whipping off the North Sea, chapping her face. Babe had packed for warmer weather. Rather than freeze in light golf skirts, she had to ask the hotel manager if he could round up some slacks she could borrow. Since she was a celebrity golfer in the land where golf was born, he had been happy to accommodate her and checked around with family and friends. As a result, she now wore a gray pair of borrowed slacks, or "slocks" as the Scots called them.

As Babe stood on Gullane Hill hitting her practice shots into the brisk wind, she paused a moment to look out across the North Sea. Before departing the United States, she had looked on a map of Europe and saw that Norway was across the North Sea from Scotland. One of the course officials had told her that Vikings raided here long ago. She tried to imagine her parents' homeland, land of those marauding Vikings, but all she could conjure up was a vision of Ole setting out on some freighter or other. Well, at least you could say he was a sailor, if not a Viking.

As Babe turned her gaze once again to the course, several plump creatures with dirty white fur came ambling into view further down on the fairway.

Babe turned to Jock, the leathery old man who had been assigned to be her caddy.

"What's up with them sheep?" she asked him. Although the caddy looked too old to haul her clubs, in his seventies if he was a day, you never knew with these Scotsman. They were a wiry lot, with their chapped red faces, as hard as dry biscuit.

"Ah, them sheep, we let them roam as they will," Jock told her. "They keep the grass down."

"Yeah, but what if I hit one?" Babe asked. She could imagine one of her drives hitting a poor creature in the head and it keeling over, dead. Well, that was one way to get mutton.

"Hasn't happened yet. They've got a sixth sense about golf balls from being around them so much."

"But what if they, uh, leave droppings?" She didn't like the idea of stepping in sheep shit.

"We've got a grounds man to take care of that."

Babe nodded. "If you say so."

Jock frowned. He didn't look all that pleased to be caddying for a woman, celebrity or no celebrity. Other than him, the Scots had been very friendly. Her room at the North Berwick Inn was comfortable, with a thick paisley quilt compensating for the radiator's inability to generate as much heat as she was used to. The breakfasts, which included the usual plus a choice of muffins and scones, were great. She really had nothing to complain about it. The only thing that was missing so far were the crowds at her back.

Babe hit a long shot down the fairway. It landed on ground still hard from the winter freeze and bounced a long way toward the green.

"Just a short wedge shot now," Babe said to Jock, who was poker faced. His only comment was to tell her to try to avoid the winds.

"The winds, how can I do that? They blow all the time."

Jock pointed to the rows of tall grass that bordered the fairway. The grass rippled in the wind as if someone were drawing an invisible brush through it.

"I'm talkin' about those grasses there, Mum," he said. "They're what we call winds."

"Oh, I see," Babe said. Grasses were called winds here in Scotland. Well, didn't that beat all? What were winds? Grasses? She shivered even though she wore a thick wool sweater.

One great thing about playing in Scotland, though, was that the sun didn't set until past midnight. As a result, Babe got in a lot of after dinner golf. One night when George called at about eleven Scotland time, she told him she had just gotten in from practicing.

"Are you crazy?" he told her. "Save your game for the tournament."

"I might as well play. The sun's still up. Got nothin' else to do."

That was one thing George didn't have to worry about, Babe playing around on him with another man. She was all business, that girl.

"Aw, honey, I wish I could be there with you," he told her. He sounded like he meant it.

"I wish you could too." Babe wondered what George would make of Jock and the sheep, but this was long distance. She would mention all that when she got home.

"Try to get some sleep now. You wanna be fresh in the morning."

"Okay, George."

Babe knew that sleep was probably what George was planning to do in a few hours back in Denver, with the aid of his friend, Jim Beam.

As she lay in bed that night, trying to get to sleep, her thoughts turned not to George but to Peggy Kirk. She wondered what she was doing now. Maybe she was out with her boyfriend, Warren. Well, more power to her if she could land a nice man. Still, it would be nice to have the company of another woman, a friend not a competitor, especially here so many thousands of miles from home.

Back in the States, almost despite herself, Babe had gotten into the habit of gazing at women in the gallery. Some of them, to her eyes, stood out. There was something different about them, not in the way they dressed or their demeanor, but in their essence. She imagined that they, these women, had thoughts like she had, that they too, longed for a woman's touch. Or maybe they had already experienced that touch, which she could barely bring herself to imagine. Sometimes these women came up to her seeking her autograph. She'd smile at them and autograph their piece of paper. There was a breath of warmth about them, a look in their eyes, a lingering sense of recognition. But what could she say or do? And what if she was wrong, like she had been long ago about Enid? Anyhow, it didn't matter. They were only fans, after all, and she was Babe Didrikson Zaharias.

40

SINCE ITS BEGINNING in 1893, no American woman had won the British Women's Amateur Championship. The great Glenna Collet Vare had come close in 1929, but after holding a large lead after eleven holes, had collapsed and lost to Britain's own great golfer, Joyce Wethered.

Now Babe was only one of three American women to enter the tournament. The other ninety-six participants were the cream of British and Irish golf. Babe's first opponent was a member of the Gullane Golf Club named Helen Nimmo, whom she easily dispatched. Although the large crowds had appeared, Babe was taken aback by their lack of noise. They were polite, intent on watching the play, but she heard more noise at a funeral.

Babe knew from the movies that the British were less demonstrative than Americans. "Keep a stiff upper lip, pip pip and cheerio, and all that Mrs. Miniver stuff." Maybe they had needed that reserve to get through the Blitz. Still, there must be a way to light a fire under them now.

"Light a fire." The expression gave Babe an idea.

That afternoon, Babe crushed another British opponent, Janet Sheppard. Though she was so far in front of Sheppard that she wasn't required to play the two remaining holes—the bye holes—as they were called, Babe decided to do so anyway, just to be entertaining. Why not? What else did she have to do? Go back to the hotel and hang around with a bunch of ascot-wearing strangers?

While teeing up on the seventeenth hole, she slipped a kitchen match she had taken from the clubhouse kitchen behind her ball. When she whacked the match and ball, her swing set off a loud snap like a firecracker. The crowd was shocked but laughed. Later, on the eighteenth green, she putted backward, between her legs. The ball went into the cup as the crowd roared.

Behind her back, some members of the club said her performance that afternoon was gauche, childish, but she had heard comments like that before and didn't mind. If you wanted to get people on your side, it wasn't enough to simply play good golf, like poor, boring Louise Suggs did. You had to have a little razzmatazz.

41

"YA SHOULD USE a three-iron instead of a wedge," Jock the caddy told Babe, who was now up against a former Irish champion, Mrs. Val Reddan. It wasn't the first time Jock had given her unwanted advice.

"I always use a wedge on short shots."

"But the wind will carry it." Jock's wrinkled features made him resemble a dried apple. "You can just run the ball up there with this iron."

Who did he think Babe was . . . a piker?

"I'll pick my own clubs," she said.

After defeating Mrs. Reddan, Babe requested and received a new caddy. Michael was only slightly younger than Jock, in his sixties if he were a day, but he kept his mouth shut. Babe then defeated a former Scottish champion, Mrs. Cosmo Falconer, before going up against the current Scottish champion, auburn-haired Jean Donald, in the semifinals. The daughter of a well-respected local doctor, ladylike Jean was a fan favorite. But she was no match for Babe. Certain of winning the match by the thirteenth hole, Babe reapplied her lipstick for the photographers whom she knew were certain to crowd around her. Someone had told her that Scottish warriors danced the Highland fling after a victory in battle, so she danced the Highland fling. Not everyone appreciated her "fling," but the photographers certainly did.

It grew warmer the morning of the final. Now Babe could finally wear some of the warm-weather clothes she had brought. To go up against Jacqueline Gordon, she wore pink and white checked Bermuda shorts and a light knit top. It would be another long day. They would play thirty-six holes—eighteen in the morning and eighteen in the afternoon.

Jacqueline Gordon, although totally unheralded in the press, had played consistently excellent golf all week and proved a tough competitor. At the lunch break, she and Babe were tied. Then the wind whipped up and the weather turned cold again. Babe took off her shorts and put on some blue slacks she had borrowed. Some people said she had changed because of the supposed jinx against American golfers.

"Naw, I was just cold," she later told the press.

The afternoon match wasn't close, with Babe pulling away from Gordon quickly and finishing ahead by five holes with four left to play.

Again, the Highland fling. Again, the swarm of reporters. When they asked her the secret of her long drives, Babe replied, not for the first time, "I just loosen my girdle and let the ball have it."

This comment was not well-received by some of the stodgier members of the British press. But then Babe was a brash Yank, and one had to give her latitude. She had not only won; she had driven the ball with amazing accuracy—out of eighty-four tee shots hit to fairways, she had only missed three. That was a driving accuracy of 96.4%, which was virtually unheard of in women's or men's golf.

"Ah'm really lookin' forward to gettin' home to George," Babe told the press. "This has been just about the longest we've been separated since we got married."

But then invitations from other Scottish golf clubs came pouring in, and she decided to spend a few weeks touring them. After all, she was in the land where golf was invented and who knew when she'd return?

"I'd be a darned fool not to travel around a bit and see the sights," she told the press and cabled George of her intentions. He cabled back in agreement. First, she had to play the Old Course at St. Andrews, the place where golf was born. Like Gullane, it also looked out over the North Sea. Unlike Gullane, this was a strictly private course, where no onlookers were allowed. But as Babe was playing, she noticed a crowd of people penned in half a football field away.

"Good gosh," she told her caddy.

She walked over to the crowd and waved them toward her. They followed her as she played her way through the course. The course overseers might not have been pleased, but who were they to challenge the great Babe Didrikson Zaharias?

42

"NOW IS THE time to turn pro," impeccably dressed, smooth talking Fred Corcoran was telling Babe and George later that week over dinner at Manhattan's 21 Club.

Fred Corcoran was Sam Snead's agent and represented Ted Williams and Stan Musial as well. To look at him now with his calm, Buddha-like demeanor, you wouldn't dream he had begun life as a fast-talking Irish street kid in Cambridge, Massachusetts, that he had begun caddying as an eight-year-old and, using a combination of wit and fists, had become a caddy manager by the time he was thirteen.

By the 1930s Fred had risen to become tournament manager of the PGA. By the 1940s, he was the PGA's promotions manager and had helped to make it a major business enterprise by creating charity matches between such luminaries as Babe Ruth and Ty Cobb. With a promotional acumen that seemed instinctive, Fred had also established the Golf Hall of Fame. It was said that he knew everyone in golf, though he was a poor golfer himself, famous for triple-putting on courses around the world.

He had met Babe and George back in 1945, when Babe entered a men's PGA event as a lark.

"I remember that day," Fred said. He had a strong Boston accent, which amused Babe. She hadn't been around many people with that accent in the course of her career.

"You certainly gave those fellas a run for their money," Fred added.

"I didn't do too bad," Babe recalled. "But I could've done better."

"You haven't seen her when she's really on," George said. "She just gets this cold look in her eye. Like a shark."

Though reluctant to entrust his wife's career to another, George sensed that Fred was a kindred spirit. Both were big men who had worked their way up from the lowest rungs of society via sports. But George had to concede that Fred operated on a higher, more sophisticated plane than himself. With his Irish charm and way with words, low-key yet convincing,

not to mention the services of an excellent tailor, the country club set
accepted Fred Corcoran without reservation.

"If you go pro, I'd like to manage you, Babe," Fred told her.

George leaned in, elbows on the table.

"You know I already manage Babe's tournament appearances," he told
Fred. For once he wasn't drinking the hard stuff, just seltzer water. He
wanted to be clear-headed when negotiating with the renowned Fred
Corcoran. It wasn't that he didn't trust him; it was just that he didn't trust
him entirely.

"You can continue to do that," Fred assured George. He knew that
George had done very well for his wife, so far. Now, however, Babe's career
was going to a whole new level.

"But with my contacts," Fred explained, "I can get Babe a lot of
endorsement deals . . . Wilson, Weathervane, Spalding . . . those companies
are ready to make offers, very lucrative offers. Plus, personal appearances
all over the country."

"Sounds great," George said, who had to admit that his contacts with
sporting goods companies were nil.

"Sounds good," Babe said. It would be wonderful to be earning her
own money again, after relying for so long on George, who often had deep
pockets and short arms.

The endorsement deals would be especially sweet—her name on golf
clubs, bags, and everything else related to women's golf. As far as personal
appearances went, she could envision long days on the road or in the air,
hotel room after hotel room. That part she could do without. And if she
had seen one airport, she'd seen them all.

Fred continued his pitch. "You know Patty Berg and Betty Jameson are
pros." He was nursing a martini.

Babe noticed his diamond cuff links, the way they glinted in the
artificial light. She was drinking a gin and tonic. George broke down and
ordered a Scotch and soda. Their meals hadn't yet come.

"They're already making deals," Fred continued. "Sportswear companies
want them, sporting goods companies want them. People are gung-ho to
spend money on stuff they couldn't afford during the war."

The food was delivered, only temporarily interrupting what Fred was
saying.

"And it's happening all over the country. People with kids don't want
to stay in the cities, so suburbs are sprouting up all over. That's bound

to mean more people playing golf, more golf courses, more professional tournaments." Then fixing his smiling eyes on Babe, he added, "It's going to be a great time to be a lady pro."

"I think so too," George said. By now he was so happy, he ordered drinks all around. Why the hell not? Everything Fred said made sense.

Fred Corcoran impressed Babe as a very smart man and better connected than George.

But never one to be buffaloed, she told Fred, "Let me play at the Broadmoor Ladies Invitational first. And then I'll decide."

George agreed with her strategy. In the taxi on the way back to their hotel, he told her, "Let Fred hang a little. If he really wants you, he can hang."

Babe won at Broadmoor, extending her streak of tournament wins to fourteen, or seventeen by George's count. She got an offer from a Hollywood producer who told her that he was willing to pay her three hundred thousand dollars if she would take part in a series of ten movies shorts about sports. Though Babe was a little skeptical of the movie offer, she realized her market value would probably never be higher.

After calling Fred Corcoran and notifying him of her decision to go pro, she, George, and Fred agreed to work out an agreement that would enable him to share management of her career with George. Then Babe sent a telegram to Charles W. Littlefield, the president of the USGA. In it she told him of her decision not to defend her title in Detroit that September, of her plans to go professional. She ended the letter by thanking him and the USGA for all they had done for her.

"Really, I did more for them than they ever did for me," Babe thought after finishing the letter.

43

"I DON'T GIVE a shit about them by-laws," George Zaharias announced at the first official meeting to create the Ladies Professional Golf Association. "Women's golf belongs to me."

"Please, George," Babe pleaded as George looked on balefully.

In addition to George and Babe, five prominent women golfers, including Patty Berg and Betty Jameson, were attending the meeting, as were a high-priced lawyer and a stenographer who had been hired by Fred Corcoran. Fred himself was presiding over the meeting, which was held around a polished conference table in a conference room in the Venetian Hotel in Miami. It was the afternoon session.

Everyone in the room now knew George was drunk, including Babe, who was mortified. It had been a big mistake to go for lunch in the hotel dining room, which of course served liquor. George had liquored up at lunch. When he liquored up, he either got soppily sentimental or ornery. Lately he had been getting ornery. His shirttail came out of his trousers. He sweated even though it was a cool day in January. He now weighed over 350 pounds. And here Fred Corcoran was, looking immaculate and cool in his blue suit.

Though Fred was diplomatic, trying his best to ignore George's more belligerent comments, Babe knew everyone else was angry, including Patty Berg. Patty had served in the Marine Corps reserve during the war, as a recruitment officer. Now she was sitting at the conference table looking grim. Even Babe didn't mess with Patty Berg.

That evening, Babe asked George if he would mind not attending tomorrow's meeting. As usual, George was watching TV, Perry Como's *Kraft Music Hall*. It was good that some of these nice hotels now had a TV in each room.

George frowned as he turned to look at Babe. "What, do I embarrass you?"

"No, it's just you got to get along better with the other people," Babe said. "Stop shouting at them. People are getting pissed off."

"Who's getting pissed off?"

"Patty, for one."

"Oh, that dyke."

As far as Babe knew, Patty wasn't a dyke. But it surprised her and made her a little uneasy that George said so. This was the first time she had heard him use the word. She had heard the word before, during, and after the Olympics, sometimes to describe herself, sometimes to describe other women athletes. To some men, Babe knew, all women athletes were dykes.

Now she did her best to ignore George's remark.

"Everyone was getting pissed off, including Fred."

George respected Fred. He was a power in the sports world; the lady golfers, even his wife, weren't. "Okay, I'll keep my mouth shut tomorrow."

He fell asleep early that evening. Babe stayed up and did needlepoint—a horse and buggy on a country road, heading past a little white church. Scenic and soothing.

Thankfully, George was more subdued at the next day's meeting. There were bags under his eyes. Hung over. Contrite. Miserable but quiet.

After a series of meetings and much haggling over laws and by-laws, the Ladies' Professional Golf Association was born. With backing from Wilson Sporting Goods, and with Fred Corcoran as its director, charter members included Babe Didrikson, Patty Berg, Betty Jameson, Louise Suggs, Marilynn Smith, and Helen Hicks. When Weathervane Sports Clothes Company also pledged thousands to fund prize money, seven more fine women golfers became charter members that fall.

Creating the LPGA was a risky proposition, with women's golf ranking low in the sporting hierarchy, but the new association had one gate attraction that transcended golf: Babe Didrikson Zaharias. Like Babe Ruth in baseball in the 1920s, her personality appealed to the masses. She did the same schtick she had been doing for years: trick shots, falling to her knees and bowing when a long putt fell into the hole, chattering to the gallery. It was said that she never met a photographer she didn't like. But like Babe Ruth, she had the skills to back up her razzmatazz personality.

It didn't hurt when in February of 1950, the Associated Press named her best female athlete of the first half of the twentieth Century. There was no one else close in the voting.

IN SEPTEMBER, BABE crushed the opposition at the U.S. Women's Open in Wichita, Kansas, winning by nine strokes. It was the LPGA's first official tournament.

Babe and the other golfers knew that publicity would keep the tour in business, so she and the others would hit golf balls at minor league baseball stadiums to drum up interest before each LPGA tournament. She and the other members also attended local women's social club luncheons to talk up the tour. When they did, it was clear that some of the fusty women she talked to had never dreamed of attending a golf tournament, but with Babe's dynamic delivery, they started to consider it. And soon other sponsors put money into the LPGA, including Spalding, MacGregor, and Golfcraft.

Babe's attempt at teamwork was erratic. One day she came over to several of the other golfers driving off a practice tee, Betty Jameson and Helen Hicks among them.

"Why are you ladies even bothering to practice?" she asked, grinning. "Everyone knows who's gonna win this event."

Not surprisingly, Patty Berg was elected first president of the LPGA, not Babe.

44

IN 1951 GEORGE heard that a golf course was for sale in Tampa, Florida. After looking the place over, he and Babe decided to buy it. They would tear down the caddy house and build their dream house in its place.

Babe had wanted to own a home for a long time. Even the Denver house, where they had lived longest, was a rental. This Tampa house would be a sprawling ranch house, which they would name Rainbow Manor because she and George had seen a rainbow when they were first scouting out the property. Here Babe could practically step out the front door onto the golf course. And no harsh winters to worry about ever again.

Shortly after she and George moved into their new home, Babe got a phone call from Bertha Bowen, who had a request to make.

"There's a young lady golfer I'd like you to look out for. I'm friends with her family in San Antonio, and she's new to the tour. Actually, she said she met you before when you were doing a Red Cross charity event in San Antonio. She was still in high school then."

"What's her name?"

"Betty Dodd."

"I don't remember her," Babe said. Betty was a common name.

"Well, she's a nice kid and talented, but kind of raw. She could use some pointers about the tour."

"Kind of raw? You mean like I used to be?"

"Well, you were a little rough around the edges . . ."

"I was a mess," Babe said, thinking back to her tomboy days. Didn't know how to dress, hair chopped off like a rag, no makeup. She was forever thankful to Bertha for setting her straight.

"When you see her, you'll know what I'm talking about."

Now Babe was intrigued. Bertha had never asked her to look after a young golfer before, though she was friendly to young golfers she didn't perceive as a threat. Peggy Kirk was her best friend on the tour. But Babe couldn't hang around with Peggy all the time, especially now that she was engaged to Warren Bell.

Babe knew that people thought she didn't care what other women golfers thought of her, of her grandstanding, but she did, sort of. Still, something in Babe resented the other golfers. She felt they had it easy compared to her. No sportswriter had ever questioned whether they were male or female, in a national publication, no less. No, they fit easily, unthinkingly, into life, like round pegs into round holes. They didn't know how good they had it.

"Sure, I'll be happy to talk to Betty Dodd," Babe told Bertha. She was curious to see just how raw this kid was.

45

BETTY DODD WAS a tall, gangly girl with freckles and a shock of coppery hair that fell in front of her dark brown eyes. She didn't care if her eyebrows needed tweezing. She didn't care a lick about makeup. She didn't care if her blouse hung out over her skirt when she wacked the ball or if her golf shoes were scuffed and dirty. She had been a tomboy all her nineteen years and didn't see the need to change. It was hard being that way in San Antonio. Her parents were well-off members of society, but Betty adamantly had no interest in church socials and debutante balls and that kind of thing. She learned to play golf at the age of twelve. Maybe that's what saved her.

Betty met Babe Didrikson at an amateur tournament in Miami which Babe attended as a spectator. She and George had recently moved into their new home, Rainbow Manor in Tampa. It was nearly three hundred miles from Tampa to Miami, but with Bertha Bowen's words in mind and with George away once more, checking out some business opportunity in Detroit, Babe decided to make the trek.

As Babe observed the younger golfer teeing off, she thought, "Bertha was right. This kid is raw."

After the round, in which Betty played well but did not win, Babe strode over to the young woman as she was heading back to the clubhouse. As she grew nearer, she could see that Betty's clothes were something less than stylish and that she needed a good haircut and permanent wave. Babe was oddly delighted.

"Hi, I'm Babe Didrikson Zaharias," Babe said. "Bertha Bowen is an old friend of mine. She suggested I introduce myself."

Betty was taken aback. "You don't need to introduce yourself. I know who you are," she said, grinning nervously.

"You do, huh? Well, I enjoyed watching you play golf," Babe said.

"Sorry you didn't see me win."

"No, but you did pretty well for a young 'un. Why not talk about it over dinner? On me."

At dinner, it was all Betty could do to keep from gaping at her idol. She couldn't eat much because her stomach was queasy with nervousness. She was lucky she didn't pour salt into her iced tea.

Babe found Betty's obvious nervousness flattering. Looking at the girl, with her shapeless hair style and boyish face, was like going back in time and looking at her twenty-year-old self.

There was no need to hurry back to Tampa. Babe would stay on in Miami for a couple of days. Maybe she would do some shopping.

"So, tell me what you've done in golf so far."

Betty told her that she had started playing when she was twelve, that she had won a few amateur tournaments in the San Antonio area.

"Did you notice anything I'm doing wrong?" Betty asked.

"A few things. But if you've got time, I can show you what I mean on a course."

"Have I got time to get a lesson from Babe Didrikson? I should say so."

Betty and Babe spent the next day playing golf together at the Bayshore course in Miami Beach. Babe had some tips for Betty. She tried to teach her the way Stan Kertes, Gene Sarazen, and others had taught her. It was nice having someone look up to her. What did they call such a person? A protégé? A fancy word—one that George would scoff at—but maybe Betty could be her protégé. She invited her to join her later that month at Rainbow Manor.

"I practically roll out of bed onto the course there," Babe told Betty.

Betty agreed.

That night Babe called up Bertha Bowen.

"Well, I've met Betty Dodd and given her a few pointers," she said.

"How do you like her?"

"She's a nice kid. Sorta reminds me of me when I was her age. You know, we Texas gals gotta stick together."

"I thought you'd get along."

Bertha wanted Babe to be happy.

Their final day in Miami, with a degree of tact unusual for her, Babe took Betty to a well-regarded beauty salon, the kind where most of the hairdressers were men. The salon, which looked like a Roman villa, was bustling with wealthy women patrons—the crème of the city, who demanded the best in terms of the three C's: cutting, coloring, and curling. Initially when Babe called to make an appointment, the receptionist had told her that they were booked up, but when Babe told her who she was, the young woman checked with her boss and then told her to come right in.

"We'd love to have you in our salon," the receptionist gushed.

"These swishes give the best haircuts," Babe advised Betty as they walked in through the glass doors. "Don't let them scare you; they're harmless." She had noticed Betty's unevenly trimmed nails. "Get a manicure too while you're at it. I'll wait."

Betty had never noticed such unusual men as the hair stylists before, all bustling and whippet thin. Babe was opening up a whole new world to her. But then, Babe had been all around the world, or at least to some of it. Babe had told Betty a lot about winning the women's tournament in Scotland, had talked about how the cold wind whipped in off the North Sea, causing her to have to borrow slacks, and about her crusty old caddy, Jock, who tried to tell her which club to use. She told her about dancing the Highland fling after she won. Betty mulled this over as a girl shampooed her hair.

Betty's hairdresser, a tall, willowy fellow named Paul, was both masterful and gentle, with long tapering fingers that held a comb and scissors like sculpting tools.

"Honey, you've got nice thick hair," Paul assured her. "I can do a lot with this."

Paul was right. Betty looked much better after she and Babe walked out of the beauty salon.

"How much do I owe you?" Betty asked.

"Don't be silly," Babe told her. "I didn't pay anything for your haircut and manicure. When you're as famous as I am, people throw free stuff at you."

Later that month, Betty joined Babe at her home in Tampa. George was away again. He had returned for a few days, the three of them had gone out to dinner together, but then he went back out on the road, this time to Tulsa. He told them he needed to check out a rental complex he had bought.

Babe gave Betty a tour of the house. Betty was impressed. Even though she had been raised in a handsome residence in one of San Antonio's wealthier neighborhoods, her parents' house had been rather old-fashioned, with dark, heavy furniture and lots of bric-a-brac. As a toddler, she had been terrified of a grimacing plaster gargoyle that her parents kept on the floor by the fireplace, a souvenir from a trip to Paris. Now that she thought back on it, who even needed a fireplace in San Antonio, let alone a gargoyle?

In contrast, Babe's house was new and airy, with plenty of light colors. The latest appliances, wall to wall carpeting, a fireplace, and handsome furniture in a style Babe said was called modern manor house.

"A lot of this stuff I got free from the manufacturers," Babe told Betty. "It's funny, now that I can afford this stuff, I don't have to pay for it."

"Did you pick out this furniture?" Betty asked.

"Yeah, along with the people at the stores. They have swishes at the stores, too, to help you decide. They got the best taste. George ain't, isn't interested in furniture."

Though he generally wasn't, they had shipped George's massive brown easy chair from Denver. That he couldn't part with. It now sat by the fireplace: a throne with a cigar burn in the right armrest.

Betty's eyes fell on the tile-enclosed fireplace.

"Who needs a fireplace in Florida?" she asked herself. She guessed it did make an attractive part of the décor. It's not what you need, it's what you want, she was beginning to realize. Also, it's what you thought would impress others, your friends, your competitors, the military brass like in her father's case, even the kitchen help. That was a big part of life, like it or not.

As Babe escorted Betty through the house, Babe recalled what it had taken her to have this kind of home. It was a far cry from Doucette Street and, she guessed, George's in Pueblo, Colorado, where he said all they had to eat was Greek bread and olive oil. She used to rib him about getting so big on Greek bread and olive oil, but she had to give him credit. He had fought his way up, just like she had. Still, respect wasn't desire.

Betty was especially impressed by Babe's trophy room. In contrast to the house in Denver, where Babe's trophies were kept in a section of George's office, there was now an entire room devoted to them and Babe's golf equipment—clubs, bags, shoes, other paraphernalia.

Babe flipped a switch and the florescent lights sizzled on in one of the trophy cases. Then she flipped another switch and the lights blinked on in another case. The silver trophies gleamed in the artificial light.

"Wow, you won all these," Betty said.

"Yep, I won 'em all. And I'm not gonna stop there. Before I'm done, I'll win everything there is to win."

Betty didn't doubt it. To her it seemed like Babe had already won all there was to win. But then she remembered something.

"What about your gold medals from the Olympics?"

"Oh, I keep them separate from these," Babe said, a frown clouding her face. "I'll let you see them some time, not now."

"Okay, but why do you keep them separate?"

"Honey, it's a long story. I'll explain it to you some time."

They were standing close together. Each could feel the other's warmth.

Babe breathed a satisfied sigh. She felt refreshed in Betty's presence. A break from the wearying grind, a break from George and Fred telling her what to do and when to do it, and from the couple's boring evenings together: George drinking and Babe watching him drink.

Betty and Babe were standing so close that their bare arms touched, and then Betty unexpectedly, daringly, slid her arm through Babe's. Babe turned to her, looked into her eyes. Now there seemed to be nothing left for Babe to do but to reach out and stroke Betty's coppery hair, now pleasingly coiffed. The girl turned to face her idol. The glass trophy case reflected their embrace.

46

AFTERWARD, AS THEY were lying in each other's arms in the guest bedroom, Babe and Betty tried to justify the astonishing thing that had just happened as something natural between women of their kind.

"We athletes are a different breed. We're bolder than the rest." Babe thought about all those silly girls she had gone to high school with. Enid Adams. What a bitch she had been. Well, now Enid was no stranger to suffering. Shortly before Mama died, Lillie had told her that Enid's husband Carter, a bomber pilot, had gotten shot down and killed over Germany. That was sad, no matter what she thought about Enid.

"What about George?" Betty asked.

Babe sighed. There was a rueful look in her eyes.

"George looked like a Greek god when I married him; now he just looks like a goddam Greek," Babe said. Then feeling disloyal, she added, "Yeah, he's my husband, but there's certain things you can't expect from men." Like tenderness, like thoughtfulness, like the ability to listen. She thought of Tiny Scurlock. "Maybe with some men, but not with George."

Betty mulled over what Babe had said. So far, she hadn't had a romantic relationship with any man and didn't expect to, though she was golf buddies with some of the fellows back in San Antonio.

"I'm not about to divorce George," Babe added. "We've been a team for a long time."

"I didn't ask you to divorce him," Betty said. Who was she to tell Babe Didrikson Zaharias what to do?

Babe sat up in bed. *She has a beautiful body*, Betty thought. A powerful body. What battles she had been through. The taut muscularity of her youth was still there underpinning everything, but with maturity had come a new fullness. If George had looked like a Greek statue in his youth, Babe still looked like one: Diana, goddess of the hunt.

Now Babe put her right arm around Betty, letting her hand fall just above Betty's breast.

"Honey, what we have," she gently said, "is going to have to be besides George. And anyhow he's not here that much."

"So, I'll have you all to myself," Betty said, reaching up to hold Babe's hand. Babe *must* prefer her to George. Hadn't she just shown it?

"Yes, you will, a lot of the time," Babe said, gazing at Betty. She was thinking about how nice it would be to have a companion on the tour.

Compared to being with Betty, George had become a bore. Not that Babe had ever given the public any inkling of problems in their marriage. They still kissed and hugged like newlyweds for the news crews. As far as the world knew, they were still the same lovebirds they had been on their wedding day.

Babe confided to Betty that she had had two miscarriages. "Swimmers," she called these lost babies because they had just flowed out of her. There had been some pain, some cramping and then the pregnancies had ended.

"Do you miss not having kids?" Betty asked.

Babe pulled up a pillow, lay her head back on it.

"It's probably just as well." Babe couldn't imagine either herself or George being in one place long enough to raise a kid, or raise one right, anyway. You had to sacrifice a lot to be that kind of parent. And she thought of George's drinking. A kid shouldn't have a drunk for a father.

Betty had another question for Babe. "Do you know if there's anyone like us on the tour?"

Babe knew right away what she was talking about. "Not really, but I think Susan and Judy might be." Susan and Judy were a couple of lesser lights on the tour, two sturdy-looking single women, New Englanders, who always roomed together.

"Yeah, I thought the same about those two." It would be nice to pal around with them a little, maybe find out for sure. But how would one go about such a thing? It was risky. What if they were totally wrong about the nature of their relationship?

Betty thought back to when she had her hair done by the swishy fellow at the hair salon. "If there's all those fellows in the hair salon, there's gotta be more girls like us."

"Yeah, we're just hidden," Babe said. With that, she pulled Betty to her, kissed her deeply. Tinged with guilt as it was, it was the kiss she had imagined all her life.

THE FIRST TWO years of the 1950s were great ones for Babe. In 1950 she racked up wins in each of the three majors. And 1951 was another banner year, with Babe winning seven of the twelve tournaments she played in. With Babe's victories, the LPGA was attracting more sponsors, and the purses were slowly but surely becoming bigger. Even though many of the women golfers on the tour still resented Babe's hard-boiled competitiveness, they couldn't dispute the fact that the sizeable galleries at LPGA events were largely due to her. Not that Babe would ever let them forget that fact.

Feeling flush over her successful career and her newfound friendship with Betty, Babe had a proposition to make her. They were having dinner together at a restaurant in Niles, Illinois, outside of Chicago, after the All-American Open, which Babe had won.

"Why don't you come live with me and George?" Babe asked.

"What?" Betty looked startled, not sure she had heard correctly.

"Live with me and George. You know the house."

"Yes, I do know the house." The thought of what she and Babe had done in the guest bedroom came back to her, the lovemaking they could tell no one about, what other people would call "sick." If they couldn't tell anyone about it, did it really happen?

"There's plenty of room. Not like some of these crappy little hotel rooms we stay in."

Betty was delighted with this invitation, but there was a question hanging in her mind. "Is it okay with George?"

Babe took a bite of prime rib. "I haven't asked him yet."

Betty was taken aback by Babe's admission. "Don't you think you should?" By now she had had been around George a few times. Her conclusion was that he was loud and bossy. Besides that, he didn't seem to treat Babe very well when there were no reporters around. She, Babe, and George had had dinner out together once in Tampa before she and Babe had become intimate. George had looked morose, paid little attention to either of them, drank too much, and grumbled replies whenever Babe asked him something.

"What's your problem?" Betty had felt like asking him. But maybe she already knew the answer to that question.

Babe had confided to Betty that she was now earning more money than George was.

"Way more," Babe had said. "I'm pulling in more moolah these days than I can spend."

Even with Betty's limited experience with men, she suspected this fact was a recipe for discord, even besides the fact that she had fallen in love with George's wife. Did she really want to become part of Babe's tense domestic scene? Not at all. Still, she wanted so much to be near her. Babe understood her like no one else did in the entire world. That was no romantic cliché—she knew no other lesbians.

"Yeah, I'll ask George," Babe told her. She just had to figure out how to ask him in the right way.

"BETTY LIVING WITH us makes sense," Babe finally told George. He was home from yet another business trip, this one to Los Angeles. The thought occurred to Babe that maybe George had women on the side. Maybe he was seeing them on these road trips. She found it difficult to imagine that some woman would be attracted to her husband, but if he slept with some cheap broad, some waitress or other, who really cared? Not her.

"Why do ya say that?" George asked.

"Then she won't have to pay for so many hotel rooms when she's playing tournaments around here. Besides, she's just a kid."

It was true. Betty had just turned twenty, and she was a young twenty at that. Gullible, naïve. She had no one to look after her best interests on the tour except Babe. And from what Betty told Babe, she had never had a social life, never dated like the other San Antonio kids she knew. She was like Babe in that regard, too.

Both Babe and George were in the kitchen. They could put a full-sized billiard table in this kitchen with room left over for the kitchen table, it was so big. And it had a beautiful view: lush green lawn rolling down to a small lake. Babe could often hear frogs in the lake, sticking their heads out among the lily pads, croaking their mating calls.

George was bent over, rooting around for something in the refrigerator, grabbing things and knocking them over in his haste.

"Where's the goddam mustard?" he asked. He preferred spicy mustard to mayonnaise on his sandwiches. Spicy mustard gave cold cuts that zing.

"Look in the door."

There was the Gulden's bottle.

"Besides, she'll be company for me when you're on the road."

George was relieved to find the mustard. He did feel guilty about being away from home so much. But he had always been a restless guy; he had explained that much to Babe early in their marriage. So, what was the harm of having this kid Betty stay with them? The house was plenty big. And the refrigerator was enormous, the biggest Frigidaire they made. Of course, they hadn't had to pay for it. The Frigidaire Corporation had given it to them in return for Babe's endorsement.

George slathered mustard on his ham and cheese sandwich, brought it to his mouth, and bit into it.

"It's okay with me," he muttered.

47

ONE AFTERNOON GEORGE came home from a long trip as Babe and Betty were sitting together on the living room couch watching the soap opera *Hawkins Falls* on TV. She and Betty had been sitting close together as they watched it, with Babe's right arm slung over Betty's shoulders. But when they heard George's car crunching in the macadam driveway, they scrambled apart. The front door opened. George seemed to fill the entranceway, sending a shadow across the wall-to-wall carpeting.

"I'm home!" he boomed.

Babe rose to greet her husband. They kissed and exchanged pleasantries as Betty sat on the couch.

"Can I get you anything to eat?" Babe asked. "There's plenty of cold cuts in the refrigerator. Roast beef, cheese, liverwurst. And that potato salad you like."

Sometimes George made his own sandwiches. Since he had just arrived home after a long road trip, Babe felt it her duty to serve him.

"Roast beef sounds good. I'm starved. Oh, hi, Betty."

"Hi, George."

After George ate his lunch, he announced he was going to take a nap and went into the master bedroom. He took off his shoes and lay down on the eight foot by eight foot bed they had had shipped from Denver.

George didn't know what to make of Betty but guessed that Babe needed company.

Women were like that. Always gabbing among themselves. They didn't have kids. If they had had kids, things might have been different, Babe would have had more company. After the miscarriages, they had tried adopting but were told they didn't qualify because they were both on the road so often. It was alright. Kids could be a pain in the ass. His brothers' kids were a pain. Cute but a pain.

George fell asleep. Tired of sitting around watching the travails of other people on TV, Betty and Babe decided to go outside and practice their putting.

When they got back, an hour later, George was up, drinking a beer, and watching TV. There was a new show that all of them liked called *I Love Lucy*. They watched it together and laughed at Lucy's antics, especially the way she would break out bawling like a baby. She drove her husband, bandleader Ricky Ricardo nuts at times, but he still loved her.

"That crazy redhead," he'd call her in his cute Spanish accent.

Later, Babe went to the kitchen to fix dinner. Betty followed her to help. She and George didn't have much to say to one another.

George drank more beer at dinner. He had switched to Michelob, the champagne of bottled beer, and consumed two cans in quick succession. After dinner, they watched more television as George drank more beer. Milton Berle was on. They loved when Uncle Miltie dressed as a woman. He made a hilariously ugly woman with his buck teeth and garish makeup. The beauty mark was the killer.

"Jews make the best comedians," George said.

"I guess they do," Babe said. "And they sure know money."

"I know money too," George said.

Then George yawned and stood up, a little unsteadily. Another show came on.

"Honey, how about we turn in now?" he said to Babe. It was only nine o'clock.

"In a little while," Babe said. Both she and Betty wanted to watch *Kraft Television Theatre*. This episode promised to be a good one, with the ghost of Abraham Lincoln confronting John Wilkes Booth.

"I'm goin' to bed *now*," George said. He said it sullenly, like a little kid.

George was still awake when Babe came to bed. He had been reading the newspaper in bed, waiting for her. He was bare-chested and hairy, having stopped shaving his torso after he gave up wrestling. After Babe undressed and put on her nightgown, George placed the newspaper on an end table and switched off the light. She still had a great body, he thought, a thoroughbred's body. Beautifully toned, no fat on her. He turned over and kissed her, moving his rough hands over her smooth, firm skin. Then, lifting her nightgown, he fondled her and pulled her on top of him. That was the only way they made love these days, with her straddling him. It still excited him to make love to an athletic woman, a champion: all that energy. Babe seemed to enjoy it, too, rocking back and forth on him, her eyes closed.

Both came, and Babe slipped off George and lay on her side, quiet, distant. A little sex was all George asked of her. Was that too much? Sure, he had put on weight, but he was still well endowed where it counted.

Then he thought maybe that was the way good women were. They didn't like sex the way men did unless they were sluts, like the women he had been with both before his marriage and several times thereafter. Some gals still chased after wrestlers, even if the wrestlers were paunchy and retired.

Then again, Babe had liked sex well enough when they were first married. Back then they had nearly broken the bed with the heat of their lovemaking. She used to fondly call George's penis "Big Pete" back then. No more. Anyhow, he and Babe had been married nearly fifteen years. Everything got stale after a while, George guessed.

George dozed off and snored while Babe lay wide awake and thinking. She and Betty would go back on tour in a couple of days, this time back to Fort Worth. She couldn't wait. She was glad that Betty's bedroom was down from theirs and on the opposite side of the hallway.

Sweet kid, she couldn't have heard anything.

48

WORD HAD GOTTEN around that Babe was being paid cash under the table for simply entering tournaments. And rumor had it the money wasn't a piddling amount—a thousand dollars for each tournament—at a time when a lot of the tour members were struggling to break even. As a result of these rumors, several members of the LPGA—Louise Suggs, Betty Jameson, Shirley Spork, and Marilynn Smith, called an emergency board meeting. Patty Berg couldn't make it—her mom was ill. Peggy Kirk Bell attended but hadn't called the meeting. Everyone around the conference table was dressed in suits. Everyone was wearing makeup. This was important business, not fun and games.

"It's not the money so much as the secrecy," Betty Jameson told Babe. "You could have at least told us about the payments." Betty was a well-liked member of the tour, a tall, willowy woman with fine features whom some members of the press had dubbed the "glamour girl of golf." Like Babe, she was from Texas.

"The money is my business, not yours," Babe replied. Though she liked Betty Jameson, thought she was classy with her UT degree, she wasn't about to let emotions get in the way of business.

Actually, it was George who had come up with the idea of charging tournament organizers an appearance fee, but Babe had readily agreed with him. He wasn't here at this meeting; he was on another of his never-ending business trips. Just as well: his presence would have only added fat to the fire. Anyway, Babe felt she could handle this little brushfire herself. Hadn't these same women elected her LPGA president for 1953? If she was such a greedy person, why had they done that?

Louise Suggs was one of the best golfers on the tour, but relatively quiet during LPGA meetings. Now she felt strong enough about the matter to speak out.

"Sometimes you treat the rest of us like pigeons," she told Babe, her face reddening.

Startled by Louise's comment, Babe frowned.

"Let me lay it on the line," she said. "You know how in show business there's a star and then there's the chorus? Well on this tour, I'm the star; you're the chorus."

Her bluntness did not go over well.

Louise rolled her eyes. "I may not have the same star power as you, Babe," she said hotly, "but I shouldn't have to remind you that I've beaten you on occasion."

Unused to such verbal sparring, the rest of the women stirred uncomfortably in their seats. They all agreed with Louise, who had every right to be proud. She had won nearly as many tournaments as Babe. She had even won the Ladies' British Tournament a year after Babe had. Unfortunately for her, not too many people had noticed because she got scant press coverage. There was nothing like being the first at something; besides, Louise just didn't have a colorful personality. She would have slit her wrists rather than whacked a golf ball with a match behind it like Babe had done at the British.

"Yeah, you're a good golfer, Louise, but I'm the marquee name," Babe said. "Without me, there wouldn't be half the tournaments we have. Without me, a lot of tickets would go unsold."

This was uncomfortably true. Like her or hate her, Babe had the common touch, at least with regards to strangers. Like some glad-handing politician, she was always ready to press the flesh and shine for the cameras. She was always on. As a result, the fans adored her.

As a close friend of Babe's, Peggy Kirk Bell was torn. She could see Babe's point, but she could also see why the other women were offended, especially Louise, whom Babe had never been friendly toward.

After the meeting was over, Peggy lingered and talked to Babe in private. Louise Suggs, Betty Jameson, and the others had already left the conference room, and not in good spirits.

"You shouldn't have said those things. I would have said them for you," Peggy told Babe.

"You would have?" Babe hadn't even thought of that, someone sticking up for her, here, among all these competitors. Maybe she was just too used to fighting.

"Yes, I would have," Peggy continued. Unlike most of the women, she sensed that a lot of Babe's boastfulness was defensive in nature. Babe was like a kid in that respect. She had been born on the wrong side of the tracks and then had a tough time breaking into the country club circuit.

People had said nasty things about her, and she had never forgotten it. You had to realize that about her.

"You're right about being the star and about some tournaments not being around except for you," Peggy explained. "But people don't like to be reminded they're not the main draw. It hurts their pride."

"Well, I was only stickin' up for myself." But she would listen to Peggy when she wouldn't listen to anyone else because Peggy was genuinely "nice."

"But I can see where Louise and the others would be pissed," Babe conceded.

"They *are* pissed," Peggy said, who rarely used coarse terms.

Now Babe regretted her belligerent tone. But she'd be damned if she'd give up asking for appearance fees at tournaments. She had worked long and hard to deserve everything she got. Anyway, George wouldn't like it if she did that.

49

"THEY'RE LESBIANS," A lesser-known golfer named Janet McDougall came right out and said in the tournament locker room one day. She had been talking with a newcomer to the tour, a fine young golfer named Betsy Rawls. Louise Suggs, who was standing nearby, smirked. She didn't know if it was true or not about Babe and Betty Dodd, but she got a sense of satisfaction from hearing Debbie's comment. Being a lesbian was a bad thing, wasn't it?

"They do seem to be close," Betsy Rawls said. As one of the youngest members of the tour, she didn't want to go shooting off her mouth and have it getting back to Babe. But another golfer, a seasoned veteran named Lyla Simpson, wasn't so circumspect.

"They're *always* together," she said with a knowing smile.

When the rest of the tour members thought about it, Babe and Betty *were* always together. They roomed together on tour, they traveled together, and they ate dinner together, though sometimes with other golfers, like Peggy Bell and Patty Berg, neither of whom were in the locker room just yet.

But Lyla Simpson wasn't finished with her remarks. "No doubt Babe's the man in *that* relationship." She giggled.

As if on cue, Babe and Betty walked into the locker room talking and laughing together, cutting the conversation dead and Lyla looking red-faced. Later, the LPGA members were left mulling over what Janet McDougall had stated and Lyla Simpson had joked about. Was Babe really a lesbian? Everyone knew she was a fantastic golfer, and Betty Dodd seemed to be a nice enough kid, if a little raw. Then there was the confusing fact that Babe had been married over ten years. She garnered some sympathy in that regard, seeing as her husband George was what he was: a loudmouth hustler who would never fit into the country club scene.

The consensus among the women was that Babe and Betty could do whatever strange, unnatural things they did together, just so nobody got the impression that all women golfers were like that, which they certainly weren't. True, they didn't have male fans throwing themselves at them, the way some male golfers had floozies—known as gallery girls—throwing themselves at them. The tour could be awfully lonely. It was hard to meet decent guys when you were on the road a lot of the time. But it could be done. Just look at Peggy Bell. She had snagged a nice, smart, good-looking guy, a real gentleman, from back in Ohio. If you were inclined to get married, there was always a way. You certainly didn't have to go lesbo.

50

GEORGE HAD BEEN home four days straight, and he was already getting restless.

"What do ya' say we go out to dinner?" he asked Babe. Business was going well, he had just signed Babe up for several more tournaments, but now it was late afternoon, time to close the blinds and call it a day.

Babe and Betty had just come in from grocery shopping, laden with paper sacks. There was a nice, new Publix just a couple miles away. It was dazzling, with long gleaming aisles, and the number of items it carried dwarfed anything they had seen before. Babe had signed some autographs at the store, something she didn't mind doing, including one for the man behind the meat counter. She and Betty came away with eight sacks of groceries, including some choice T-bone steaks.

"You really want to go out with all this food we bought?" Babe asked her husband.

"It'll take you a while to cook. I'm hungry now," George said.

Betty fully expected him to stamp his foot on the floor, like a little kid would.

"If you help us unload this stuff, we'll go," Babe said.

George did help with the food, carrying three sacks at a time to the kitchen, then three more.

"Did you get the donuts?" he asked.

"Yep. I think they're in that sack."

George rooted through a sack on the kitchen floor and pulled out the donuts. They were the powdered kind that came a dozen to a box. He put one in his mouth, chewed, and swallowed it.

"Don't spoil your appetite," Babe warned him.

He ignored her comment and polished off a second and then a third and fourth donut.

THE THREE OF them went to an Italian restaurant—Natali's—that evening. Though Babe and Betty talked with each other about recent events on the tour, George didn't have much to say. Tuning out the girls, he lit a cigar and took a swallow of Jim Beam. He loved the bitter burning sensation of the liquor going down.

It wasn't like the old days, he mused, when he was surrounded by his wrestling buddies—managers, promoters, trainers, and hangers-on who were all eager to rub elbows with a pro. Those were the days, when he was a young stud earning big bucks by knocking guys around the ring. Of course, he got knocked around too, but that was all part of the game. Afterward, as reward for all his labors, there'd be a pretty girl in his bed at night, so soft, so eager . . . So what if she was a bore the next morning? Often, he'd be on his way to another town after breakfast.

George kept drinking during dinner. As he did, his mood went from bad to worse.

"You know, I get tired of hearin' you girls gab about the tour," he stated.

Babe and Betty stopped talking. Babe regarded him with raised eyebrows. If he was bored, he didn't have to be rude about it.

"Well, why don't you say something then?" Babe finally said. "We're all ears."

There was an uncomfortable silence as George glared at them. He took a roll from the breadbasket and bit off a hunk.

"Nothin' I'd say would interest you girls."

"Try us," Babe said. "You're on the road so much, you must have something to talk about."

This only made George angrier. One of his recent investments, an apartment complex in West Hollywood, had been giving him problems. He had had to fire the property manager for doing a lousy job. He shouldn't have hired him in the first place, but he had fallen for the man's hard luck story about being out of work for a year. No wonder the guy had been out of work. He was a lazy bastard.

"You think you're hot stuff for makin' a lot of dough," George accused Babe.

So that was it. Babe sat back in her chair, her shoulders slumped.

"Aw, George, I know I couldn't ah done it without you. All this money, I'm, we're makin', none of it would've happened without you." She reached out to touch his hand. "You're my rock, honey!"

"And never forget that." George returned to his meal. "This chicken is raw. I don't eat raw chicken."

"Then send it back," Babe said.

George called the waiter over. He told he didn't want the chicken cooked any more, that he now wanted veal scallopini instead. That maybe the chef could keep from messing that up.

Knowing who George and Babe were, the waiter quickly, servilely agreed, taking the offending plate and bowing his way back to the kitchen.

It was awful, Babe thought, what money did to people. Not that she didn't like special treatment. But sometimes it got embarrassing, the way people fawned over her and George, as if they had no self-respect. Luckily, she had been born with talent, so she didn't have to live like that.

George looked across the table at Babe, continuing to glare. "Who told you this restaurant was good?"

"It got a good write-up in the paper," she replied. "And my Alfredo is pretty good."

Betty was about to say that her meal was good too, but Babe's calm reply seemed to anger George all the more.

"Well, it's no damn good. Whoever wrote that write-up don't know nothin'."

A lot of writers don't know anything, Babe thought. Like they didn't know the truth about her and George. They thought their relationship was all lollipops. Well, she was partly to blame for that. But what choice did she have?

Through all this, Betty sat quietly.

George picked up his cigar and clamped it with his teeth.

"Why don't you tell Betty about your wrestling days?" Babe suggested.

"I'd like to hear about that," Betty said.

"Naw, you don't wanna hear that stuff," George said. "You'd think it was boring."

"Sure I want to hear it."

George felt they were trying to humor him. In a way, it was pleasant feeling sorry for himself, stewing in his own juices like a steak.

"Naw," he said. He drank more bourbon. Before they left, he wiped his mouth on the tablecloth.

After they got home, George headed for his office. Betty suggested that she and Babe practice playing harmonica and guitar together. They had been doing this whenever they could, working up a selection of country and western songs, mostly to entertain their friends on the tour.

"Okay, but we better go out on the patio, so we don't disturb you know who," Babe said. The patio was screened in, and it was a pleasant night—mild, not stiflingly humid.

"You know I still remember when I bought this harmonica," Babe told Betty. "It was about thirty years ago in the Woolworth's on Main Street."

"And I can still remember when I bought this guitar," Betty replied. "It was way, way back, about three years ago at a music store near the Riverwalk."

"You kid!" Babe laughed, swatting at her.

LATER THAT NIGHT, Betty could hear George and Babe arguing through their bedroom door. Loud arguing, mostly George's voice. Was it her imagination or did she hear a clatter and something thump against the wall? Should she go over and knock on Babe's bedroom door? No, that would be intruding. She was a guest here. She wasn't supposed to hear anything.

The next morning Betty entered the kitchen to find Babe sitting alone at the kitchen table, a cup of coffee in front of her. There were a few dirty dishes and a crumpled table napkin where George had sat. It was a beautiful kitchen, with patterned yellow and white wallpaper and the latest gleaming appliances. The kitchen table was bone white Formica and chrome.

"Where's George?" Betty asked, pulling out a chair and sitting down next to Babe.

"He left for LA. He'll be gone a week."

"Thank God for small favors," Betty said. "What happened last night?"

"Oh, you heard." Babe frowned. "Me and George had a little, old fight. Sometimes he gets mean when he drinks."

"He drinks a lot and he's mean a lot. I heard a thump. Did he hit you?"

"No," Babe said, avoiding Betty's eyes.

"Are you sure?"

"He pushed me against the wall, and my arm knocked over a lamp."

"Damn him. Did he hurt you?"

Babe hesitated, and then unbuttoned her blouse to reveal a black and blue mark the size of a tea rose, just under her right clavicle. Her back was bruised, too, where she had hit the wall.

Betty winced. "Bastard! Bastard."

"He was drunk. He apologized this morning. He was real sweet."

"So what," Betty cried. She found the thought of George Zaharias ever being sweet unimaginable. Maybe once upon a time but not now. He hadn't even bothered to clear his dirty dishes. "Why don't you divorce him? You told me you're making tons of money. You don't need him anymore."

"I'm thinking about it," Babe said, buttoning up her blouse.

She had already spent a lot of time thinking about divorcing George, going over and over it in her mind until her brain was buzzing like a saw. This wasn't the first time George had hit her. And she didn't like to be hit.

But what would everyone say about her? That she wasn't woman enough to please a man? That George had good reason to hit her? You bet your life, that's what some people would say. She was still grateful to George for rescuing her from all the innuendos about her sexuality. He had been her knight in shining armor, driving up that evening in his late-model Caddy to take her out to dinner and dancing at the Cotton Club. He, at least, was big enough, man enough to see her as a woman and not as a threat.

"This coffee is getting cold." Babe rose to refill her cup from the plug-in percolator near the stove.

"I think you should divorce him," Betty told her.

But Babe felt uneasy even thinking of divorcing George. Being married to George was protection against slander. On the other hand, couples got divorced every day, especially in show business. Look at Joan Crawford, look at Lana Turner . . . seemed like that broad got a divorce every week. And Betty was so much nicer to be around than George. But if she divorced George, what would the tattle sheets say? That she and Betty were lovers? Even the legitimate press would have to cover it, old friends like Grantland Rice and Tiny Scurlock.

Babe knew that George wouldn't want a divorce, that he still wanted her to himself. Like he owned her. Yes, the kind of gossip George could spread if he wanted to would ruin her career, and Betty's too, while it was still getting off the ground.

"I love you," Betty told her. "You don't need to be George's punching bag."

"Let me make you some eggs," Babe said, suddenly standing up. "Sunny side or scrambled?"

Betty looked up at her. Babe did love puttering around her bright new kitchen.

"Scrambled," Betty said.

ONE THING THAT Babe didn't mention to Betty was the reason for George's beef with her. He told her he was tired of having Betty around, that he couldn't relax around her. She wanted to spare Betty that hurt.

"She gets on my nerves," George had told her in their bedroom.

"Why, she hardly says anything when you're around," Babe said.

"That's the trouble. She just looks at me with those big eyes of hers. Like she don't like me."

"She likes you," Babe lied. "It's just she just doesn't know what to say to you."

"But she sure seems to have a good time with you."

His comment alarmed Babe. How much did he guess about their relationship? He couldn't know for sure; she and Betty had been careful about that. No cute notes, no touching when George was at home. Anyway, was it really any of his business? She and Betty's closeness was on a different level than her relationship with George. He had been sweet and considerate when they were dating and when they were first married, but his attentiveness had dropped off a table since then. Now he was now more like her boss than her lover, always telling her what he had planned for her, the tournaments she had to play in. And now that Fred Corcoran was managing her too, having her travel from exhibition to exhibition, it was like she had two husbands. Anyhow, Betty gave her what George couldn't.

Babe continued to reflect on last night's fight with George.

"Betty's nice to talk to," Babe had told him.

"And I'm not?"

"Come on, George. When you're around here, you're drunk a lot. It's embarrassing."

It was then that George pushed Babe into the wall. Hard.

Though he immediately apologized, reaching out to help her regain her balance to keep from falling to the floor, the damage was done.

Babe muttered, "Bastard." She looked behind her. There was a dent in the wall where she had hit, which would have to be repaired. A pretty lamp overturned on the floor. Babe picked the lamp up, with its shade dented, and placed it back on the dresser.

"I am a bastard," George said. Then he flopped down in the bed, pulling the covers over himself. Babe got in beside him. Soon she heard him snoring.

Even at eight foot by eight foot, the bed felt too small.

51

ON A BRIGHT, sunny day a few weeks later, a delivery truck pulled up in front of the Zaharias residence, and two beefy men got out, one white, one Negro. They were delivering two new beds: a double bed for George and a single bed for Babe, along with two new mattresses. The delivery men broke down the old eight foot by eight foot bed and took it away with them. They told Babe they had never seen such a large bed. Babe noticed one of the delivery men wink to the other fellow.

"They're probably wondering what's going on with me and George," Babe thought. Well, let them wonder. They're hauling furniture for a living. They ain't gonna blab to the press.

While all this was happening, George was away, tending to his investments.

A few days earlier, Babe had talked with Betty about the upcoming delivery. It was just after breakfast. They were practicing together, at the Tampa Golf and Country Club adjacent to Rainbow Manor. The course wouldn't open to outsiders for another hour. It had rained overnight, and droplets of water still dripped from the trees. The grass was wet, dampening their shoes and making a squishing sound as they walked. Birds sang. Squirrels chirped and scampered. Butterflies and bees danced.

"George and I agreed we needed separate bedrooms," Babe said.

"He agreed to that?" Betty asked, incredulous.

Babe nodded. "I think I get on George's nerves as much as he gets on mine."

Betty found this hard to believe. But maybe it was true. They had been together for years before she came on the scene. What did she know about being married? By now marriage wasn't something she ever considered for herself.

"Anyhow, I told him I can't sleep anymore with his snoring, that it didn't use to bother me, but now it does. And now that I'm doing all these exhibitions, I need all the sleep I can get. Of course, it's more than the snoring, but . . ."

She left unsaid the fact that George had hit her before. She had even talked over that matter with her older brother, Louis, who had done some amateur boxing.

"Couldn't you beat up George for me?" she had asked him.

"Even though he's a fat slob, I don't think I could beat him up," Louis had said. "Sorry, Babe. Get a divorce."

In addition to George's bad temper, there was the fact that he no longer aroused desire in her. When they had first gotten married, she had looked at him standing there in their bedroom in the nude and thought, yes, he is what a man should look like. Like one of those muscular Greek statues she had seen pictures of in her World History textbook back at Beaumont High. But after he retired from wrestling, he had let himself go to hell in a handcart.

On the other hand, Babe considered, maybe George was angry with her a lot of the time because he knew she loved Betty. Any way you looked at the situation, it was a hot mess.

"Well, I'm glad you're going to have your own bedroom," Betty said. Then, looking around to see if anyone was watching, she took a step closer to Babe and put a hand on her shoulder.

"You don't have to sleep with him," she said.

"Not often, anyhow," Babe said.

52

ONLY TWO MILES from downtown Seattle, which was booming due to the post-war aeronautic industry, Broadmoor Country Club was a different, bucolic world. Its stately Douglas fir trees, some as tall as forty feet, lined the fairways and its rolling topography made the course challenging for even the best golfers. On some tees, golfers could look out into the distance and see the snow-topped Cascades, while on others, the shimmering expanse of Lake Washington shone blue and placid in the sun.

Hoping for a dominating performance, Babe whacked the ball on the first tee at Broadmoor. But the ball traveled not even two hundred yards. Good enough for a lot of golfers but pathetic for her.

"Shit," Babe muttered. If this drive was a sign of things to come, she was in big trouble.

She looked toward the gallery, where George was standing under a cluster of fir trees, a puzzled look on his face. She hadn't done well in her previous two tournaments at Bakersfield and Fresno. It was the pain that was shooting up from her left hip. The pain came and went. When it came, George told her to soak in a hot saltwater bath, but that provided only temporary relief.

Now, as Babe strode along the links at Broadmoor, she felt the pain getting worse. She told herself she shouldn't have entered this tournament; now, she just hoped she could finish it.

She did, barely, finishing in eleventh place.

By the time she woke up next morning, she had to lean on George to get to the bathroom. When she finished in there, George ordered room service for them both. No going out today.

"You gotta go see a doctor," George urged.

Betty, who was also playing in the tournament, agreed. While George went down to Los Angeles to handle some business, Babe and Betty drove together to Salt Lake City. Now Babe was in agony each time the car hit a bump in the road and often when it didn't.

"Screw this driving," Babe told Betty through clenched teeth. "Let's get a plane."

So they turned in the rental car at the Salt Lake airport and flew back to Beaumont, where Babe saw her old family doctor, eighty-year-old Dr. W.E. Tatum, at Hotel Dieu Hospital.

Dr. Tatum had seen Babe and her siblings through many an illness, from ringworm to measles to scarlet fever. He had been comparatively young, in his early forties, when he treated Babe after she jumped off a half-built house and cut open her leg. He had treated her again after she broke her ribs on another jump.

"You've got a strangulated femoral hernia," old Dr. Tatum told her. "It's a protrusion that's stopping the flow of blood. You need surgery right away."

Without surgery, he explained, Babe could lose her leg or die.

Betty Dodd was there with Babe.

"You gotta have it," she said.

"You're also anemic," Dr. Tatum added. He explained this was due to exhaustion. "So, we'll wait a few days to build you up. Give you some vitamins and food that has lots of iron, like liver and spinach. Then we'll operate."

Liver and spinach? Babe would eat dog food if she had to. But hearing the word *exhaustion*, she thought of all those tournaments, all those road trips, all those hotels. She had been pushing herself too hard. Or maybe George and Fred had been pushing her. She loved playing golf, but between all the tournaments and exhibitions, exactly what was she running herself ragged for? She was already a household name. And how many fancy outfits could she buy? How much steak could she eat? After the surgery, she would have to mull this over as she recuperated back at Rainbow Manor.

"How long will it take for me to recover?" Babe asked.

"At least a few months," the old doctor said, his wrinkles deep enough to hide a coin in. "You could be ready by late summer."

On the way home from the doctor's, Betty drove, and Babe sat silently gazing out the car window at the familiar streets of downtown Beaumont. The city was still doing pretty well, considering, although with the postwar boom, white people were starting to move out to the suburbs, leaving some streets down at heels. Babe had been told by Lillie that "the colored" were moving in more and more.

"If you have money, you move out," Babe thought. She had done the same. Maybe Lillie and O.B. would, too, eventually.

They passed the Jefferson Theater, where Babe had had the abortive encounter with Enid. After all these years, that still rankled. But life went on. She noticed the people lined up to see the feature: *Sudden Fear* starring Joan Crawford and Jack Palance. Sudden Fear? She had a sudden fear herself.

Babe would be staying with Lillie and her family in the old house on Doucette Street for a week after the surgery. So would Betty. That was fine with Lillie, who still adored her little sister, Babe, and liked Betty.

Betty cast a quick look at Babe, who had little to say on this drive.

"I'll drop out of the tour for a while to help you," she volunteered.

Babe turned to her. "You don't have to do that."

"I know I don't have to, but I want to."

Betty reached out to take hold of Babe's hand. Babe turned to her and grasped her hand tightly.

"Maybe stay with me a week or two and then go back out on tour."

A MONTH AFTER her surgery, Babe consulted with a doctor in Tampa that Dr. Tatum had recommended. This doctor told her she wasn't nearly ready, that she must wait until at least July, maybe August. Babe liked the layoff at first, but then it bored her. True to form, George left on a business trip soon after she got out of the hospital, an absence that didn't bother Betty at all.

She and Babe could relax now. They watched *The Guiding Light* and *Search for Tomorrow* on TV and cuddled and played their harmonica and guitar together, learning a few new tunes.

They played cards: hearts and gin rummy, until Betty came to realize that Babe was a poor loser. An intense competitor at everything, she'd go into a sulk after she lost. Like now. She was pulling a long face just like George did when he didn't get his way. Betty had just trounced her at hearts.

"I don't wanna play anymore," Babe said, scowling.

"For crying out loud, Babe, it's just a game," Betty said. They were sitting at a wicker table on the back patio, drinking Dr. Pepper on ice.

"I don't care. I wanna win."

"You can't win all the time."

"You can't but you sure can try." Babe put the deck back in its box. "Let's go play some golf."

After a few weeks, with Babe's blessing, Betty went back on the tour. Tiny Scurlock and Bertha Bowen called. Bertha drove over from Fort Worth, stayed for four days, then left. Since Babe hadn't really had time to develop friendships with the neighbors, she had few people to talk to. There was the cleaning lady, a middle-aged Mexican woman named Lupe. Lupe was nice, but she spoke little English.

Feeling better day by day, Babe practiced her putting and chipping. When Betty stayed over between tournaments, they played a few holes together, nothing taxing.

Finally, Babe got the green light to fly up to Chicago to play in the World Championship at Tam O' Shanter. Babe was more than a little concerned over the reception the girls would give her. She knew she had bruised their feelings at times, boasting the way she had. And that whole thing about her getting appearance fees at tournaments had left a bitter taste in everyone's mouth. She winced when she remembered that she had called them the chorus. Maybe they felt she had deserved to be sick, that it was her comeuppance for all her boasting.

Babe paused before entering the locker room, steeling herself, then walked briskly in.

"Hey everybody," she said, all smiles.

There was dead silence as her sister golfers turned to look at her, blank faced. For an anguished moment Babe thought they all hated her. But then everyone burst out in greetings, even Louise Suggs. Some of the girls, like Betsy Rawls and Patty Berg, went over and hugged her. Of course, Peggy Kirk Bell hugged her, and Babe grew teary-eyed to see them all again. It was hard to stay mad at her for all the bragging she did. She *was* like a kid in some ways.

Although Babe started off strong at the World Championship, she ran out of gas on the back holes and finished third behind Betty Jameson and Patty Berg. Since she had won the tournament all four times it had been played, this was a big letdown. It broke her streak.

"I thought I was ready," Babe told Betty when they were back in their hotel room. "But I guess I wasn't."

"Relax, honey," Betty consoled her. "You'll be back to your old self soon."

Babe did return to form in the Women's Texas Open at River Crest Country Club near Fort Worth. There she to beat the up-and-coming golfer, Polly Riley. The victory was especially sweet since it was the site of the 1947 loss that had ended her fourteen-tournament winning streak.

Polly was a tough little Texas firecracker, all of five-feet-two inches. She had beaten Babe in another tournament. But she folded like an accordion this time. Babe trounced her, winning the final round 7 and 6. As a result of these lop-sided scores, Polly accused Babe of piling on.

"You didn't have to rub my nose in it," she admonished Babe within earshot of the press.

Despite Polly's ire, or maybe because of it, Babe was amused.

"Don't squawk, kiddo," Babe told Polly. "If you had the chance, you know you'd do the same to me."

53

STILL, BABE DIDN'T feel right. When she returned to Tampa that winter, the energy she had felt playing the Texas Open was gone. When she woke up, it seemed a challenge just to get out of bed and get dressed, and when she practiced, her drives lacked their usual Zaharias z-z-zing. She decided to skip all the winter tournaments.

"Do what you want, honey," George said, genuinely worried about her by now. More than worried; he was frightened but tried to hide his fear from Babe. "You'll be raring to go in the spring."

But in the spring Babe failed to win any of the three tournaments she entered. Lately, after playing golf during the day, she didn't even have the strength to go out to dinner. One evening she and Betty ordered room service, which they ate off a coffee table in their hotel suite. George hadn't come to this tournament, too much work at home he said. As she and Betty sat together, the late afternoon sun seemed to hang suspended in the air. The venetian blinds were partially closed, casting stripes on the furnishings.

Babe was picking at her dinner plate; her roast chicken lay almost untouched.

Betty, who was devouring her meal, looked at Babe. Was it just her imagination, or had Babe lost weight? Her clothes seemed to fit her loosely, and her coloring was wrong, pallid, yellowish as old lace.

"Come on, eat, eat," Betty said. "That hernia thing really took it out of you."

Babe chuckled a little. "Maybe it's not the hernia thing. Maybe I have cancer."

She said the word *cancer* offhandedly, like you would mention having indigestion or a head cold. Her dad had died of cancer. People in Beaumont died of cancer. It was something people whispered about. They didn't even like to say the word, using euphemisms like "malignancy" and "a serious illness," but word got around. Doctors said they had treatments for cancer. Yeah, treatments like carving people up like Thanksgiving turkeys and giving them radiation burns. And all the while the patients would grow weaker and weaker, shrinking down to skeletons before your eyes like Pop had. And after all that fancy, not to mention expensive treatment, the patient still died.

Betty's fork hung in midair. "Don't even say that. Just get a checkup, *please.*"

But Babe put off getting a checkup for weeks, until she was back in Beaumont once again, this time for the inaugural Babe Zaharias Open. It was an ordeal to play in this tournament; she felt winded and her muscles felt strangely numb as she walked the course, but she used all her willpower to narrowly beat Louise Suggs. Realizing Babe was struggling physically, the other golfers, her erstwhile rivals, cheered her one-stroke victory. Even Louise seemed less put out than usual by Babe's victory.

"Something's wrong with that girl," Louise told herself.

Babe hadn't told anyone she had noticed blood in her stool. This was such a frightening development that she tried to deny the fact, even to herself. Who knew? Maybe the blood was from a hemorrhoid. She had hemorrhoids, which flared up occasionally.

A few days later, Babe and George sat beside each other in a proctologist's office in Fort Worth, where they had been sent by Dr. Tatum. The biopsy had been completed and the results were in.

"Babe, you've got rectal cancer," Dr. Mitchell said.

Babe felt lightheaded and electrified at the same time, as if she had accidentally touched a live wire. If she hadn't been sitting down, she might have fainted. She had known something dreadful was coming. How do you know when something dreadful is coming? Some animal sense, you just do. Like dogs know when they're about to die. They just go off somewhere and you never see them again.

George gaped and gripped Babe's hand, tightly.

The doctor went on. "You'll need surgery as soon as possible."

Then he showed Babe and George a flip chart that showed what the surgery would involve.

"Your rectum and part of your colon are going to have to be surgically removed," Dr. Mitchell said, pointing to the full-color cutaway diagram of a human torso on a chart. The colors on the chart were vivid: purple for the ascending colon, Kelly green for the transverse colon, deep orange for the descending colon, a lighter orange for the sigmoid colon, and baby blue for the rectum, that little troublemaker.

"Then what?" Babe asked.

"You're going to need a colostomy."

"I don't know what that means."

"I do, sort of," George said. He remembered the word from when one wrestler had accidentally gotten stomped too hard in the gut and needed one because the stomping had messed up his intestines. But he didn't mention all that now. Dr. Mitchell explained the procedure.

"The surgeon will cut out the cancerous growth and divert a piece of your colon to your abdomen," he told Babe. "In that way, the unaffected part of the colon will be able to bypass the damaged portion to excrete waste. This means you'll have to wear a colostomy bag at all times, which will have to be emptied and cleansed several times a day. I estimate the recovery time will be two to three months."

He showed them some photographs of people with colostomies, which to Babe looked like having an asshole coming out your side, and photos of people's sides, not their faces just their sides, wearing colostomy bags. He went into detail about maintaining the colostomy, assuring Babe and George that tens of thousands of patients had adjusted quite nicely to them. From his point of view, colostomies were miracles of modern medicine. Then he handed them detailed instructions to look over when they got back home.

Despite himself, George felt a wave of disgust at all this. The photos of the stoma looked so hideously red, red as an open wound, which, when you thought about it, it was.

Babe thought, "To collect my crap. I'm going to have to wear a bag around my middle to collect my crap. Probably for the rest of my life."

"Will people smell it?" Babe asked. She could imagine becoming a pariah.

"Not if it's maintained properly," Dr. Mitchell assured her. "People won't know you're wearing it."

This was reassuring, slightly. It was sort of like being on the rag, only worse. Then Babe asked the ultimate question: will I live?

Dr. Mitchell said yes. He told Babe that rectal surgery would remove the cancer.

"Okay, so another question: will I be able to play golf again?"

"You may be able to play golf again, but perhaps not on the level you're used to."

"You mean I won't be able to play tournament golf."

"I don't know," Dr. Mitchell told her. "Possibly not."

WHEN BABE AND George got back to the Bowens' home in Fort Worth, where they were staying, Babe bluntly told Bertha the news, while George went out back onto the patio and sat down heavily in a chair by the pool. There was a plastic raft in the pool, and George watched it glide soundlessly in the breeze.

"B.B., I've got rectal cancer," Babe said.

The two women sat on the sofa. It was a well-padded sofa, engulfing. Bertha hugged Babe and held her while Babe told her that she would need a colostomy. She could barely get the word out. No one she knew had ever had such a humiliating operation, not even her Pop, who had had a different type of cancer. She told Bertha about having to wear a bag strapped around her middle to collect her waste.

"The thought of it makes me sick," Babe said.

"What does all that matter, honey?" Bertha assured her. "As long as you're alive."

Babe hung her head. "I don't want to talk about it anymore. I want to lie down."

"Of course," Bertha said.

As Babe lay down in the guest bedroom and stared at the rose, green, and white floral walls, she thought of how she had often played golf matches to benefit the American Cancer Society and the Damon Runyon Fund. And before that, she had played in lots of charity events to benefit the war effort. She had even taught those kids swimming back in Denver. She had always tried to do the right thing.

But maybe this cancer diagnosis was punishment for her pride. She had always been cocky. Well, why not? Sports was a show. You wanted to entertain people. She hadn't meant anything by her boastfulness; it was just that she had been given all this talent, and she was just pointing it out to people. She had made people happy by getting them involved in her play. That was why the gallery loved her; she didn't give them the cold shoulder. And they weren't the only ones: her family loved her, B.B. and R.L loved her, Peggy Kirk Bell, loved her, George loved her, in his own way, and of course Betty loved her. So why had this happened to her? Then again, why did it happen to anyone?

Dr. Mitchell doubted she would ever play tournament golf again. You could see it in his eyes. Maybe she wouldn't. But she would sure as hell try. Her set of golf clubs was still in the trunk of George's Cadillac.

"Let them stay there for now," Babe thought as she drifted off to sleep.

OUT IN THE living room after Babe had gone to nap, Bertha Bowen called her husband R.L at his office and told him to come home at once. Even though she had tried her best to be reassuring to Babe, she needed reassurance herself. Rectal cancer. Had the cancer spread? If so, could it be stopped? The same feeling came over her as when the doctors told her that her son had a heart defect. It was like walking into a tunnel with no light at the end.

George shuffled into the room. He looked even more disheveled than usual. Bags under his eyes. He looked like he had been crying.

"Sorry to bother you B.B., but you got any Scotch?" he asked her.

Bertha went to a cabinet in one corner of the room, took out a bottle and a glass, and poured him a Scotch. Then, hesitating only for a second, she pulled out another glass and poured one for herself.

54

A LARGE PRESENCE loomed one morning in the doorway of Babe's room, Room 201 in Hotel Dieu Hospital in Beaumont. The large figure wasn't her husband.

"Hi, Tine," Babe called weakly from her bed. "Come in and pull up a chair."

"Hi, Babe." Bill "Tiny" Scurlock shambled in, kissed Babe on the cheek, and pulled up a chair. He already knew that Babe's operation would take place at two that afternoon—Friday, April 17, 1953, and he had come at her request. She wanted him to write a story about her for the *Beaumont Journal.* She said she was sick and tired of the way people whispered about cancer. Why, no one ever said that Babe Ruth had throat cancer until after he died. Babe had met the Bambino on several occasions and liked him. They were cut from the same cloth . . . outgoing, brash, supremely talented. But with his last appearance at Yankee Stadium, you could tell something bad was happening with him, that he didn't have long to live. Still, he never came right out and said what was ailing him.

It was stupid, pussyfooting around like that, especially with so many people nowadays getting the disease. It wasn't like it was contagious, and it shouldn't be shameful.

"Can I mention the type of cancer you've got?" Tiny asked, pen and notepad in hand. His hairline had receded a bit, but he was the same big man he had always been, shoulders as wide as the doorway.

"Sure," Babe said. "Write that I've got cancer of the rectum. Most people have rectums, don't they? Anyhow, there's so many people out there with cancer, they shouldn't feel ashamed of it. Who knows? Maybe what I'm going through will help them."

She heaved a sigh as a thought crossed her mind: she couldn't be open to Tiny about Betty, but at least she could be open about with him about cancer. Wasn't that strange?

Tiny took notes about the doctor who would be coming in to perform the surgery, Dr. Robert Moore, of the University of Texas Medical Branch in Galveston.

"He's supposed to be topnotch," Babe said. "That's what I want."

Tiny wrote that Babe's brothers Ole Jr. and Louis, who had the same blood type as their sister, had donated pints of blood.

Tiny noticed the golf bag and clubs in a corner of the hospital room. Babe followed his gaze.

"Betty Dodd brought 'em," she told Tiny. "I don't know if I'm ever going to play golf again, but I hope to."

"Is there anything more you want to say, Babe?" Tiny asked gently. He couldn't take things for granted, ever, but he didn't want to go all soppy in front of Babe.

"Yeah," Babe said. "Tell people that instead of sending me flowers an' fruit baskets, make donations to the American Cancer Society."

Tiny jotted that down. Then he bent over and kissed Babe's cheek.

"I'll see you soon, Babe," he said in a quavering voice.

Babe smiled at his words and gave his shoulder a playful little nudge. "And for God's sake, Tiny. Get the story on page one."

55

SEVERAL HOURS AFTER the operation, George sat by Babe's bedside. Betty had gone to the hospital cafeteria to get some dinner.

"How are you feeling?" George asked.

Babe lay there, groggy from the anesthesia and painkiller, a tube up her nose and the colostomy bag planted on her like a saddle bag.

"Lousy," she murmured.

George didn't know how to respond. Ever since they had met, she had been in terrific shape. Like a beautiful deer, his deer. Now her condition was tearing at him. He felt bad about hitting her. In deference to Babe's illness, he had cut down on the drinking. He had recently been diagnosed as diabetic, so now he had a double reason to cut down. He wasn't smoking cigars in the hospital. He was antsy.

"You'll feel better soon," he said.

The next day he brought Babe a newspaper. He told her what was happening in the golf game, who had beaten who.

She smiled at his fumbling efforts. A few days later, she actually did feel better and said so.

George was relieved and began spending less and less time at the hospital. The way he saw it, it didn't matter. The kid Betty was there, and Babe's siblings were popping in and out. Later on in the week, Peggy Kirk Bell stopped by. Bertha Bowen spent time there, and Patty Berg even dropped in. Good old Patty. Short and stocky, with that snub nose and freckled face. Like a kid in the funny papers, but strong. Almost as good a golfer as Babe.

"Well, well," Babe said to Patty Berg when Patty popped her head in the hospital room. "My old rival. Just come by to see if the rumors are true, eh? That I'm on my last legs?"

"So, Mrs. Z, when will I have the pleasure of beating you again?" Patty asked, nodding to Betty and pulling up a chair.

"You beat me. That's a laugh." Babe cackled. She was feeling better today and eating better. The sun was shining, and she wasn't dead. She looked at the golf bag in the corner of her room. The afternoon sun was shining on the golf bag and clubs, haloing them in light.

"Well, I hope I can beat you real soon," Patty said. "It would please me a lot."

After Patty left, Tiny returned to Babe's hospital room, with his wife Ruth this time. They reminisced about the old days in Beaumont. Tiny brought flowers, peach-colored roses. Their smell was wonderful. Ruth gave Babe a wrapped gift, a slender book of poetry by a fellow named Robert Frost.

"Robert Frost, I've heard of him," Babe said as she looked over the volume.

"He used to be a farmer," Ruth said. "You might like his work. Even Bill here likes his poetry."

"Ever the English teacher. Still tryin' to spoon feed me lit-ra-chure," Babe cracked. "Don't you know I'm a lost cause?"

Still, she promised to read the book.

IN ABOUT A week, Babe's appetite came roaring back, and she was telling visitors, "I feel a whole lot better."

She was a bit reluctant to eat big meals because of the colostomy. Waste coming out a hole in her side? It was disgusting, but she guessed she would have to get used to it. The colostomy bag was strapped around her middle with an elastic belt. The bag encircled the stoma tightly.

George wanted no part of the colostomy bag. It wasn't that he didn't want to help Babe; it was just that he feared messing things up. What if he didn't do it the right way? What if he wound up hurting her?

But Betty Dodd was confident.

"I've seen colostomies before," she told Babe. "I worked summers as a nursing assistant at a hospital when I was in high school."

Upon receiving instructions from a nurse on how to change the colostomy bag and how to irrigate it, Betty assured Babe that when she went home, she could take care of it. The hospital staff was letting her do it now at the hospital every other day. They knew she was like a daughter to Babe.

Babe gazed at the bouquets that people had sent, even though she had told them not to. Luscious roses, pretty lilies, and pink, red, and white carnations. The aroma of the roses and lilies filled the room, helping to blot out the antiseptic hospital smell.

Get well cards were piling up, too. Fortunately, Lillie and some other family members promised to help Babe reply to them. It was Lillie who had brought a few cardboard boxes to keep them in. Sometimes she and Babe read through the cards together. There were ones from old friends like Stan Kertes and Grantland Rice and George Aulbach, as well as celebrities like Bob Hope, Groucho Marx, and Bing Crosby. Even the great Ted Williams, whom she hardly knew but who was active in the Jimmy Fund in Boston, had sent a cheerful note.

Babe opened one envelope that contained a blue note card expressing the sender's wish for a speedy recovery. It was signed Paul Gallico.

"Drop this one in the trash," Babe told her sister.

Only one of Babe's sponsors showed up to visit her. This was Lew Serbin, the president of Serbin of Florida sportswear. Blouses and dresses in his casual clothing line had Babe's signature on their label. Lew stayed for over an hour. He would have stayed longer, but he was worried about tiring Babe.

"Good old Lew," Babe thought when he left. "My other sponsors must not think I'm worth much now."

Babe had been in the hospital over three weeks. It was morning and she had just had a bath and was feeling all clean and relaxed when she stood up and excrement spurted from her side.

Unthinkingly, Betty reached out her hands and caught it.

"Oh my god!" Babe cried.

"It's okay, I got it," Betty said, not batting an eyelash.

Before the nurse came, Betty had deposited the waste in the toilet and thoroughly washed her hands. Then, as she had been instructed, she cleaned Babe up, reaching into her incision with rubber gloves to irrigate it.

"Damn, Betty, I don't know how you can be so calm doing that," Babe said.

"Don't be silly. I'd do anything for you."

WHAT NO ONE told Babe during this time was that when Dr. Moore opened her up, he discovered the cancer had spread. There were the tell-tale metastases. Immediately after the operation, Moore called George and Betty into his office and told them this grim news.

"Can't you take out all the cancer?" George asked.

"It's too late," Moore said. "The rectal operation will give her some relief. But the cancer will give her more trouble within a year."

After overcoming his initial shock, George did his best to blot out the bad news. "Some relief," the doctor had said. Maybe a year—a year in which Babe could become active, maybe play some golf. He pictured her smiling out on the course. They could still have some good times together.

Betty, on the other hand, was frustrated by the news. She had done all she could for Babe. But now the doctor was asking her and George to do something more.

"I think it's advisable not to tell Mrs. Zaharias," Dr. Moore said. "She's got enough to handle right now, just getting used to the colostomy."

George quickly agreed. Betty agreed, too. What choice did she have? But later she wondered if she had done the right thing. Didn't Babe have a right to know? After all, it was her body, her life. Betty could imagine Babe's reaction to hearing her cancer had spread. She *would* be devastated. She might well give up. Betty guessed the doctor was right. If Babe had a year, maybe something would happen in the interim. Doctors were always coming up with new treatments, weren't they?

56

"I THINK OF this operation as just another setback," Babe told the gentlemen of the press, who were gathered in and just outside her hospital room. "Like when I was stripped of my amateur status in 1935. It's best not to cry about things. You just have to face your problem and figure out what to do next."

The reporters dutifully scribbled Babe's words and took her photo, with George and Betty Dodd flanking her bed. Babe was wearing a new pair of pink silk pajamas, which Bertha Bowen had bought for her. Neiman Marcus all the way.

"Any word about whether you're going to return to tournament play?" one reporter asked.

"It's too soon to tell," Babe said. "All I know is I'm gonna try my darnedest to get ready."

Tiny Scurlock, who was standing nearest Babe's bed, asked, "Any words to other cancer patients?" He knew Babe had walked around and seen the other patients in the hospital's oncology ward, offering them encouragement. One, a nun named Sister Tarsisis, who had refused a colostomy operation and was wasting away, seemed especially encouraged by Babe's visit. After talking with her for some time, she told Babe she would have the operation.

"Yes," Babe told the press. "When I'm on the golf course, I use my physical muscles to hit the ball. But now I'm using my spiritual muscle to stay in touch with God. I'm not gonna give up, and I hope that others in the same boat as me won't either."

As cameras clicked, she put on a cowboy hat and held up a toy six-shooter in each hand. George had given her both props for the reporters.

"We Texas gals are used to scrappin'," she said.

57

BY LATE JULY, Babe was on the LPGA tournament circuit again, this time back at the All-American at Tam O' Shanter in Niles, Illinois. The tournament directors had agreed to let Betty Dodd be paired with her once Babe explained that Betty could help her if she had any trouble. By this time, just about everybody in America knew that Babe had battled cancer.

Once again, Babe teed off, hitting the ball hard, though the drive barely cracked two hundred yards. She trailed throughout the first day of the tournament, tiring on the back nine. The next day was no different: start off strongly but fading to the middle of the pack. She, who used to have such energy. By the last day of the tournament, Babe was three-putting. After missing an easy putt only a few feet from the cup, she hung her head and wept. As the gallery murmured in unease, Betty Dodd walked over to her and whispered in her ear.

"Quit," she said. "Everybody will understand."

But Babe thought of all the cancer patients whom she had told never to quit. She was their inspiration now.

"No," she told Betty. She brushed away her tears.

Praying for the strength to continue, Babe finished the tournament, placing fifteenth out of thirty.

"Well, you have to look on the bright side," Babe thought. At least the colostomy bag had held tight and was unnoticeable under her loose-fitting blouse. She had had nightmares about it springing a leak in front of everyone, but it hadn't. She guessed that was a victory for all the people living with one of the damned things.

Patty Berg, who won the tournament, came striding over to Babe afterward.

Babe spoke before her rival could. "Congratulations, Patty. You played terrific." Saying the words felt strange to her. She was used to them offering her congratulations.

"You're all grit, girl," Patty replied, as she looked into Babe's hazel eyes.

Babe held her gaze for a long moment. Both women knew what few others did: what it took to be a champion—the endless practice, the self-denial, the loneliness traveling from hotel room to hotel room across the country. While one part of you told you that you should be lounging by a swimming pool somewhere or else having loads of kids, letting a man support you, another voice was driving you on. Why? Because you had been given this wonderful ability, and you might as well use it to its fullest because it wouldn't last forever. That's why.

"Thank you, Patty," Babe said.

58

"WE'LL PLAY BETTER a week from now," Betty Dodd told Babe as they sat that evening in the Tam O' Shanter dining room. George was with them. He had sheltered Babe with a huge umbrella when it began to rain that afternoon, and he had looked on in consternation as Babe momentarily broke down on the course. Betty hadn't played well during the tournament either. It was hard for her to concentrate, seeing what Babe was going through. All three of them were subdued. George, for once, was drinking ice water, not liquor.

"Don't get sad, honey," he told his wife. "The doctors said it would take a while to get your strength back."

"Sure," Babe replied.

That was what everyone had been telling her for months. Everyone was encouraging but cautioning, encouraging but cautioning; it got on her nerves. Unless you had cancer, you had no idea what it was like—the bone weariness, the feeling of all those nasty white cancer cells multiplying, clawing at your insides, sapping your strength. An enemy takeover.

Not to mention all that hospital stuff, the pills and needles and all—the strange, hushed, half-lighted nights in the hospital that made you feel suspended between life and death, the nurses coming in at all hours to take your vitals. It felt like prison. Thank God Betty had been there, sleeping on the cot in Babe's room. She didn't know if she could have stood the loneliness otherwise. It felt good to hear her soft breathing, her occasional turning in her sleep.

Well, Babe would try to get plenty of sleep tonight because she was dead tired. She and George were sharing a hotel room this time. Betty was in a room just down the hall, ready to come in and replace Babe's colostomy bag when needed.

AT THE WORLD Championship, which was played at the same course a few days later, Babe did play much better. No three putts. However, she tired a little on the final nine, and Patty Berg once again won.

"Damn you, Patty," Babe mock complained to her rival back in the clubhouse. "You gotta stop showing me up."

"Ha, fat chance," Patty said. "I beat you now when I can 'cause I know you'll be back at full tilt soon."

Despite Babe's disappointment at her third-place finish, which felt like last place to her, the press was ecstatic. Everybody loved a great comeback story. Reporters swarmed her as if she had won the tournament. *Time* magazine wrote a nice story about her, which they entitled "The Babe is Back," complete with a photo of her at the World Championship.

Babe read the story, then tossed the magazine aside.

"It's all bullshit," she told Betty. "I won't be back until I've won another tournament."

"Don't you think you're being a little hard on yourself?"

"No, I've always demanded the most from myself. That's how I got to be where I am."

But where *was* Babe, Betty wondered, thinking of what Dr. Moore had said about the cancer giving her more trouble within a year.

About a week later, Babe got a phone call from her co-manager, Fred Corcoran. Fred always sounded so cheery, she liked talking to him.

"How'd you and Betty Dodd like to be on Ed Sullivan's *The Toast of the Town*?" Fred asked.

"What? Why?"

"Ed Sullivan knows about you playing the harmonica and Betty playing the guitar. He thinks having you and Betty on the show will help the fight against cancer. You know, he'll say a few words about your recovery."

Babe quickly agreed, telling Fred that she and Betty would fly up to Manhattan.

The Toast of the Town, which was hosted by Ed Sullivan, was easily the most popular variety show on TV. All the top entertainers wanted to be on it.

"Now we really gotta practice," Babe told Betty. They practiced when they weren't playing golf. They liked sitting on the couch in blue jeans playing music together. A new song they were learning was "Begin the Beguine."

"Ah, Babe, we have such fun when George is away," Betty said.

"I know we do," Babe said.

"So . . ."

"So what?"

Betty hesitated to say what she felt she must say. "Have you thought any more about divorcing George?"

She felt like she was being pushy, but this relationship was putting her in a bind, too. It was so secret it was stifling.

Babe had a hawk's eyes: great adjusting to distance, homing in on whatever she needed to do to crush her opponents. However, that skill was useless here—with someone she loved. Now she just looked confused.

"Oh, George," Babe said.

Sometimes she had bad dreams. People were wielding swords against her; she was the monster they were trying to kill. What's worse, she was stark naked!

The dreams weren't so far-fetched. She had read in *Time* magazine that President Eisenhower, "Ike" for whom she had voted, had thrown all the homosexuals out of the government. With the Red Scare taking over, they were considered a security risk, not fit to serve their country. Babe didn't consider herself a homo because she had married George and lived with him for a long time. But she knew most people would think her one if she divorced George and lived openly with Betty.

"Well?" Betty asked.

"I don't know . . ." Babe said.

She didn't really want to keep on being with Betty behind George's back. It would be better, more honest for all concerned to divorce him. But did she have a choice? She told Betty her fears.

Betty realized that Babe might be right. If Babe divorced George, rumors might fly about her and Babe. She had already noticed some funny looks in the locker room when she and Babe walked in together. She could only imagine what the ladies were saying behind her and Babe's back.

"Do you think all that would really happen?" Betty asked.

Babe told her about the old Paul Gallico piece.

"That one hurt real bad," she admitted. And Gallico hadn't been the only one to call her sexuality into question. Babe told Betty about another article, which stated, "Don't let your daughter grow up to be a muscle moll," with Babe as the obvious bad influence.

"I don't want all that stuff happening again," Babe told Betty.

"Who can blame you?" Betty said. To be a target like that. Babe must have felt like the loneliest person in the world. Even the Negroes, downtrodden as they were, had others of their race to rely on. Not Babe.

Betty put an arm around Babe. "Well, whatever happens, you're not alone now."

59

BEFORE A STUDIO audience and millions of TV viewers, Ed Sullivan introduced the great Babe Didrikson Zaharias and her protégé Betty Dodd.

"The whole nation was shocked to hear Babe had cancer," Ed told his audience. "But now I want everyone to see how she's licked this thing."

With that, the audience applauded, and Babe and Betty came out and did their bit. Though Betty was nervous, Babe wasn't at all afraid. After winning her gold medals at the Olympics, she had briefly headlined in a theater in Chicago. They had her running on a treadmill and stuff, showing off her athletic prowess. Bright lights came naturally to her.

Babe and Betty played "Begin the Beguine." It was hokey but fun. The audience applauded warmly. Who didn't like Babe Zaharias? She was an inspiration.

There were also two Negro performers on the same show as Babe and Betty, two big names: Nat King Cole and Ella Fitzgerald. Nat sang his hit "Unforgettable," while Ella sang "Trying." Ed Sullivan was well known as for his willingness to spotlight Negro performers. This rubbed some people the wrong way, especially in the South, but he would not back down.

"We've never had any trouble with our Negro guests," Ed Sullivan told the press.

From the green room, where they had a TV tuned to the show, Babe and Betty watched as Ed shook hands with Nat "King" Cole. Later in the show, Ed took Ella Fitzgerald by the hand and gave her a peck on the cheek after she performed.

Now, back at their swank mid-town hotel, Babe and Betty got into their pajamas, lay in bed together and caught part of *What's My Line* on TV.

Somehow the conversation shifted to the two Negro performers they had seen on the Sullivan show.

"That Nat King Cole sure has a beautiful voice," Betty said. "So does Ella. I wish I could sing like that."

Betty sang a little, accompanying herself on the guitar, but she was no Ella Fitzgerald.

Babe thought over Betty's remark, which reminded her of something. "When I was growing up in Beaumont, we had the KKK," she recalled. "The Klan said colored people were lazy and shiftless and dumb and all the colored men wanted was to rape white women. That's how I was raised. Until I got older, I never thought colored people could be good at anything."

Babe recalled the time she had thrown ice water on her two brown-skinned Olympic teammates as they lay sleeping in their berth on the train out to Los Angeles. She didn't tell Betty that story. It was too shameful.

"You didn't think they were good at *anything*?" Betty asked. She had grown up following the exploits of Joe Louis on the radio. Like many Americans, she had been thrilled when "The Brown Bomber" whipped Hitler's favorite fighter, Max Schmeling, in the first round of their second bout. In fact, Joe Louis was kind of a hero to her. "So, what do you think now?"

Babe shrugged.

"They're great singers and all, but I don't think Ed should have kissed Ella."

"Why not? I love Ella."

"Ella's fine, but that kissing bit was going a little too far. It'll rile people up down South." Babe thought of people like her brothers Ole, Louis, and Bubba, who still said the word "nigger" on occasion. Everything was still segregated down there, from washrooms to movie theaters and restaurants to schools. "No, Ed shouldn't have kissed her."

Betty mulled this over. Unlike Babe, she had not grown up in the South. She had been born in Portland, Oregon, and the family traveled frequently because her dad was a general in the United States Army. He had been a commander in Germany during and after the war. As a result, he had mentioned some things to his family—things about a place he had seen called Dachau, with its piles of corpses and walking dead.

Maybe it was General Dodd's influence or maybe it was something innate, but when the Dodd family settled in San Antonio after World War II, Betty never quite felt like she belonged there, never felt a part of the South's prevailing attitudes. They just felt wrong to her. The kind of thing ignorant people did.

"Ah, you're old fashioned about Ella and Ed," Betty told Babe.

"Maybe I am," Babe said. Betty, being twenty years her junior, had different attitudes toward things. She already knew Betty was happy when Jackie Robinson broke the color line in baseball. Maybe it was a good thing.

Babe felt like pulling out a Pall Mall, but Betty didn't like her smoking in bed. Maybe she would smoke in the bathroom later on. There was a ceiling fan in there.

Another thought occurred to Betty.

"You know, these same people who called Negroes bad names, what nasty names do you think they'd call us?" Her voice rose as she continued. "What we're doing would probably rile people as much as Ed Sullivan kissing Ella Fitzgerald . . . if they knew about us."

"But they *don't* know about us," Babe said.

It was a disturbing thought, especially since she had already been called bad names—the insults stung like hornets, back before she married George. She was desperate to keep her relationship with Betty a secret, hiding in plain sight. They always got hotel rooms with two beds and messed up the covers on one to make it seem as if it had been slept in. Didn't want any chambermaids blabbing. To the outside world, Betty was Babe's protégé, that was all.

"Well, *if* they did," Betty continued.

"Well, they won't," Babe said. "So let's not talk about it anymore."

Now she really would have to have a cigarette, to settle her nerves.

Betty knew better than to pursue the subject.

What's my Line was ending.

"Let's turn this baby off and get some sleep," Babe said.

As she and Betty lay together in bed, Babe thought, "Of course she's right, darn her." If people knew the truth about her and Betty, they would despise them just liked they despised Negroes. Maybe not everyone, but a lot. Maybe her own family.

60

BABE SIGNED UP for the Florida winter circuit. Though she felt her strength returning, she lost the first two tournaments she played in: the Tampa Women's Open and the St. Petersburg Open. It galled her because these were local tournaments that, she felt, she should have easily won. A consolation: though she finished seventh at the Tampa Women's Open, she finished second at the St. Pete. She was on the upswing.

"I can't say how pleased I am that you're playing today," Lew Serbin told Babe at the Bayshore Golf Course in Miami Beach. To Lew, who had also risen from poverty and whose sportswear company sponsored the Serbin Open, hardscrabble Babe was the personification of the American Dream.

"Well, Lew, we'll see if I'm really recovered," Babe said. "The proof is in the pudding, as they say."

Though Lew had to be neutral as sponsor of the tournament, he had seen Babe, weak and wan, in her hospital bed.

"Best of luck, Babe," he told her, giving her a hug.

Throughout the tournament Babe and Patty Berg were tied round after round. Babe knew Patty wouldn't let up because of her recent illness, not that Babe wanted her to. They were like two racehorses, straining down the home stretch.

"That damn broad," Babe said to herself when Patty made a marvelous shot to escape a bunker. "I couldn't have hit it better."

On the last hole of the tournament, a 430-yard par 4, Babe's drive went long but directly into a stand of palm trees. To get over the palm fronds and past the bunker that lay before the green, she would have to use her four-iron to blast her way out. Would she have the power? Before she had gotten ill, she would have said something funny to the gallery at this point, talked about how she would loosen her girdle and bust one. Now, not sure what her body would allow, she said nothing, just focused on what she had to do. For a few seconds the world dropped away, and she was totally alone, in that liminal spot between defeat and victory. She swung fiercely, and the ball carried to within one hundred yards of the green. She used her nine-iron to land the ball on the green, and then sank a long putt to win the tournament, beating Patty Berg by one stroke.

"You know I have mixed feelings about losing this one to you," Patty remarked afterward, a wry smile on her round, freckled face. "On the one hand, I wanted you to do well, but on the other . . ."

"Yeah, yeah, I know," Babe said. "You're a killer, same as me."

Patty did not deny it.

Babe had no mixed feelings about accepting the first-place trophy and a kiss and hug from Lew Serbin. The trophy was a diamond-encrusted metal golf ball mounted on a podium.

"What do they say?" Babe chuckled. "Diamonds are a girl's best friend."

61

BECAUSE PRESIDENT DWIGHT D. Eisenhower was an enthusiastic golfer—to his political opponents it seemed like all the old general did was play golf—it seemed logical to Babe that he should invite her to kick off the American Cancer Society's annual Cancer Crusade. The word came to her from the Society's president: there would be a ceremony and a luncheon at the White House. Of course, she would accept the invitation.

"Imagine a little gal like me from Beaumont gettin' to meet Old Ike, the president of the United States," Babe said.

George looked over at her.

"Why not?" he asked.

He and Babe were sitting in the living room at Rainbow Manor, him in his big brown easy chair and she on the couch. They had been watching *Make Room for Daddy* with Danny Thomas—when the phone call came. They now had a Zenith TV with a huge 21 inch screen in the living room—their old TVs being relegated to two of the bedrooms.

"You met pretty much everybody else," George continued. "Ed Sullivan, all them movie stars, etcetera . . . the president ain't such a big deal."

Babe dismissed what George was saying. She knew he was as thrilled by the presidential invitation as she was. He just liked to lowball events, to not show how excited he was, except for the ones he himself was promoting.

"I voted for Ike," Babe reflected. Adlai Stevenson had been too much of a talker for her. Always bellyaching about what was wrong with America; never pointing out what was right. She liked that Ike was an optimist.

There was no tournament this weekend, and Betty was off somewhere in the used Lincoln convertible—forest green—she had purchased with a loan from her parents. Betty liked to get out and just drive along the Gulf coast with the top down. One afternoon she got up her courage and parked across the street from a bar in Tampa that stood on the corner of Polk and Morgan. She had read somewhere that the bar was a "haven" for homosexuals. She didn't even get out of her car, just stared at the bar's clapboard façade, trying to imagine the wondrous nightlife within. But no good loitering here. You never knew who could be watching.

62

IT WAS LATE afternoon when Babe, George, and Betty flew into Washington, D.C. As the chartered plane circled the city before landing at National Airport, everyone got a kick out of seeing the Washington and Lincoln Monuments from the air. It was Betty who spotted the White House, surrounded by its beautiful lawn, so well-tended that it could have been a putting green. The sun was low in the sky, bathing everything in a glow the color of honey.

"We'll be inside that house tomorrow," Betty said.

Babe had kept her word to Ruth Scurlock and read some of the poems in the book her ex-teacher had given her. Now, looking out over Washington, D.C., she recalled one of the poems and said it aloud: "Nothing gold can stay."

Betty turned from the plane window. "What?"

"It's from a poem by Robert Frost." She recited the poem in its entirety—only eight lines.

"That's beautiful," Betty said. She wasn't big on poetry herself, but she had to admit the truth of that poem, sad as it was. She and Babe were sitting together, while George was sitting up near the pilot, chatting him up a little. Betty recalled what Babe's doctor had told her about Babe's cancer spreading.

"Within a year," the doctor had warned. *Nothing gold can stay.* Did Babe already realize that?

As a military band played "Hail to the Chief," President Eisenhower strode into the East Room and greeted Mildred Ella "Babe" Didrikson Zaharias. For once in her life, Babe felt intimidated. Who wouldn't be? Here was the man who had launched the D-Day invasion, the Supreme Allied Commander. That feat impressed Babe the most, more than all the political stuff in the world.

As they shook hands, the President mock whispered to her, "We'll talk about golf a little later."

While Ike shook hands with those in the receiving line, Babe gazed around the august room, took in the crystal and gold chandeliers and the full-length oil paintings of George and Martha Washington, the antique furniture, and the long gold window treatments. During her golf career, she had become used to fancy places, but this room had an element of history she wasn't used to. Who else had stood in this room? Lincoln, all kinds of people you read about in the history books.

Now it was time for the President to flip a switch and light a seventy-foot Sword of Hope, the symbol of the American Cancer Society, in Times Square, where millions of people would see it.

Presenting Ike with a miniature Sword of Hope, Babe said her carefully rehearsed piece. "Mr. President, on behalf of the hundreds of thousands of volunteers of the American Cancer Society and of the thousands like myself who have had cancer, who have known its terrible threat, and have been able to get back to our normal life, I present you with this sword of hope."

Formalities done, Babe and the President talked golf for a few minutes, with Babe demonstrating a grip on the Sword of Hope as if it were a golf club. Ike was a good guy and a knowledgeable golfer, even if he did look a little older than Babe had expected, his face lined with wrinkles you couldn't see on TV.

"I didn't take up golf until I got older," Ike explained to her. "But now I love to play it, even in winter."

Then he explained how he had his golf balls painted black, so they'd show up in the snow.

"I should've thought of that one when I was living in Denver," she told him. "It would have helped."

The cameras clicked like cards being shuffled as Ike and Babe chatted about golf. How many people would see these photos? Millions.

At dinner that night at a fancy restaurant on DeSales Street, George was holding forth on politics.

"That Ike, he's no commie," George was saying. "He cleaned all those Reds out of the government, just like he did with the homos."

Here he cast a significant look at his wife.

"Right," Babe said, uneasily. She guessed Ike had to get all the homos out of government because they were a security threat, subject to blackmail. They were threats, not her. Who cared what some lady golfer did in her private life?

Later, back at their hotel room on Lafayette Square, Babe got a call that made her shout, "I'll be down tomorrow!"

"Who the hell was that?" George was watching boxing on TV—*Pabst Blue Ribbon Bouts.*

"Peggy Kirk Bell!" Babe shouted. "She just had her baby and it's a girl."

"That's nice," George said. "Peg'll make a good mom. You're gonna visit her, right?"

"Yep."

That settled, George returning to watching the fight. He missed the stink of sweat and cigars and spilled beer, the strain of muscle against muscle, the managerial machinations before each wrestling match. Watching boxing on TV was a substitute.

"The ref better stop this," George said as blood from an open cut ran down the younger boxer's face. He had no desire to see anyone killed in the ring.

A thought came to George.

"I guess Betty'll go with you?"

"Yeah, probably."

George had lost some of his resentment toward Betty. What if she and Babe were a little too close for comfort? What if George suspected there was a physical element to their friendship? Just how that could express itself, he didn't want to think about. The kid was taking care of Babe's colostomy, something he didn't feel able to do. She was like a live-in nurse.

The referee had finally stopped the fight. Thank God. Maybe the kid would get over being shellacked.

CARRYING A LARGE bouquet of pink and white carnations topped by a pink helium balloon, Babe stormed into Peggy Kirk Bell's hospital room while the newborn was taking suck from a bottle.

"Hey, Peggy. Oops."

Babe stopped abruptly.

"Sorry, I don't want to interrupt."

"That's all right," Peggy said, looking up. "This baby could drink through an air raid siren. Thanks for flowers. They're lovely."

"Where should . . . ?" Babe asked.

Peggy pointed to the radiator. All the other surfaces were festooned with flowers and cards.

"You can put them over there. Betty get yourself in here."

Betty, who had been lingering in the doorway, came in.

"Hi, Peggy," she said. She liked Peggy Kirk Bell, too. Everyone liked Peggy.

Fortunately, there were two chairs in the room.

Babe and Betty agreed that Peggy looked fine. It was good for a change, seeing someone in a hospital bed who wasn't deathly ill.

"Aw, she's darlin'! So, are you gonna name her Babe Bell?" Babe asked, only half kidding.

Babe was such a card, sometimes, Peggy thought. Like a little kid in her enthusiasms. You had to take her with a grain of salt.

"No, honey. We're calling her Bonnie."

"Well, that sounds good. 'Bonnie Bell wins the Open.' That'll do."

As she sat there gazing at mother and child, Babe felt a sense of satisfaction. Since she couldn't have kids herself, it was nice that one of her closest friends and a fine golfer to boot, had a girl. Although Peggy said she had wanted a boy, Babe told her it was better to have a girl.

"Boys have already done all kinds of things in sports, while we girls are just getting started," she told Peggy.

"That's true," Peggy said. It hadn't been so long ago—only a few years— that Babe and the others had started the LPGA.

"You got that right," Betty added.

Babe went on. "Warren's an athlete and you're an athlete—I predict great things for this kid. Say, where is the proud papa?"

"He went out to do some grocery shopping. He'll be back this evening."

A nurse came in to take the baby, who had finished her bottle.

"Good-bye, sweet cakes," Babe said.

As the nurse and baby left the room, Peggy turned to Betty Dodd, who had said little. "So, Betty, how are you doing?"

She knew that Betty had moved in with Babe and George. Everyone knew George could be difficult. Peggy wasn't a gossip, but she heard things. She had even heard rumors about Babe and Betty being lovers, but she didn't believe them. They were just close friends. You needed a close friend or two when you were married to someone like George. Even if you weren't.

"Me? Oh, I'm fine," Betty said. "I like being on tour. And one of these days I'll win a tournament."

Babe turned to her. "You will."

Betty volunteered no further information. What could she say? She sat uncomfortably in her chair.

But Peggy was gracious enough not to press Betty, especially for information she did not necessarily want to know.

"Bonnie and I are going home tomorrow," Peggy finally announced. "And it'll be a good thing. It's been two days and I'm already tired of lying here in this hospital bed."

"I know how you feel," Babe said.

Did she ever.

63

THE 1954 U.S. Women's Open was to be played on Saturday, July 3 at Salem Country Club in Peabody, Massachusetts.

"If I can win at Salem, I can win anywhere," Babe told herself.

She knew it was a par 72 course, a long course. Sometimes she felt fatigued, even when she hadn't particularly exerted herself. Was it the cancer coming back or was she just getting old? She wasn't a kid anymore; she was forty-three. Forty-three years of nonstop motion, it often seemed to her. Well, that was the way she had wanted it. Mama once told her that she used to move around a lot even in the womb. And when she was a kid, she had so much energy she could hardly wait for the sun to rise, especially on weekends when there was no school, and the streets and dusty lots of Beaumont beckoned. Running, jumping, swimming, playing any game with a ball—she was the best at them all, always first to be picked for a team. She always felt indestructible.

Now, she knew she had to pace herself, taking care not to practice too strenuously, taking naps more than she used to. Having had cancer was like living with a slumbering beast. You didn't want to be overconfident, to awaken the beast; on the other hand, you didn't want to give up what you loved doing. That would be another kind of death.

The thought occurred to Babe that maybe people were granted only a certain amount of mileage in their lifetimes, like cars. Maybe, with her constant activity, she had already exhausted her mileage, compressed it into a shorter span than most people. That was why she had been stricken now. Well, no sense dwelling on that.

Since Babe was unfamiliar with the Salem course, she, George, and Betty flew up there five days early, to get the lay of the land, so to speak. Beautiful, historic clubhouse with a prominent white cupola. And Babe and Betty were tickled by the fact that the club had a witch on a broomstick as its insignia.

New England had different kinds of trees than Florida: no lazy palm trees waving in the breeze; instead, stout sycamores, birches, and maples, chestnuts standing majestically, like town elders. Even if they did represent hazards on the golf course, it was lovely to be among them, especially after being cooped up in a hospital room for so long.

"Under the spreading chestnut tree," Babe said to herself.

She had had, under duress, to recite the Longfellow poem back in junior high school. Now, as she practiced at Salem, she wished she had learned the names of more trees. After all, she had spent half her life on golf courses, surrounded by them. They, casting long shadows on the fairways, had always borne witness to her victories and defeats. And yes, the trees would be here long after she was gone.

Babe got off to a quick start on the first day of the tournament and never looked back. Although she did tire somewhat on the last eighteen holes, she had built up such an insurmountable lead that it didn't matter. She scored 72-71-73-75 during the tournament's four rounds and left her nearest competitors far behind. The gallery was ecstatic; so she knew, were the sportswriters who followed her progress around the course. The bigger the comeback, the better the story.

This time on the eighteenth hole, Babe felt that her victory, now assured, called for a certain gravity. Rather than performing one of the antics she was known for, like dancing a jig or getting down on her knees and salaaming to the hole, Babe simply took off her straw hat and bowed deeply to the gallery. Then she slowly raised her right hand in victory, letting the applause wash over her.

It had been barely fifteen months since her surgery, and she had won by twelve strokes over a fine golfer, Betty Hicks. Ever competitive Louise Suggs had finished third, while a tall, blond newcomer out of Stanford, nineteen-year-old Mary "Mickey" Wright had tied for fourth with Betsy Rawls. Babe had been paired with Mickey.

"Wow, that Mickey Wright," Babe gushed to reporters at the close of the tournament. "Don't you think she's got the most beautiful swing? I predict she's gonna be a champion before long."

There was a press conference in the Salem Country Club, with reporters falling all over themselves to commend Babe for her incredible victory. More than a few of them had doubted she would ever play golf again after her cancer diagnosis, let alone win a major tournament by a record-setting margin.

"I promised to God that if He made me well," Babe told the press, "I'd do everything in my power when I got out to help the fight against cancer."

After the press conference, she called her surgeon, Dr. Robert Moore, back in Texas. "Thank you for helping me. My win is your win, too."

"You did it yourself, Babe," Dr. Moore told her. "Your faith and your courage."

"Nah, I didn't do it myself, Doc," Babe said. "All of us in this fight against cancer helped make me strong."

"It's remarkable," Dr. Moore told himself after speaking with Babe. He thought about his diagnosis of Babe's rectal cancer, that the malignancy had spread. Well, it had, he was sure of that as he was sure of his own name. Chalk it up to sheer willpower that Babe had battled back and won the Women's Open. She truly was Texas tough.

64

"I'D BE ONLY too happy to escort you around the hospital," Monsignor Paul Di Genova told Babe, who earlier in the day, had opened the Babe Didrikson Zaharias Chapter of the American Cancer Society in Seattle. Di Genova was an administration at Seattle's Catholic Hospital.

Babe had gotten quite used to Catholics since her early days, when she had viewed practitioners of the religion as suspiciously un-American.

"They follow the Pope, not the president," her nominally Lutheran father had once told her.

But now, because of her illness, she knew that Catholics ran many fine hospitals—Hotel Dieu in Beaumont, and Saint this and that elsewhere. It was okay; they didn't try to convert you or anything. She also knew that a monsignor was kind of a superior priest, someone who had risen through the ranks. As Babe now saw it, Catholics were a lot like Protestants. But, of course, their priests couldn't marry. That must be hard for them. On the other hand, not all marriages were happy.

As Monsignor Di Genova and Babe walked through the cancer ward, Babe popped her head into rooms, introduced herself, and chatted with the patients. Many of them brightened when she talked with them.

"I don't know if you know my story, but I had cancer surgery not too long ago. It was rough." She didn't shrink from going into the details of her type of cancer. She guessed that everyone had gory details of their own.

"I felt so bad, I didn't think I was going to make it," she told them. "But I just won the Women's Golf Open a couple of weeks ago. So, don't ever give up hope."

One of the patients, a shriveled man with mottled skin who had just had his voice box removed, couldn't talk, but gave her a thumbs up.

Some of them were too far gone to even recognize her. Some were virtually comatose, with half-open mouths and unseeing eyes, family members huddled around them in tableaux of grief. Babe didn't linger long with these people. They were experiencing something she had no words of comfort for.

"You are doing God's work, Mrs. Zaharias," Monsignor Di Genova assured Babe.

"Thanks, Monsignor," Babe said. She was still a bit uncomfortable around religious people. Now Di Genova was trailing her like a bird dog.

"Why do so many of these hospitals have the same color paint?" Babe wondered. A sickly green color. Mold green, she called it. And some of it was peeling in corners and around the ceiling. She felt like offering to pay for a paint job of the entire oncology ward, but that would probably have offended the Monsignor. People were protective of their own turf, she knew that by now.

It was worse visiting the kids. Babe had to steel herself to stay strong for them. A lot of them had bald heads from the new treatment they were getting, which was being injected with powerful chemicals in hopes of killing the cancer cells.

"Chemotherapy," the doctors called it.

The kids were waxen looking, with yellowish complexions. Some of them had chubby, balloon-like faces. If you didn't know better, you'd think it was the chubbiness of good health, but it wasn't. It was the chubbiness of water retention.

Still, some of the kids smiled up at her and seemed to enjoy it when she pulled out her harmonica and played a few tunes. They liked "Old Susannah" and "When You Wish Upon a Star."

Babe sat at the foot of one little boy's bed. He was so weak he couldn't smile, though Babe could tell he was trying to, that he thought it was expected of him. His eyes were dead-looking, flat as old pennies. In the bed beside him was a stuffed Mickey Mouse doll with a chewed left ear.

Tousling the boy's lifeless hair, Babe tried hard to keep from weeping. Sometimes she felt like she was selling these kids a bill of goods. How many of them would really recover?

Monsignor Di Genova introduced her to a portly young doctor named Frederick Pappas, who had just entered the room. Pulling him into the hallway, Babe asked him how effective their treatments were now.

"Our rates of recovery are going up," Dr. Pappas told her, smiling.

Babe brightened.

"Childhood leukemia used to be a guaranteed death sentence. But we're finding that we can get more and more of these kids into remission with chemotherapy."

"So what are their odds now with this new treatment?" Babe asked. From years of golfing, she was used to weighing the odds of using a certain golf club in a certain situation. One club might be safer; on the other hand, another was riskier but could get you further to the cup. Maybe chemotherapy was like that.

Dr. Pappas's smile disappeared.

"About ten to fifteen percent will go into remission and live as much as a year or two longer," he said. "A few may live a normal lifespan."

Babe said nothing, grim-faced.

As if reading her mind, Dr. Pappas went on. "But we're only at the beginning of using chemo to fight cancer. We're experimenting with new combinations of drugs—folic acid, ACTH, cortisone. And with every advance we make, the survival rates are improving. That's why people like you, Mrs. Zaharias, who raise money for cancer research are so important."

"I'll do my best to raise money," Babe assured him. She knew she wasn't alone in that regard. Up in Boston, Teddy Ballgame was doing great work for the Jimmy Fund.

Still. Babe looked at the children around her, yellowish, waxen. What good would slow advances do these kids in this room right now? Still, there was always hope. And they had today. It got boring lying in a hospital bed day after day, she sure as hell knew that.

She took up her harmonica and played them five more songs before leaving. From Seattle she would catch a plane to St. Louis's Children's Hospital, which she had promised to visit next. After that, she would fly over to St. Joseph's Hospital in Philadelphia, which had also sent her an invitation, before heading home. She had a stiff drink in the airport lounge before boarding her plane.

65

"YOU WOULD BE proud of me," Babe told Betty upon getting home to Rainbow Manor.

Betty was sitting at a wicker table on the back patio, leafing through *Sports Illustrated* and drinking a Coke. George wasn't around. They didn't know where he was, exactly.

After kissing Betty, Babe sat down at the table and looked out across the lawn that rolled down to the small lake.

"Why?" Betty asked.

"When I was in Philly, I went to the wing for colored patients and said hello to them."

Betty looked at Babe, wide-eyed. She had gotten used to thinking of Babe as rather behind the times in matters of race.

"That was nice of you. What made you do that?"

"Well, I saw this little colored nurse walking down the hallway and when I asked a doctor about her, he said that she was headed to the hospital's Negro wing. I was surprised to see a colored nurse, though I guess I shouldn't have been."

It had only lately occurred to Babe that Negroes were segregated in different hospitals or on different floors of white hospitals. What she didn't mention to Betty was that she thought the nurse was very cute, possibly one of their kind. There was just something about her.

"Yes, there are Negro doctors and nurses," Betty said. "They're not all maids and street cleaners."

"I know that," Babe replied, a little irritated by Betty's lecturing tone. "Anyhow, then the doctor asked me if I wanted to tour that part of the hospital. At first I didn't, but then I thought why not, the colored get cancer too, and so I said yes."

"So, what was it like?" Betty asked. She herself had never been in a colored wing of a hospital before.

"Well, I was nervous," Babe continued. "I didn't know if they would like me, you know, me this big ole white lady. But I plunked myself down in that pediatric cancer ward, there were a lot of beds in there kinda crammed together, and a lot of the kids looked startled at first—like I was strange. Then I played them a few tunes on my harmonica, and, you know, they looked kinda pleased."

Babe recalled the colored children she had seen . . . same bloated faces, same tubes attached to machines, same bald heads. There had been one especially cute little girl—she hadn't lost her hair yet and she had pig tails and huge brown eyes who had called her Miss Babe. The little girl's name was Rosalind, and she appeared to be about six years old.

"Miss Babe, can you play 'Old MacDonald'?" Rosalind had asked. Rosalind had the kind of clear, piping voice that some little kids have, like birds. So Babe had played the tune for her, even getting the rest of the kids to join in with the barnyard sounds, and Rosalind looked so happy and full of spirit. Maybe, Babe thought, she would be one of the ones to make it. One of the few.

"Thank you, Miss Babe," Rosalind had said, as if Babe had done something great for her.

"You're welcome, Rosalind," Babe had replied. "It was sure nice meeting you."

Babe had needed another stiff drink that night before going to sleep in her hotel room.

"I am proud of you," Betty said. "But I think it's dumb to have a separate ward for Negroes."

"Maybe so." Babe shrugged. "But you know that's what some people want. They'll get up in arms if you try to make changes."

"A good excuse for doing nothing."

"Maybe," Babe replied. "But some of those good ole boys are mean."

It was sad the country was like that, but it was. Babe thought uneasily of little Rosalind in her too-crowded hospital ward. Yes, it was very sad.

SOME DAYS BACK in Tampa, Babe didn't feel so good herself. Everything ached, from her legs to her hips and up her back. Pain exploded up and down her body and a worrisome fatigue made it seem futile to get out of bed. On other days she felt fine. Noticing Babe's listlessness, Betty suggested a fishing trip to Port Aransas, Texas, on the Gulf Coast. The small city wasn't far from Beaumont, so they could stop in and see Babe's sister, Lillie.

"Let's rent a cabin," Betty said. Port Aransas on Mustang Island was famous for its fishing. "They've got tons of tarpon down there." Even FDR and his friends had fished for tarpon in Port Aransas.

"Tarpon?" Babe said. "Those suckers reach two-hundred-and-fifty pounds. I don't think I can hoist one of them out of the water."

"Then we'll fish for something else," Betty said. "There's plenty of fish down there."

"Well, then, let's go."

A FEW DAYS later, Babe, Betty, and Betty's younger sister Margie, laden with luggage and fishing tackle set out for Port Aransas in Betty's Lincoln convertible. With Babe's approval, Betty had invited Margie, who was on spring break from high school. Her presence meant that Betty and Babe couldn't be as free around each other as they would if they were alone together, but taking Marge along was a good deed. Besides, they knew that Margie had no inkling they were lovers. Lots of people were like that: they only saw what they wanted to see.

"Ever been to Port Aransas?" Babe asked Margie.

"No, I haven't," Margie said. She was the opposite of Betty, quiet and bookish, not athletic. "I haven't done much fishing."

"Well, we'll show you how it's done," Babe told her.

They took turns driving up through the Florida panhandle, with its dense pine forests and cypress swamps, stopping for a night in a motel on the outskirts of Tallahassee, then through the southern tips of Alabama and Mississippi, bypassing New Orleans, and then down past Houston. Since it was early spring, the heat wasn't yet oppressive. Three days of steady driving—they weren't pushing it—with a couple of stopovers including Beaumont, where they stayed in a downtown hotel while paying a visit to Lillie.

"My, my, you look so good." Lillie wrapped her arms around Babe as she stood in the doorway at 850 Doucette. The visitors had timed their arrival for after dinner. As they sat down in the old familiar living room, Lillie offered them all refreshments. Babe, Betty, and Peggy and Lillie's husband, O.B. Grimes, opted for beer. Lillie took a Dr. Pepper.

"Where are the kids?" Babe asked.

"Out back," Lillie told her. "I'll call them in so they can say hi."

"I'll see them before I leave," Babe told her. Let's just us grownups talk for a while."

There was a pause in the conversation until Lillie burst out with, "You got your color back." The last time she had seen her youngest sister was a month or so after her cancer surgery when she had still looked as pale as the sheets. "How do you feel?"

"Some days good, some days not so good." Babe didn't tell her about the pain in her back and legs that came and went. No sense worrying her.

Lillie filled her in about the rest of the siblings, who were all doing reasonably well. Her husband, O.B., didn't contribute much to the conversation. He had been employed as a ship builder during the war. Now he worked making widgets in a machine shop owned by the Hughes Corporation.

"It's so good Betty and Margie could come with you," Lillie told Babe. She knew that Betty had helped Babe with her colostomy. She was such a nice girl, helping that way, and her father was a general. Yes, the Didriksens had come a long way in the world even if most of them did stay close to their roots in Beaumont.

"Any more tournaments in the works?" Lillie asked.

"Yeah, but not until late April," Babe replied. "The Peach Blossom in South Carolina. We'll probably drive up there for that."

Betty caught the tiredness in Babe's voice, even if Lillie didn't. One more tournament. She had been playing golf a long time, almost since before Betty was born.

"Remember the time I let that dog eat the stew meat?" Babe asked Lillie.

"Lord, what made you think of that?"

"I don't know. It just came into my mind."

She would never forget the look of frustration on her mother's face when she had returned home without the meat. That and the whacks she gave Babe. The good old days.

"I still miss Mama a lot. She gave me a good whipping for that, but you know what? I think she could have whipped me harder. I think she was pulling her whips."

O.B., who didn't smile often (bad teeth) smiled at Babe's comment . . . pulling her whips. She was a card, that one.

"She probably was," Lillie said. "You always were her favorite."

Lillie said this without resentment. Babe was everyone's favorite. Had always been, would always be. Her success was their success.

"Good old Mama," Babe said. "I hope I gave her some pleasure with all the problems I caused. Like the time I broke my ribs jumping off that roof."

Betty looked surprised. "You jumped off a roof and broke your ribs?"

"Yep, I was a hellcat," Babe told her.

"You gave Mama a lot of pleasure, honey," Lillie said. "You paid for that new kitchen and other things."

"Yeah, I know," Babe said. "She still had a hard life, comin' over here and all."

"Well, she adjusted. We all adjust." Lillie thought about what O.B. had told her about *his* family: hard-drinking father, mother dead of a stroke when he was ten. Though he never complained, O.B. had had to adjust something awful. Then, switching the subject, Lillie reminded Babe of when she used to jump all the hedges on the street, practicing for the Olympics when they were kids.

"You knew even then you were going to the Olympics," Lillie said. "Did you know that, Betty? Babe used to jump every hedge on this street."

"I can imagine." Betty smiled.

"You sure kept me moving." Lillie sighed, as if even the thought tired her.

Before she left, Babe beckoned Lillie out to the car and gave her sister a wad of bills to pay for an air conditioner, maybe two.

"Tell O.B. it's a birthday present from me to you," Babe said.

"But it isn't my birthday for a couple of months."

"Hold it then," Babe said. "For the summer heat."

66

THE NEXT DAY Babe, Betty, and Margie took the auto ferry and crossed onto Mustang Island. After disembarking, they drove over a few streets and pulled up at the cottage in Port Aransas they had rented. The cottage was a neat, red, clapboard, two-bedroom affair with a little wooden porch out front and a pebble lawn. It was in a row of other rental cottages of various bright hues—mango, turquoise, egg yolk yellow, Kelly green, coral pink—that you rarely saw on the mainland, as if island living had given people liberty to drop their inhibitions and indulge themselves in riotous color.

"This is cute," Babe said. "You done good, Betty."

After they unpacked and took out their fishing gear, they fished from a pier until late in the afternoon, catching a few redfish and enough flounder to feed all three of them. They threw back the redfish and put the flounder in a cooler to cook for dinner.

Although their cabin came equipped with a stove and refrigerator, they got out the small metal grill they had brought, set it in the small backyard, loaded it with charcoal, topped that off with scraps of newspaper, and cooked the fish. Before boarding the ferry, they had bought fresh corn and tomatoes at a local market on the mainland, beer at an ice house, as well as fresh baked biscuits and butter and beer to go with the fish.

"Ahh, this is the life," Babe said. The Gulf breezes were blowing, and the sunset cast a blood red glow over the expanse of water. You couldn't smell the fumes from the refineries down here, either. Just clean salt air.

It was funny: this was the first time Babe spent relaxing on a beach since her Hawaiian honeymoon with George. Since then, she had been far too busy with golf to relax by the water, and George was never big on the beach.

"How about we go swimming tomorrow?" Margie suggested.

Babe and Betty exchanged looks.

"Oops, I forgot," Margie said. "Sorry." Betty had told her about the colostomy bag.

Ruth Rouff

"That's okay, kid. I can go swimming," Babe said. She wore a smaller colostomy bag when going in the water.

That night, Babe and Betty slept on twin beds in one bedroom while Margie had the other bedroom to herself.

The next day they swam in the morning and early afternoon. When she wasn't in the water, Babe lay on the beach getting a tan and reading Babe Ruth's autobiography, *The Babe Ruth Story*. Fred Corcoran had suggested she write her own book. He said he could arrange for her to work with a ghost writer, just as the Bambino had worked with one. Why not?

Sometimes the thought crossed her mind that the doctors hadn't gotten all the cancer, that it was still swimming around in her bloodstream the way fish swam in the water. From her experience touring cancer wards, she knew that doctors tried to put a rosy face on things, sometimes at the expense of the truth. Who knew how much time she really had left?

Done with the beach, they tried fishing from a different pier in mid-afternoon, parking Betty's Lincoln on the sand at the base of the pier. This pier, Keepers Pier, jutted out over a thousand feet into the Gulf of Mexico, and it was said you could catch the same fish there as you would if you had taken a boat ten miles out into the Gulf.

They did well, with Babe catching a twenty-five inch speckled sea trout and Margie catching a red drum. This time they decided to keep each of the fish and save the red drum for lunch tomorrow. But when they returned to the base of the pier, ice chest in hand, they discovered that the car had sunk into wet sand from the high tide. As Betty floored the accelerator, the Lincoln's back wheels made a whizzing noise and only spun deeper into the sand.

"Shit!" Betty exclaimed.

"Only thing left to do is push," Babe announced, setting the metal ice chest on the ground.

Together she and Margie got behind the car and leaned their full weight into its rear.

Two men stood about twenty yards away, watching their efforts. One was beefy and suntanned, with a stubbly white beard and a tanned belly hanging out over the front of his Bermuda shorts. The other fellow was short and scrawny, with bowed legs and a reddish tan that made him look boiled like a lobster. They seemed highly amused by the women's struggles with the car and didn't offer a hand to help them.

"Goddammed idiots. Who needs them?" Babe said of the men. It was always the idiots who were the bastards. "Probably both got tiny peckers and ugly wives."

Margie grinned. Forget about college; this trip was an education.

The Lincoln's back whitewalls kept spinning.

"One big push," Babe said. She and Margie gave a mighty heave.

The back tires skidded again but the heavy car finally rose out of the wet sand with a bounce. The women cheered. Margie remembered the ice chest.

Babe scowled as they drove past the two men who had failed to help them. She wanted to give them the finger but felt they didn't deserve even that recognition. She needn't have worried. Betty gave them the finger instead, raising her middle digit in a brisk salute. It was amusing to see the men's open-mouthed reaction. In a few seconds, they were far enough away that they couldn't hear what the men were shouting after them.

That night an acute pain, like something was clawing through Babe's insides, spread out from her back through her buttocks and legs.

"Maybe pushing the car out hurt my spine," Babe thought. "Maybe I slipped a disc." She didn't want to think it was the cancer coming back. She didn't want to wake Betty, who was sleeping in the other bed, so she tried muffling her groans in her pillow.

It didn't work. Betty turned on the lamp. The clock face read 3:26.

"My God, what's the matter?" she asked, bleary-eyed. Babe's face was almost as white as her pillowcase.

"My back is killing me."

"I'll give you some aspirin," Betty said.

But the aspirin didn't help.

Early that morning Betty called Dr. Mitchell, Babe's proctologist in Galveston, who told her to get Babe to the clinic on the island.

The clinic was little, three rooms in a small lime green building on the main street of Port Aransas. Someone had hung a pastel of a conch shell on one wall of the waiting room.

They were ushered into the examination room.

As Babe sat on the examination table, the doctor gave her an injection of Demerol.

"When you get off the island, see your regular physician as soon as you can," he told her. She told him about pushing the car, but he offered no diagnosis.

"I will, doctor," Babe said. She was praying that it was a slipped disc. As the potent drug kicked in, the pain subsided, and Babe felt drowsy. "That's the stuff," she told Betty on the short drive back to their cottage.

When they got back to the cottage, Babe was nearly dead on her feet, so Betty and Margie helped her into bed. An hour later, Betty checked on Babe, who was sound asleep. Her profile was thin and hawk-like, her mouth cast in a frown, her complexion gray under her suntan.

"In about a year," Betty was thinking. That was what the doctor had said. "The cancer would cause more trouble." Well, it had been over a year, closer to two years, actually. But who was counting?

They decided to stay in Port Aransas for the rest of the week, as the pain pills the doctor prescribed made Babe feel groggy but almost back to normal. Why not stay? It was Margie's spring break and they didn't want to shorten it. Besides, if Babe hooked a big one while fishing, one that might strain her back, she'd simply hand her rod to Betty or Margie and let her land it. They could return to the first pier they fished at. That way they wouldn't run into the two men who had laughed at them.

"What if we do?" Betty remarked.

"Well, we'll just have to give them the finger again," Babe said. "This time I'll join you."

"You could just tell them who you are," Margie suggested. Surely the men would be impressed when they learned who they were messing with. Just the greatest woman golfer that ever was, that's all.

"It's not worth it," Babe said. She didn't have the energy anymore to try to impress bastards. Anyhow, from experience she knew that low-class men like those two weren't impressed with women no matter how much they accomplished.

ON THEIR WAY back from Port Aransas, Babe stopped in Galveston to see Dr. Mitchell. He ordered another round of tests, but none of them revealed any sign of cancer.

"Maybe it was just a strained muscle," Babe thought. But she had strained muscles before and never experienced that kind of knife-like pain.

By late April, Babe was feeling well enough to play in the Peach Blossom Open in Spartanburg, South Carolina. She still didn't feel energetic, though, not like the old days when she felt she could walk through a wall.

At times the pain in her lower back would flare up, and she'd have to take more Demerol, like it or not.

At the Peach Blossom, Babe started off poorly, for her, missing easy putts and slicing some of her drives. As a result, a young golfer named Marilynn Smith took a one-hole lead against her with nine holes left to play. With her friendly grin and effusive personality, Marilynn was widely respected for her willingness to talk up the LPGA tour at luncheons and lectures and wherever she possibly could. Babe appreciated Marilynn's commitment to the tour, but she was damned if she would let personal feelings influence her. The way she looked at it, she wasn't just playing for herself; she was playing for cancer survivors and those who were fighting the disease—the people in the hospital beds. Maybe if she could emerge victorious, they could too.

Babe's pain came flaring up her spine on the back nine. But she gritted her teeth and came roaring back. She hit the longest drives of the tournament, and her short game was "on" as well. Meanwhile, Marilynn's game fell apart. She missed easy putts, something she couldn't afford to do against someone like Babe. As a result, Babe won the tournament by four strokes. She didn't feel at all guilty about beating Marilynn, who was nearly twenty years her junior. Marilynn had many more years left to play.

After winning the Peach Blossom, Babe felt more fatigued than ever, and the pain in her back returned even with painkillers, so she and George returned to the hospital in Galveston.

67

"THE DOCTORS THINK I'm nuts," Babe told Betty from her bed at John Sealy Hospital. Betty had stayed with the tour for a few more weeks before cutting things short and heading down to Galveston.

"George is really pissed off," Babe continued. "He wants to punch them all in the mouth."

"Why?"

Babe took a sip of water. She looked even worse than when Betty had last seen her.

"The docs think I'm making up this stuff about being in pain just to cage more pain killers. Can you believe that?"

"I think they're the ones who are nuts," Betty said. Babe was the most uncomplaining, self-disciplined person she had ever met, except for her father, the General. No, she wasn't about to go soft for painkillers.

George overheard Betty's remark as he walked into the room. "The doctors are the crazy ones. Babe is a champion, always was, always will be. There is no way in hell this is all in her head."

After kissing his wife on the cheek, he sat down, took out a stick of Spearmint gum, and popped it in his mouth. He had taken to chewing gum because more than one of the nurses gave him a dirty look when she saw him smoking in Babe's room. Not only did cigars smell up the place, but there was a rumor going around that some doctors believed there was a link between smoking and cancer. That was disturbing.

Although all this wasn't enough to make George give up cigars entirely, he feared that Babe's cancer had come back, just as Dr. Moore had warned. But what could he say to her? The doctors told them both that they had found no visible evidence of it and suspected that Babe's pain was imaginary.

Then a young psychiatrist on the hospital staff, a Dr. Grace K. Jameson, was invited to sit down with Babe and ask her a series of questions. Babe was surprised at first to see a lady doctor.

"You're a head shrinker, right?" Babe asked.

"I'm a psychiatrist," Dr. Jameson said, amused but not surprised by Babe's colloquialism. "And I'd like to ask you a series of questions."

"Are you trying to find out if I'm crazy?"

"I wouldn't put it that way," Dr. Jameson replied. "But the attending physicians here asked me to help evaluate your situation."

"*Evaluate* . . . that means to figure out if I'm crazy. Anyhow, Doc, ask me the questions, and I'll try to answer honestly."

This Dr. Jameson seemed nice enough. And it was a novelty being questioned by a young woman.

From her responses, Dr. Jameson concluded that Babe wasn't neurotic in the least. If anything, she seemed rather embarrassed by the fact that she was in so much pain.

"Patient exhibits no signs of delusional thinking," was the way Dr. Jameson put it in her report.

When Jameson spoke privately with Betty Dodd, she was much less clinical.

"She's no more addicted to drugs than I am," she told Betty. "That girl is in pain."

But Jameson was overruled by the rest of the attending medical staff, who decided to wean Babe off painkillers.

This resulted in excruciating pain for Babe, and the doctors put her back on painkillers.

Not knowing what else to do, they then operated on Babe for a ruptured disc.

It didn't help.

As Babe's sister Lillie, who had been following her sister's situation, put it, "That girl don't have a ruptured disc any more than I do."

It wasn't until the end of July 1955 that the doctors found a cancerous lesion on Babe's sacrum, in the back of her pelvis.

"At least they know now I'm not crazy," Babe said. After all she had gone through in the past few months, the diagnosis came as a perverse kind of relief.

Cancer was a tricky little beast, Babe thought. Sneaking around like that, dodging and feinting, lulling you into a false sense of well-being, then coming at you just when you let down your guard. Damn! She had been enjoying herself so much at Port Aransas before the pain kicked in. Well, nothing gold could stay.

After this latest cancer diagnosis, something else was bothering Babe. She and Betty were sitting alone in Babe's hospital room. There were the usual flowers and cheery get-well cards. Babe was starting to dislike the smell of lilies. It was a cloying, syrupy smell, almost nauseating. And Babe was already having trouble with eating. She would have told Betty to toss the lot of them, but she didn't want to seem unappreciative.

"I have something to ask you," Babe told Betty, frowning. She was again wearing the fancy silk pajamas that Bertha Bowen had given her. For luck?

Betty steeled herself.

"What do you want to ask?"

"Did the doctor tell you my cancer would come back?"

Betty could not look Babe in the eye.

"Dr. Moore told us it might come back after you had your colostomy."

She couldn't bring herself to tell Babe what Dr. Moore had really said, that the cancer *would* come back and cause her "problems," but Babe guessed as much. Betty was a lousy liar.

"I see. And did George know too? He must have if you knew."

"Yes, he did. I'm so sorry, Babe," Betty said. Tears welled in her eyes. "I hoped it wasn't true. We thought you had enough to deal with, just recovering from the colostomy."

Babe sighed and laid her head back on her pillow. She felt betrayed. Her muscles had lost their tone by now. Useless. But then she thought about all she had done, the tournaments she had won after the cancer operation. Winning the U.S. Women's Open had been the crowning achievement of her career, and she knew from the cards and letters people sent her that her victory had inspired them. Could she have done that if she had known the cancer would come back? Probably not. And could she have done it all without Betty's loving help? Hell no.

"Don't blame yourself, honey. I shoulda known," she finally told Betty, who was by this time blowing her nose into a Kleenex. "Stage 4 rectal cancer—what they say I've got—is about as bad as it gets. Is there even a Stage 5?"

"I don't know," Betty mumbled.

"Stage 5 is probably you're dead."

"Don't say that. There's always other treatments. What do the doctors recommend?"

"They said radiation."

Who knew? Maybe radiation *would* help in her case. What did she have to lose?

THEY WERE STILL holding hands, with Betty leaning very close to Babe, when George strode into the room. His eyes went wide. For a moment he was tempted to walk right back out again, but Babe, dropping Betty's hand, told him to come in and sit down. There was a threatening look in her eyes as she did so, as if she was daring him to say one word about her and Betty, just one word.

"Betty was just telling me how sorry she is that the cancer came back," Babe explained.

"I'm sorry, too," George said. It was almost a plea.

"Well, that's the rub of the greens," Babe replied.

68

A GIANT METAL machine resembling a reflecting telescope loomed over Babe as she lay on her stomach on a ceramic-topped metal table. Her hospital gown was open in back, revealing the spot on her lower back that the machine was focused upon. Babe had been told exactly what the machine was designed to do, but she still felt like a cut of meat at a butcher shop.

"Hey, Doc, is this thing gonna drill a hole clear through me?" she cracked.

The doctor in charge, a radiologist by the name of Wilkins, chuckled. "No, but it's going to give that cancer a megavoltage dose of x-rays."

Despite what the doctor said, Babe imagined the x-rays going through her, through the table, through the floor and all the way to China. As kids, she and her siblings had tried once to dig a hole to China, where they thought they would see Chinese people wearing funny straw hats and pulling rickshaws. How dumb they had been.

George and Betty were watching the procedure at a safe distance, from behind a glass window. Babe could see them from where she lay, each giving her a thumbs up. Their faces filled the window like balloons. George looked a lot older lately, his brown eyes tired, his hair graying, the lines in his forehead etched deeper. He could be a bastard at times, but all this stuff was hard on him, too. She shouldn't forget that. Betty looked tired, too. Although she never complained, sleeping on a hospital cot night after night couldn't be pleasant.

The doctor stood back behind a metal barrier and pressed a button. There was a clicking noise from the machine, and the procedure was over in a few seconds. It was a little anticlimactic in that regard, Babe thought. She had expected a more dramatic noise, like a dentist's drill or at least a popping sound, something loud to show that something was definitely being accomplished.

Dr. Wilkins told Babe she would get another treatment in a week's time. He and the other doctors said they had learned to space the treatments to give surrounding tissue damaged by the radiation a chance to heal.

"I see," Babe said.

She was remembering the radiation burns on cancer patients she had visited, lurid things they were. She also knew what the survival rates were for rectal cancer . . . piss poor. On the other hand, she felt that a lot of people with cancer were counting on her to put up a good fight. She thought of Sister Tarsisis, who was still doing well after Babe had convinced her to have a colostomy. She had gone into remission, the doctors said. Some patients did. Maybe Babe would, too. Whatever happened, she would certainly put up a fight. Fighting was something she knew how to do.

An orderly wheeled Babe back to her room after the procedure.

Betty and George were waiting for her there and watched as the orderly, a powerfully built man wearing a crucifix around his neck, gently helped Babe back into bed. Babe thanked him.

"My pleasure, Mrs. Zaharias," he said. "God protect you."

"I'm praying," Babe told the orderly.

"Well, that was quick," George said. "Did it hurt any?"

"Naw," Babe said. "It was just like gettin' an x-ray."

"That's good."

Babe didn't tell George that the doctor said the treatment would sting later.

George took out another stick of Wrigley's and started talking sports. By now he had blotted out the sight of seeing his wife and Betty so close. The pennant races were heating up, and it would soon be World Series time.

"Looks like the Dodgers and Yanks again," George said.

"Again," Babe said. She still followed sports in the newspaper.

Betty was a Dodgers fan. "Jackie's got so much grit."

Babe did not dispute her comment. Someone had told her she had grit a while back. Who was it? Oh right, Patty Berg.

As Betty and George talked over the pennant races, Babe's mind drifted to a pleasant thought. Just two days ago, she got a card. It was nothing special, just a simple get-well card with a bouquet of pink and yellow flowers on the front. But inside it read:

Dear Mrs. Zaharias—you always told me to call you "Babe,"
You may not remember me, but I used to be a waitress as the
Riviera Country Club in Los Angeles. I have fond memories
of waiting on you there, along with Mr. Kertes. Well, I'm no
longer a waitress. When my mom died and left me some
money, I went back to school and became a registered
nurse! I work at a hospital in Fresno, in the maternity unit.
Anyway, I'm proud to have known you and think it's very
courageous of you to spread the word about cancer. I'll
always cherish the memories I had of meeting you at the
Riviera. My prayers for your speedy recovery.
    Yours truly,
    Kathy Lopez

Babe remembered Kathy well. How could she not? She had been the
first woman Babe could discern who had ever been attracted to her. She,
with her brown eyes sweet as dark chocolate, a wonderful smile . . . And
she, timid jackass that she had been, had done nothing in response. Just
sat there like a bump on a log. The bitterness of a lost opportunity had
weighed on Babe until the day she met Betty Dodd. Even her marriage
to George had never completely lifted the memory of Kathy, even though
she and George had been happy at first. The memory and the need it
signified had simply been pushed to the back of her mind, like old papers
in a drawer.

"This could be the year the Dodgers win it," Betty was saying.

"Could be," George said.

Now Kathy's get-well card was sitting on the nightstand to her right,
along with some others. She wouldn't throw that one out, no sir. She
would bring it home with her and keep it in a secure place. She would
cherish it. But before that, she would write Kathy Lopez a thankyou note.
She hoped she would realize that Babe regretted not getting to know her
way back when. And she hoped that Kathy had found someone the way
she had found Betty.

PRIOR TO BABE'S stay in the hospital, Fred Corcoran had suggested
she write her autobiography. Although he was a kindly man, he was also
a businessman. Things could go south soon for his greatest female client,

so he got a ghostwriter for her, a sportswriter. Babe would dictate into a machine, and the writer would write the book.

Babe enjoyed reminiscing about her career. It was like reliving it. And now that she could no longer play golf, the book project was giving her something to do while she was sick. She would begin the book with starting work at Employer's Casualty Insurance.

"You never saw anybody more excited than I was that night at the railroad station in Beaumont, Texas, back in February 1930," Babe dictated into the machine.

She would go on to talk about her Olympic victories, her barnstorming days, and the long wait she had had before she could again play amateur golf.

Of course, there were things she wouldn't mention. Like the truth of her relationship with Betty. It wasn't that she didn't want to. The relationship made her so happy she felt like crowing about it.

But what would her friends think about that? What would the world think? That she was betraying George? Well, he never even tried to make love to her anymore, being intimidated or maybe even disgusted by the colostomy. And it wasn't like she had taken up with another man. Besides, Betty still had her best years ahead of her. Her career would be ruined if Babe let on that the two of them were lovers.

Not that there weren't other female homosexuals on the LPGA tour, Babe was convinced of that by now. It was obvious with some of the women, no matter how hard they tried to hide it. It was like a sixth sense you developed, knowing which girls were like you. No, she and Betty were far from alone. Nonetheless, it was best to build a wall around their relationship, or a castle with a moat, to keep enemies out.

69

AFTER THE ROUND of radiation treatments was over, Babe was released from the hospital and returned to Rainbow Manor with George and Betty. It was great being home, with the green grass surrounding her and the pleasant smells and the chirping birds flitting from tree to tree; even the frogs that croaked in the little lake at the base of their property seemed cheerful. She missed all of that in the hospital, with its antiseptic walls and hovering nurses. Forget all that for now. Betty had been instructed in how to administer her painkillers, what dosage to use, so she was like a nurse to Babe.

As usual, George was in and out. He must suspect by now that Babe and Betty were lovers, but he did his best to be agreeable. Maybe he had a girl on the side? Babe sometimes wondered about that. She wouldn't mind, really, if he did.

He bought her a cute, turquoise, three-wheeled electric golf cart from E-Z-Go to help her get around the course by their house. Because her feet were so swollen, she couldn't fit into golf shoes, so she wore loafers that were a size bigger than what she normally wore. Babe hated even to look at her feet by now, which were shapeless. Sometimes they became so painful that Betty would have to knead them, like bread dough, to ease the pain.

"You're a saint doing all this," Babe told Betty. She was sitting on the couch and Betty was sitting on the floor in front of her, assiduously massaging her feet.

"You'd do the same for me," Betty said.

"I guess I would."

But would Babe really? She doubted it. She had always been solely focused on winning. She had never been forced to take time off from her career to care for somebody. There were always other people to do those things, like the way her sisters helped her parents when they got old and feeble. But what if she hadn't had sisters? What if it was just her? Would she have dropped golf and come home to nurse them? That would have been so hard. As Betty sat before her, diligently easing her pain, Babe looked down at her and concluded that Betty was a better person than she was.

ON GOOD DAYS Babe and Betty would shuttle around the course near Rainbow Manor in the turquoise cart, with Betty doing most of the playing and Babe observing her and making a few comments. She didn't like to meddle too much in Betty's game. She knew that each golfer had a different way of doing things that worked for her. Babe's own swing was powerful, but she knew it wasn't classic, not one to emulate. This new kid from California, Mickey Wright, now she had a swing like butter. It was like the ideal of a golf swing . . . it couldn't be improved upon. Even Ben Hogan said as much.

Nonetheless, Babe's swing worked for her, and she had learned to compensate for its occasional errancy by developing a remarkable ability to scramble out of bunkers. It was up to Betty to discover what worked best for her. And she had to do this by continuing to play tournament golf.

"You'll see," Babe told Betty. "You'll start winning that big money soon."

Babe knew by now that Betty should be as free as the birds, going about their business on this beautiful day. Soon it would happen.

A FEW WEEKS later, Peggy Kirk Bell came to visit, having left baby Bonnie with Warren and a nanny.

George picked Peggy up at the airport and drove her to Rainbow Manor.

"Here's Peg!" George boomed as the two came through the door. He hoped Peggy would cheer his wife up. He had never seen her this down before and it made him nervous, as if a bigger disaster were looming right around the corner.

Peggy and Babe hugged. Peggy looked at her long-time friend, who seemed to droop and sag like a plant that hadn't been watered in weeks. Give her some water. Holy water. If only it were that simple.

"You look good," Peggy said.

"Cut the crap, Peg," Babe said, not unkindly. "I know what I look like."

"Well, at least she's still got spirit," Peggy thought.

Later, on the golf course, when Peggy hit one of her characteristic 170-yard drives, Babe cracked, "Peggy, you must be the greatest golfer in the world. How do you break a hundred driving this far?"

Peggy laughed. She had always loved the cut-up in Babe. She left unmentioned the fact that the pop was gone in Babe's drives. Now, most times they traveled, bleakly, just about as far as her own.

As they were playing, George appeared with another man, one who was pulling a Spalding golf bag on wheels. As the two drew closer, they could see that the man was wearing a white polo shirt that bore three words: Alpha Cadillac Oldsmobile.

Introductions were made.

"Nick here wants to play a couple holes with you," George announced to his wife and Peggy.

George had befriended Nick, who owned a car dealership in St. Petersburg, while both were attending the dog races in that city. The two had hit it off over drinks after the races.

"It's always been a dream of mine to play with you, Mrs. Zaharias," Nick said, proffering his hand.

Babe shook it, trying to hide her displeasure with George for springing a stranger on her. With his narrow shoulders and paunch, Nick didn't look like much of an athlete, but how could she refuse this man his dream?

"Okay, but we're only playing three or four holes today," Babe lied. They had planned to play nine, but Babe didn't want Nick buzzing around after them for that long. He sold cars? Well, then he was a talker, and she wasn't in the mood for small talk.

True to her observations, Nick wasn't much of a golfer. In fact, one of his drives quickly plopped into a small pond on the course.

"Forget about that one," Babe told Nick. Her legs and feet were throbbing by now. "Here's another ball. Start from the water's edge."

Nick looked at her gratefully. It had dawned on him that he was interrupting Babe and Peggy's game.

"Yes, I don't want to hold you ladies up," he said.

Later, on the way back to the house after Nick had departed with her autograph, Babe remarked to Peggy, "Sometimes George doesn't use good sense."

Peggy said nothing but thought that if Warren ever foisted a stranger on her while she was engaged with an old friend, she would slap him silly.

70

BY EARLY DECEMBER, Babe was in so much pain that she told George to take her back to Sealy Hospital. Despite the radiation treatments, the cancer was spreading throughout her body, like one of those flaming maps the western movies used to signify the spread of trouble. All the doctors could do was give her stronger painkillers and send her back home. There, she felt woozy a lot of the time.

Christmas promised to be miserable, but then the Bowens invited Babe and George to spend the holidays with them in Fort Worth. Something to look forward to, especially since Betty would be visiting her folks in San Antonio.

R.L. chartered a private plane for Babe and George. When the flight landed at Love Field, George popped out of the plane first, then gently helped Babe down the metal steps, where she practically fell into Bertha's waiting arms. R.L., who was waiting to drive them to the Bowens' house, nearly wept when he saw Babe's appearance.

As they pulled up to the house in one of Fort Worth's wealthiest neighborhoods, Babe recalled how she had once been afraid to enter it. With its Georgian stonework, white portico, and columns, it looked so grand, too grand for the likes of her, who had shared a bedroom that was actually an enclosed porch with two of her sisters.

The Bowens had set up a ten-foot Balsam fir in their living room and festooned the tree with hundreds of ornaments and colored lights. With Bertha by her side, Babe stood by it for a moment, savoring its decorations and its piney smell. The Bowens, or their help, had even strung popcorn on it, like the Didriksens used to at home, elbow to elbow with needles and string at the kitchen table. Now, the sight of the splendid tree and its fragrant odor reminded Babe that this would most probably be her last Christmas.

While R.L. and George were playing billiards in the den, Babe and Bertha sat on the sofa. Babe was drinking water, while Bertha had her usual Scotch on the rocks. Hors d'oeuvres lay on a silver serving tray on the coffee table in front of them, nibbles of cheese and smoked salmon and artichoke. Babe and Bertha sat close to each other as Christmas music played on the stereo console: Nat King Cole singing about roasting chestnuts. Although the house had a fireplace, there was no fire burning in it right now. Maybe if the temperature dipped below forty, they would light it.

Babe was telling Bertha of the cancer foundation she and George had started—the Babe Didrikson Zaharias Cancer Fund.

"We're gonna help people who don't have the money to find out if they have cancer," Babe told her. "People who wait around and wait around and when they finally find out they have it, it's too late."

Babe didn't tell Bertha that she herself had waited until it was too late. Why? It wasn't that she didn't have the money. She was scared stiff, of course, of what she would learn. She, who had always prided herself on her courage. Well, now she knew there were all different types of courage. Parents and nurses and doctors who cared for sick kids had courage. The kids themselves had courage. And yes, you could be courageous as hell in sports and still be timid as a mouse in other ways.

"We're raising money to start a tumor center at the UTMB."

"That's wonderful, Babe," Bertha said, "R.L. and I will certainly donate. But how have you been feeling?"

"Not too bad today. But you can see what I look like," Babe said.

"You look okay, honey," Bertha said. "Considering all you've been through."

"You're a lousy liar, B.B." She wanted to tell Bertha that she knew she looked like crap, but she watched her language around B.B. Always.

Babe took a sip of water and gazed at the hors d'oeuvres, picked one up, and nibbled on it. Dinner was on the way, and she didn't want to ruin what little appetite she had. One side effect of the painkillers was nausea, a churning in her gut that often made even the thought of food loathsome. Today wasn't so bad, though.

"Anyhow I want to thank you for all you've done for me."

Bertha didn't like hearing these words. There was too much finality in them.

"What I did for you," Bertha said, "was nothing. What you did for me was more than I can say."

"You really mean that, B.B.?"

She meant it. Bertha told Babe that she had been like a daughter to her, and it had been one of the main satisfactions of her life that Bertha was able to help further her career. What a great career it was. When one really thought about it, there was none better in the entire history of sports. Maybe as good as, but not better.

"Aw, come on now," Babe said. "You did a lot for me. I was a mess before you showed me the ropes."

"Pshaw! You just needed a little guidance," Bertha said.

Babe laughed hollowly. "A lotta guidance. Remember that first time you took me to Neiman?"

"As clearly as if it were yesterday."

They both sat reliving that day. The excitement of the experience—it wasn't just about clothes; it was an adventure. Bertha was like the fairy godmother in Cinderella. She had waved a charge plate and transformed Babe's ragged, tomboy image into one that enabled her to become a star of the golf world. And Babe's image had never changed back, Babe made darn sure of that.

"That was the first time I ever saw someone use a charge plate," Babe admitted.

"It was well-used," Bertha said.

From the living room, they could hear the clicking of billiard balls in the den. So neat, so matter of fact, over the smooth green surface of the table. Click, clack, and the ball falls in the pocket. Cause and effect. They could hear George's booming voice, though they couldn't make out what he was saying. And the smell of the men's cigars wafted into the room along with the sound of the billiard balls.

"Yeah, well now I've done the same thing for Betty," Babe said. "I took her out shopping and I took her to a good hair salon and . . ."

What else had she done for Betty? She hesitated as Bertha waited for her to continue. She felt like telling her all about she and Betty's love for each other, but there were no words for that, no acceptable words. Babe felt very sad that she couldn't tell Bertha. Did her expression show it?

Finally, she continued, rather anticlimactically. "I helped Betty fit into the tour, but she's done a lot for me too. In fact, I don't know how I would have gotten along without her . . ."

"She's a fine young woman," Bertha said. "I thought you two would get along."

There was another pause. Babe noticed Bertha's eyes were warm and large. If there were things you couldn't talk about, maybe it didn't mean others weren't aware of them. The thought crossed Babe's mind that maybe Bertha already knew about her and Betty, *everything* about them. Babe didn't dare ask Bertha if she knew, and Bertha couldn't tell her. It was not what a Texas society matron, even a liberal one like her, did. Ever. Still, the thought that Bertha might know was satisfying to Babe.

"Well, dinner should be ready in a few minutes. I hope you've got some appetite," Bertha said at last. "Yolanda is making Crown Roast of Lamb. It's a specialty."

"That Yolanda, she's a pro," Babe said.

71

BABE AND GEORGE returned to Rainbow Manor from Fort Worth after New Year's Day. Betty joined them there. One day Betty walked into the trophy room to find Babe gazing into one of her trophy cases. The glass reflected Babe's own dull image. By now, appalled by what she saw, Babe couldn't look at herself in a mirror.

"What are you thinking?" Betty asked.

"Oh, just remembering how I got these trophies."

A thought occurred to Betty. "You never did show me your Olympic medals."

Babe turned to gaze at Betty with a look that Betty had never seen before, as if Babe were studying her from Mars or Jupiter or even farther out in the Solar System.

"You want to see them?" Babe finally asked.

"Of course." Although Betty had been only a year old at the time of Babe's great track and field victories, everyone who followed sports knew she had starred in the 1932 Olympics.

Babe beckoned Betty to the kitchen, where she opened a cabinet and pulled out an old red Hills Brothers coffee can. She handed the can to Betty.

"Open it," she said.

With difficulty, Betty pulled off the metal lid and lifted out the medals. They were impressively heavy: two gold and one silver. She wondered when Babe had last looked at them. Not lately, given how difficult it had been to open the coffee can. Betty had almost torn a nail doing so.

"The silver one is 'cause the judges said I didn't use a standard jumping technique on the high jump," Babe explained. "I actually jumped as high as the other girl. I was kinda cheated, even Granny Rice told me so, but it's water over the dam now."

"They're beautiful," Betty said as she examined the medals. She had never touched Olympic medals and doubted if she ever would again. To her they were evidence of immortality, or as close as any athlete could ever come to it.

"Why do you keep them in this old can?"

"They brought back bad memories."

"What on earth do you mean?"

Babe offered a wry look. "Let's sit down at the table. My feet are killing me."

"Of course. I'll give you a foot rub in a minute."

Babe sat down heavily at the kitchen table. The cancer had affected her sciatic nerve and pains shot down her leg to her foot. Although she tried to do without one for as long as she could, she knew she would need another painkiller before long.

"I was a tough kid, real tough, and I didn't treat people nice back then," Babe explained to Betty. "And a lot of people didn't treat me nice either. They said I was 'barroom tough.' That's a laugh 'cause I was never in a barroom in my life. How could I be? I was never interested in men, aside from George. And I was scared to go into the other kind of bar. Our kind."

She told Betty of how she had acted on the train out to the Los Angeles Olympics, pulling girls' pillows out from behind their heads when they were trying to nap and throwing ice water on those poor colored girls. That had been beyond the pale.

She also told Betty what people had whispered about her at the Olympics and after.

"They said I should have to take a test to see if I was really a girl," Babe said.

Whatever the dumb and mean things she had done, they shouldn't have said stuff like that. Even now, more than twenty years later, that sex test stuff and the names they called her hurt.

"You're all woman and you earned these medals," Betty said, taking Babe's hand. How weak it had grown when it had once been so strong. You needed strong hands to play golf, especially the aggressive way Babe played it. Drive long, win big.

"Yeah, but it's still hard for me to think about that stuff," Babe replied. "Taking up golf is when I changed for the better. I had to."

Betty didn't know what to say. Treating those Negro girls so shabbily had been mean. But she couldn't imagine people saying bad things about Babe now, especially with all the work she had done to fight cancer. And she was womanly, through and through. Just a different kind of woman. One who loved women. Was that so terrible?

Betty carefully placed the medals back in the Hills Brothers coffee can and pushed the lid back on.

"Thank you for letting me see these," she said.

"You want 'em?"

"What? Don't you?"

"Naw, you take 'em. I want you to have 'em."

Babe was thinking of George. If she should die soon, what would he do with them? She knew they would be safe with Betty.

"Of course, I want them, if you don't."

"Okay. But can you help me back to bed and give me that foot rub? My feet feel like they're on fire."

72

THE NEXT TIME Babe returned to John Sealy Hospital in Galveston, in March 1956, was her last. The pain got so bad that even morphine didn't work, so the doctors suggested performing a chordotomy. This involved severing certain nerves high up in her spinal cord, so Babe could not feel pain, so she would have no bodily feeling whatsoever.

They conferred with George and Babe and Betty about the chordotomy.

"I'm sick of moaning and I'm sure these two are sick of hearing me moan," Babe told the doctors. Betty had once again been sleeping on a cot in Babe's room.

"I'm not," Betty said, though it was indeed awful to hear Babe moaning and not be able to help her. This wasn't garden variety pain. Sometimes Babe's moans edged over into wails. As long as she lived, Betty would never forget those wails.

George didn't hear Babe wail or moan so much, since he didn't sleep in the hospital room with her. In fact, days went by when he didn't visit her. He just couldn't handle it. Sometimes you'd be talking with her and she'd let out one of those moans. It was awful.

"Whatever she wants, I'm fine with," George told the doctors. He would go out later and have a stiff drink or two, doctor be damned.

"Do the operation," Babe said weakly.

She was wheeled into the operating room with Betty and George by her side. The chordotomy eased the pain but made her unable to relieve her bladder—she was now on a catheter—and gave her phantom feelings, as if her legs were moving when they weren't. With her once wonderfully responsive body now helpless, she felt like a vegetable, even if her mind was still alive.

When Lillie came to visit her, she was appalled by Babe's skeletal appearance.

"They're keeping her alive because she's Babe Didrikson," Lillie thought. "It's because a lot of people look up to her. But what good do a few more weeks do anyone?"

Tiny Scurlock visited Babe once more and was also appalled. In fact, after talking with her a bit with Babe's attention fading in and out, Tiny burst into tears after leaving the room. Then he took a pill for his bad heart.

Still, Babe was alert the last time she talked with Betty, though her voice was a whisper. Betty had to lean close to hear what she was saying.

"I want you to go back to the tour," Babe told her.

"I want to be here with you."

Babe could not raise her head from her pillow. Her once glorious eyes were dim, and her chestnut hair was lank and dying. Though she could feel no pain, she knew the cancer cells were coursing through her body, invading each of her organs. If her body was a battle ground, the enemy had long ago routed the field.

"I don't want you to see me die."

Betty sobbed, repeating her desire to stay by Babe's side.

"No, no, honey," Babe told her as if talking to a child. She was sad about Betty being so sad. "It will make me feel better knowing you're on tour."

Betty finally agreed. If she could never be the golfer Babe was, at least she could get a full taste of the life Babe had lived: the fierce competition that was leavened with clubhouse camaraderie, even hilarity; the beckoning fairways and the roughs and the greens, the oohs and aahs from the gallery, the thrill of being on the leader board and maybe even winning some trophies, all that went into the LPGA tour. And through it all, she, like Babe, would continue to be a different kind of woman.

Before departing, Betty pressed her lips to Babe's and told her she loved her. Neither George nor the nurses or doctors were around, so she could.

"I love you too," Babe murmured through cracked lips.

Later, walking out to her car, Betty thought she would have kissed Babe on the lips even if multitudes had been watching.

As Babe closed her eyes and eased into death, she dreamed of green. Acres and acres of green fields and green trees, and her friend, her lover Betty beside her. Then slowly everything was green, a soothing green, a sweet and peaceful green, green like the sea, and Babe didn't wake up.

BETTY WAS ON tour when she got a phone call from Bertha Bowen telling her of Babe's death. Bertha and R.L. and George had been by her side when she passed. Bertha told her how Babe's breathing had gotten shallower and shallower and had finally stopped. Her passing was on the front page of all the major newspapers and on the TV news. President Eisenhower even mentioned it during a news conference, telling the world what a loss Babe's passing was.

Before she died, Babe had told Betty not to attend the funeral because of the press. As Babe's protégé, she would be in the spotlight. They might ask her some questions that would make her uncomfortable. And George probably wouldn't want Betty there either. He would want free reign to arrange the funeral. Anyhow, she would find out all about it from Bertha.

Bertha and R.L Bowen, Peggy Kirk Bell and Patty Berg attended the funeral, which was held in a Lutheran church in Beaumont. Tiny and Ruth Scurlock were there, as were many members of the press. All the Didriksen siblings and their husbands, wives and older children were there, filling the pews. Stan Kertes sent a beautiful flower arrangement, as did Lou Serbin, Fred Corcoran, and others who had fond memories of Babe. Louise Suggs wasn't there. Sensitive Louise had never completely gotten over Babe's disrespectful treatment, but she had sent flowers.

As Bertha Bowen later told Betty, George made a jackass out of himself at the funeral.

"He was sobbing and wailing, on his knees before the coffin," Bertha said. "At one point he even tried to get into the coffin with Babe. The ushers had to rush over and pull him away."

"Oh my God," Betty said.

Both speculated how much of George's behavior was real and how much was put on for the press.

"I don't think he knows anymore," Bertha said.

AFTER THE BURIAL, Bertha related to Betty how they all went out to eat at a homestyle restaurant in Beaumont.

"It felt good to do that," Bertha said. Patty Berg and Peggy Kirk Bell told stories of Babe from the old days: about the time she lost and told the press that she couldn't hit an elephant's ass with a bull fiddle. About all the fantastic shots she used to make. And all the times she used to say, "The Babe's here. Who's coming in second?"

"It used to make me mad when she said that," Patty Berg admitted. "But then I realized she was playing a mental game, trying to intimidate us. Anyhow, I beat her enough times."

When Babe was in Sealy Hospital that last time, Patty had taken to calling her every week, just to chat and fill Babe in on what was happening on the tour.

"It's fitting she won the last tournament she ever played in," Peggy Kirk Bell said.

Everyone agreed.

73

FREED FROM BABE'S sometimes overpowering presence, Betty won her first tournament and then others. Even though she didn't win a great number of tournaments throughout her career, not nearly the number Babe had, she often finished on the leaderboard. She also became more friendly with the other LPGA members, including Louise Suggs.

"For a long time I didn't think you were that friendly," Louise admitted one day in the clubhouse. "But you are friendly."

Betty laughed. "That's funny, I thought the same about you."

AFTER A COUPLE of years, Betty visited Babe's gravesite in Beaumont's Forest Lawn Memorial Park. She saw what was written on the grave marker under Babe's name and the date of her birth and death: "The world's greatest woman athlete." Well, that was true enough.

But there was another marker a few yards away, a three-foot high marble statue in the shape of an open book. It was engraved with the words: "It's not whether you win or lose. It's how you play the game—Babe"

"What horse shit!" Betty thought. Since Babe never said those words, she wondered why on earth George had them engraved on the monument. If anyone was all about winning, it was Babe, who was her own idol. Betty guessed that George thought the words conveyed a genteel image of his wife. If so, it was a false image.

Well, at least George was still out there, promoting Babe's memory and helping to raise funds for a museum dedicated to her in Beaumont. When Betty heard news of the planned museum, she got in touch with George and told him she would give him Babe's medals to display in it.

"Thanks, Betty," George had told her. "Everyone should know what a great Olympic star Babe was."

On that they could agree.

Much later, when Betty visited the Babe Didrikson Zaharias Museum and saw the Olympic medals displayed there, she thought about why Babe had been so keen on changing her image that she had disavowed her wild, Olympic days. Maybe Babe changed too much, Betty reflected. Like sometimes Babe wore the most frilly, feminine clothing, stupid stuff that didn't look good on her. Like she tamped down her spirit to conform to what the world thought she should be. Like she was always telling the press how George was such a great husband when Betty knew firsthand that he wasn't. And, of course, there was their intimate relationship—which Babe would never tell anyone about. How honest was that? Of course, Betty knew that Babe felt she had no choice in hiding that. But what if she and Betty had gotten together with the other lesbians on the tour? Could the press ruin the reputations of all of them? Maybe, maybe not. It was a moot point. Back then, no one wanted to stick her neck out.

New women athletes were coming along, Betty was pleased to see, who didn't care so much about what the world thought of them. These women stars, who were making big money now, would be damned if they girly-ed themselves up the way Babe felt she had had to. Betty and her new partner liked to watch them on TV and sometimes in person. They included women like Billie Jean King and Martina Navratilova, both champions, both out-of-the-closet, as the kids said nowadays. Feminine, but in a different way. And though no LPGA member had as yet come out as gay, Betty suspected that was just a matter of time.

But it was a far different world, Betty knew, back when Babe had come up. Even heterosexual women who played professional sports were viewed as strange. A woman's place was in the home and all that. And back then they didn't have people like Gloria Steinem and Betty Friedan talking up women's rights. And you definitely couldn't have a sports career if you were a lesbian, a working-class lesbian at that. You had to hide everything, maybe your best part, stuff it in an old coffee can and then shut it up in a kitchen cabinet.

Betty thought of what she would have put on Babe's monument if she had had the chance. Honestly, she *should* have had the chance. She had been Babe's intimate in the last years of her life far more than had George. It was she who had taken care of her in her final illness, cleaned her colostomy, rubbed her aching feet, slept on a cot in her hospital room, listened to her final, agonized moans, kissed her on the lips that one last time.

Finally, Betty decided how the monument should have read. It was something she had heard Babe say more than once, something that summed up her character. What Betty thought should be on the monument were these words: "You can't win them all, but you can try."

Ruth Rouff is a freelance writer living in Collingswood, New Jersey. After earning a BA in English from Vassar College and a MS in Education from Saint Joseph's University, she taught for a number of years in Philadelphia and Camden NJ. Her work has appeared in various literary journals, including *Exquisite Corpse, Philadelphia Poets*, and *Wilde*. In addition, she has written two young adult nonfiction books: *Ida B. Wells: A Woman of Courage* and *Great Moments in Sports*.

www.ingramcontent.com/pod-product-compliance
Lightning Source LLC
Chambersburg PA
CBHW031946090426
42739CB00006B/108